D0811328

This edition published in 2011

Copyright © Carlton Books Limited 2011

Carlton Books Limited
20 Mortimer Street
London W1T 3JW

All rights reserved. No part of this publication may be reproduced, stored in
a retrieval system, or transmitted in any form or by any means, electronic,
mechanical, photocopying, recording or otherwise, without the
prior permission of the copyright owner and the publishers.

A CIP catalogue record for this book is available from the British Library.

10 9 8 7 6 5 4 3 2 1

ISBN: 978-1-84732-890-8

Editor: Martin Corteel
Project Art Editor: Luke Griffin
Designer: Sailesh Patel
Picture Research: Paul Langan
Production: Maria Petalidou

Printed in Dubai

NOTE: All statistics are up to date as of the end of 2010.

Above Mean machine: A bird's-eye view of Sebastian Vettel's Red Bull Racing RB7
Renault at the 2011 Spanish Grand Prix.

WORLD FORMULA 1 RECORDS 2012

BY BRUCE JONES

SUPERFAST FIRST | EDITION

CONTENTS

Contents pages **Legends of F1:** (*main image*) An atmospheric view of the Grand Hairpin at Monte Carlo, with David Coulthard in the lead during the 2004 Monaco GP; (*inset top left*) Lewis Hamilton in hot pursuit of the race leader at the 2011 Spanish GP in Barcelona; (*inset top right*) Ayrton Senna in 1989; (*inset bottom left*) Michael Schumacher wins the 2004 Japanese GP at Suzuka; (*inset bottom right*) Jim Clark leads the 1967 Spanish GP at Jarama.

Overleaf **On the charge:** Red Bull Racing's Sebastian Vettel leads the field away at the start of the 2011 Australian Grand Prix, with Lewis Hamilton in second place for McLaren.

MONTE CARLO GRAND HOTEL

INTRODUCTION

All sports produce record and statistics galore, from goals scored to matches won to titles collected, and motor racing has its own measures of excellence, whether it's races won, pole positions collected, fastest laps, races started or even laps led.

Examine the tables of who has done what, or which team, and you will be looking at a list of the best of the best. However, as you go through this book you will find anomalies aplenty, such as the greatest names from the early days of the Formula One World Championship languishing far further down the lists than you might expect. That's simple to explain, as they contested far fewer races each year in the 1950s, sometimes as few as six per year and, sadly, they also had a tendency to be killed in action as cars and circuits were far less safe back then. That's why Juan Manuel Fangio, a five-time World Champion, has just 24 grand prix wins to his name, leaving him only ninth in the all-time list at the start of 2011. Mind you, that was 24 wins from just 51 starts, whereas Rubens Barrichello has more than six times that number of starts and fewer than half of the number of wins, emphasising how Fangio's hit rate, at 47 per cent, is something that will probably never be matched.

Such has been the longevity and success of Michael Schumacher's career – with first Benetton and then, chiefly, with Ferrari – that he tops pretty much every category of records. Indeed, even if Fernando Alonso, the most successful of today's heroes, starts winning every grand prix from 2012 on, it will be late in the 2014 World Championship before he topples the German's remarkable tally of 91 wins.

What leapt out as I complied the figures and wrote the stories for this book is just how much the tide has flowed between success and failure across the years as the World Championship accelerates into its seventh decade. For example, teams that once had the world at their feet, such as Cooper, Lotus and Brabham, have long since shut their doors for the final time.

I've had great fun compiling this book. Hope you enjoy wallowing in the statistics!

BRUCE JONES
May 2011

Right **Owning the podium:** Michael Schumacher celebrates yet another F1 victory for Ferrari, this time at the 2004 Malaysian GP at Sepang.

PART 1

F1 ALL-TIME RECORDS

Formula One, the world's fastest-moving sport, has been exciting and entertaining fans around the globe since the World Championship began in 1950. The drive to win is as strong as ever, but Formula One has changed dramatically over the past 60 years. The cars have been transformed into high-tech missiles with incredible acceleration, cornering and braking capabilities. The circuits are bigger, better and considerably safer. So, with every grand prix, the records keep on being added to in a blaze of glamour and speed.

Heavy traffic: Nico Hülkenberg shows how frantic the action can be in the midfield as he leads Sébastien Buemi's Toro Rosso, Adrian Sutil's Force India, Nico Rosberg's Mercedes, Vitaly Petrov's Renault and Vitantonio Liuzzi's Force India at the start of the 2010 European GP at Valencia.

DRIVERS

Michael Schumacher's dominance from 2000 to 2004 means that his name is at the top of virtually every list of driver achievement. But some of his rivals and those who raced before him certainly made huge contributions to the colourful history of Formula One, including greats such as Alberto Ascari, Juan Manuel Fangio, Stirling Moss, Jim Clark, Jackie Stewart, Niki Lauda, Alain Prost, Ayrton Senna and Nigel Mansell.

Unstoppable: Juan Manuel Fangio and Mercedes were all but unbeatable in 1955, emphasizing his ability to get into the right car at the right time.

CHAMPIONS

THE LION'S SHARE

Every now and again, a team or a driver, occasionally both, hits the sweet spot and dominates F1. Take Michael Schumacher's run at the beginning of the 21st century, when he was world champion from 2000 to 2004. His team, Ferrari, won a record-equalling 15 grands prix, both in 2002 and 2004. Of those, Michael won 11 in 2002 and all but two in 2004, leaving teammate Rubens Barrichello with the scraps. When McLaren won 15 out of 16 in 1988, the wins were split seven to eight between Alain Prost and Ayrton Senna.

 ### NUMBER 1 ON THE NOSE

The world champion has the honour of carrying the number "1" on his car for the following season. Michael Schumacher has raced with this number for the longest spell, from the beginning of the 2001 season to the end of the 2005 season.

 ### BRITISH DRIVERS COME OUT ON TOP

British drivers, teams and engine suppliers top many tables of F1 statistics, which is a fact that would have amazed onlookers in the 1950s as the dark green cars made up the numbers behind the best from Italy and Germany. Yet Britain has claimed more drivers' titles than any other country, 14, and more world champions too, 10, namely Mike

Above **British drivers come out on top:** Mike Hawthorn was Britain's first world champion, in 1958. *Below* **The lion's share:** Michael Schumacher claimed his third world title in 2000, and then drove in the No. 1 car for the next five years.

Hawthorn, Graham Hill, Jim Clark, John Surtees, Jackie Stewart, James Hunt, Nigel Mansell, Damon Hill, Lewis Hamilton and Jenson Button.

 ### WINNER BY A FRACTION

Some champions win by a clear margin, others just scrape home. Lewis Hamilton in 2008 and Kimi Räikkönen in 2007 both won by a point.

Mike Hawthorn also edged home by the same margin in 1958, but his championship win required an act of fair play from Stirling Moss who stopped Hawthorn from being disqualified from the Portuguese GP, verifying that Hawthorn's Ferrari hadn't been given a push-start. The closest championship finish was in 1984, when Niki Lauda beat his McLaren teammate Alain Prost by half a point.

Above **Privateers strike a blow:** Jack Brabham celebrates after winning the 1959 British GP at Aintree as Cooper came good.
Below **Playing dirty:** Michael Schumacher's Benetton is flipped on to two wheels after turning in on Damon Hill's Williams.

TOP WORLD CHAMPIONSHIP-WINNING DRIVERS

1	Michael Schumacher	7
2	Juan Manuel Fangio	5
3	Alain Prost	4
4	**Jack Brabham**	3
=	Niki Lauda	3
=	Nelson Piquet	3
=	Ayrton Senna	3
=	Jackie Stewart	3
9	Fernando Alonso	2
=	Alberto Ascari	2
=	Jim Clark	2
=	Emerson Fittipaldi	2
=	Mika Hakkinen	2
=	Graham Hill	2
15	Mario Andretti	1
=	Jenson Button	1
=	Giuseppe Farina	1
=	Lewis Hamilton	1
=	Mike Hawthorn	1
=	Damon Hill	1
=	Phil Hill	1
=	Denis Hulme	1
=	James Hunt	1
=	Alan Jones	1
=	Nigel Mansell	1
=	Kimi Räikkönen	1
=	Jochen Rindt	1
=	Keke Rosberg	1
=	Jody Scheckter	1
=	John Surtees	1
=	Sebastian Vettel	1
=	Jacques Villeneuve	1

 ### BREAK CLEAR

Michael Schumacher achieved the largest title-winning margin in the history of the F1 World Championship in 2002. He won by 67 points over his Ferrari teammate Rubens Barrichello. It outstripped the 58-point margin over McLaren's David Coulthard he achieved the previous year and Nigel Mansell's 52-point win over his Williams teammate Riccardo Patrese in 1992.

 ### PRIVATEERS STRIKE A BLOW

Jack Brabham and Cooper struck a blow for the little guys when they won both the 1959 World Drivers' and Constructors' Championships together. This made Cooper the first specialist racing-car manufacturer to beat the established automotive marques such as Alfa Romeo, Ferrari, Mercedes and Maserati, which ran their F1 teams alongside their established road car business.

PLAYING DIRTY

Damon Hill had every reason to feel aggrieved in the season-ending finale in Adelaide in 1994. Michael Schumacher seemed to have left a gap; Hill dived for it, not knowing that the German had just damaged his car against the wall. Schumacher then turned his Benetton across into Hill's Williams and the resulting clash caused irreparable damage to Hill's car and he had to retire from the race. Schumacher claimed the World Championship by a point. Damon's father Graham also lost a title through dastardly deeds. This happened at Mexico in 1964 when Ferrari's John Surtees beat him to the title by a point after his teammate Lorenzo Bandini tipped Hill into a spin.

HOP, SKIP AND A JUMP

Aside from Giuseppe Farina's record in winning the inaugural World Championship in 1950, the smallest total number of grands prix contested by a driver before becoming world champion is Juan Manuel Fangio, who won the title in 1951 for Alfa Romeo after competing in just 12 grands prix. Drivers these days contest many more grands prix than that in just one season alone.

WORST TITLE DEFENCE

Alberto Ascari won two World Championships in a row in 1952 and 1953. However, his second title defence was a disaster. His Lancia wasn't ready and Ascari didn't race until late in the year, failing to finish any of his five races in 1954 and scoring just 1.14 points by setting one fastest lap and sharing another. More recently, Jody Scheckter had a nightmare defending his 1979 crown. Scheckter's Ferrari 312T5 was uncooperative and his full campaign produced just two points.

JUST ONE WILL DO

Anyone who watched Keke Rosberg race will know that he was a driver who raced to win, a driver full of on-the-limit aggression, yet he claimed his world title for Williams in 1982 with just one win. That was Mike Hawthorn's tally too when he was crowned in 1958. Jack Brabham (1959), Phil Hill (1961), John Surtees (1964) and Denny Hulme (1967) all managed to win the title with just two victories.

KEEP IT IN THE FAMILY

The Hill family has a proud boast. Despite F1 being littered with sons following their fathers into the sport, Graham and Damon are the only father and son to both win the F1 title. Graham won in 1962 for BRM and in 1968 for Lotus while Damon was crowned with Williams in 1996. The Andrettis and Scheckters failed to match their feat, while the Piquet and Rosberg dynasties are still aiming to emulate them.

WORLD CHAMPION PAIRINGS

The 2010 McLaren partnership of Lewis Hamilton, winner in 2008, and Jenson Button, the current incumbent, is the eighth time that a team has fielded a pair of world champions. The previous occasions were: Alberto Ascari and Giuseppe Farina at Ferrari in 1953 and 1954; Jim Clark and Graham Hill at Lotus in 1967 and 1968; Emerson Fittipaldi and Denny Hulme at McLaren in 1974; Alain Prost and Keke Rosberg at McLaren in 1986; and Alain Prost and Ayrton Senna at McLaren in 1989.

TWO WHEELS TO FOUR

John Surtees – who was the world champion for Ferrari in 1964 – has the distinction of being the only motorcycle world champion to hit world title-winning heights after transferring to car racing. Fellow motorcycle world champions Mike Hailwood and Johnny Cecotto also made the move to four wheels, but "Mike the Bike" peaked with a best finish of second place in the 1972 Italian GP, ironically racing for Surtees's team, while Cecotto's best result was a sixth position at Long Beach for Theodore in 1983.

Above **Worst title defence:** Alberto Ascari (34) struggled in 1954, failing to finish a single race. Here, he runs second behind Juan Manuel Fangio at Monza.
Top **Keep it in the family:** In 1996, Damon Hill, son of Graham, leads Williams teammate Jacques Villeneuve, son of Gilles, during the year he became the first second-generation world champion.

WITH ROOM TO SPARE

The driver who clinched the World Championship with the most races still to be run was Michael Schumacher during his runaway success for Ferrari in 2002. There were 17 rounds that year and the German was world champion by the 11th race, the French GP at Magny-Cours, which he won.

I'LL TAKE THE FASTEST CAR

Juan Manuel Fangio was undoubtedly a maestro behind the wheel, but he was also a master at making sure he had the right machinery beneath him and he moved teams to ensure this, which explains why he won the World Championship with more teams than any other driver. He was champion with Alfa Romeo, Mercedes, Ferrari and Maserati.

THE FIRST WORLD CHAMPION

Giuseppe Farina was the first F1 world champion in 1950 at the age of 44. The Italian achieved his final win three years later just a few months short of his 47th birthday and, in so doing, became the second-oldest F1 race winner ever. These days, most of the drivers' fathers are younger than that.

COMING BACK FROM RETIREMENT

Niki Lauda had two World Championship titles to his name when he quit before the end of the 1979 season. Like many before and after him he couldn't stay away and was back in 1982, racing for McLaren. In winning the title in 1984 he set the record for the longest gap between titles – seven years.

ADDING TITLES TO TITLES

Fernando Alonso set a record when he won his second consecutive World Championship in 2006, as he became the youngest double world champion at the age of 25 years and 85 days. Ayrton Senna was the youngest triple world champion, at 31 years and 227 days.

Right Drivers who competed in most races before winning first World Championship: Jody Scheckter took 97 races to be champion, but Nigel Mansell took 83 more. *Below* I'll take the fastest car: Juan Manuel Fangio smiles with delight as he wins the 1957 German GP after hunting down the Ferraris in his Maserati.

DRIVERS WHO COMPETED IN MOST RACES BEFORE WINNING FIRST WORLD CHAMPIONSHIP

1	Nigel Mansell	180
2	Jenson Button	170
3	Kimi Räikkönen	121
4	Mika Hakkinen	112
5	**Jody Scheckter**	97
6	Alain Prost	87
7	Mario Andretti	80
=	Alan Jones	80
9	Ayrton Senna	77
10	Fernando Alonso	67
=	Damon Hill	67

RUNNERS-UP

FIRST OF THE LOSERS

Nobody wants to finish second in a grand prix. In F1 it's referred to as "the first of the losers". So, imagine how drivers gnash their teeth at ending the year as the championship runner-up. It's even worse if they trip up in the final round and let the title slide from their grasp. The most extreme example of this was when Lewis Hamilton blew his chance of winning the title at his first attempt in 2007 at the Brazilian GP when gearbox problems affected his race and he could only finish seventh. Ferrari's Kimi Räikkönen powered to a race victory and the title.

LAUDA PIPS PROST

Being faster and scoring more wins is one thing, but master tactician Niki Lauda taught his McLaren teammate Alain Prost a lesson in consistency in 1984. Prost settled in quickly after joining from Renault and won the opening round, then added six more wins, including three of the final four races. However, Lauda kept racking up the points, including five race wins. Lauda won the World Championship by half a point, courtesy of only half the points being awarded when the Monaco GP was stopped prematurely because of a heavy rainstorm when Prost was leading.

CHASING THE DREAM

Rubens Barrichello ran second behind Ayrton Senna in the 1993 European GP at Donington Park in his Jordan in only his third grand prix, a month short of his 21st birthday. Yet, for all this promise, Barrichello has now contested the most grands prix without clinching a World Championship, having raced 306 times by the end of the 2010 season.

Above **Chasing the dream:** Rubens Barrichello had passed 300 grands prix before contesting the 2010 Brazilian GP for Williams. This outing, his 305th, failed to yield a win. *Below* **If at first you don't succeed...:** Nigel Mansell had his first title in his sights in 1986, but had to wait to 1992 to claim it.

POINTS DON'T MEAN PRIZES

Rubens Barrichello has the dubious honour of not only the most grand prix starts to his name without winning the World Championship, he has also scored the most points, with a tally of 654. David Coulthard is the next runner-up in the points chart, with a career total of 535.

INSTANT IMPACT

Jacques Villeneuve and Lewis Hamilton are the only drivers to finish their debut seasons as World Championship runners-up. Villeneuve achieved this for Williams behind Damon Hill in 1996 and Hamilton for McLaren in 2007. However, both drivers did win the title a year later.

IF AT FIRST YOU DON'T SUCCEED...

Nigel Mansell would have been world champion in 1986 but for his blowout in the Adelaide finale that left him ranked second behind Alain Prost. But he persevered and was runner-up twice more, in 1987 and 1991, before it all came good and he finally landed his World Championship crown for Williams in 1992.

DRIVERS WITH MOST CAREER RACE WINS WITHOUT WINNING WORLD CHAMPIONSHIP

1	Stirling Moss	16
2	**David Coulthard**	13
3	Carlos Reutemann	12
4	Rubens Barrichello	11
=	Felipe Massa	11
6	Gerhard Berger	10
=	Ronnie Peterson	10
8	Jacky Ickx	8
9	Rene Arnoux	7
=	Juan Pablo Montoya	7

Above **Drivers with most career race wins without winning World Championship:** David Coulthard is second only to Stirling Moss for races won without a title. *Below* **Always the bridesmaid:** Stirling Moss won four races in the 1958 World Championship – including the British GP – but lost the title to Mike Hawthorn, who won but once.

SO YOUNG AND SO CLOSE

Lewis Hamilton was fresh-faced when he ended his 2007 F1 campaign one point short of the title, but Sebastian Vettel was almost six months younger still when he finished as runner-up to Jenson Button in 2009. He was just 22 years and 122 days old, but became the youngest ever world champion a year later.

IS SEVEN A LUCKY NUMBER?

Three drivers who became or had been world champion hold an unwanted record in that they managed to win the most races in a season, seven, without taking the title. Alain Prost did it in 1984 and 1988, Kimi Räikkönen in 2005 and Michael Schumacher in 2006.

ALWAYS THE BRIDESMAID

Stirling Moss will be remembered as the best driver never to have been world champion. Four times he finished as runner-up, three of those behind Juan Manuel Fangio, his one-time mentor at Mercedes. On the fourth occasion he lost out by a single point to Mike Hawthorn, despite winning more races that year. Alain Prost was also runner-up four times, but he could balance those against his four World Championships.

WINS

FERRARI TO THE FORE

Combine the fact that Ferrari has been racing in F1 for longer than any other marque (going back to the inaugural season in 1950) with the fact that the most garlanded winner, Michael Schumacher, scored the bulk of his 91 wins with them, and it's not surprising that it tops the charts for the most wins, with a tally of 215 wins by the end of 2010.

McLaren lags 46 wins behind, but it did fleetingly nose in front in the late 1990s before Schumacher and Ferrari dominated.

MR CONSISTENCY

Perhaps the most impressive of Michael Schumacher's many, many records is that once he started winning in 1992 he kept going, claiming at least one grand prix win in all of the next 14 World Championship seasons through to 2006, but he wasn't able to add any in his return in 2010.

13: UNLUCKY FOR EVERYONE ELSE

Michael Schumacher wasn't the sort of driver troubled by superstition. There were no habits such as always getting into the car from the same side or wearing odd boots (like Alexander Wurz), or a lucky pair of underpants or gloves (David Coulthard). But, it seems, 13 was a lucky number for him, as his record of 13 wins from 18 grands prix in 2004 gave him his seventh and final F1 title.

RULE BRITANNIA

Not only are British drivers the most successful in landing World Championships, they've also won the most grands prix. They have 208 wins shared between 19 of them, with Nigel Mansell at the top of the pile with 31. This is good only for fourth in the overall wins table, though, far behind Michael Schumacher's 91. That said, Britain's overall tally is 100 more than the next most successful country, Germany, with Brazil third on 101.

Right **Rule Britannia:** Nigel Mansell is one of 19 British drivers to have won a grand prix. *Below* **Mr Consistency:** Michael Schumacher gave Ferrari almost half of its record-breaking 210 wins, but Felipe Massa and Kimi Räikkönen carried on the habit for the Italian team, as they showed in the 2007 Brazilian GP.

ON A ROLL

If one win upsets a driver's rivals, just think what a string of wins does. King of the rolling wins is Alberto Ascari, who hit the most vivid of purple patches in 1952 when he won the Belgian GP and carried on winning through the next eight grands prix, with the last of these being the Belgian GP the following year. Not surprisingly, he was world champion both years. Even the great Michael Schumacher peaked at seven straight wins in 2004.

 ## EVERYONE HAS A GO

The 1982 season was extremely competitive as 11 drivers took at least one win in the 16 grands prix. Keke Rosberg ended the year as world champion ahead of Didier Pironi and John Watson (both of whom scored two wins), with Michele Alboreto, Rene Arnoux (two), Ello de Angelis, Niki Lauda (two), Riccardo Patrese, Nelson Piquet, Alain Prost (two) and Patrick Tambay also enjoying victories.

 ## KEEPING IT TO THEMSELVES

The opposite of sharing around wins is what happened in the 1950 and 1952 World Championship seasons, when only two drivers claimed victories. In 1950 it was Giuseppe Farina and Juan Manuel Fangio, with three each, and in 1952 just Piero Taruffi, once, and Alberto Ascari, six times, who were triumphant. (This doesn't include the standalone Indianapolis 500 that was then nominally part of the World Championship.)

 ## TOO GOOD TO BE A FLUKE

When a driver dominates, a lot of F1 fans point to the merits of the car. So, perhaps one of the best ways to prove that a driver's input is vital is to find the driver who has won for the most different teams. Step forward Stirling Moss, who won for five marques – Mercedes, Maserati, Vanwall, Cooper and Lotus. Juan Manuel Fangio and Alain Prost both won for four teams.

 ## HOME IS WHERE THE HEART IS

With a little help from having two grands prix held in Germany most years during his career, the inimitable Michael Schumacher holds the record for the most wins at a driver's home race, adding five wins in the European GP at the Nürburgring to his three in the German GP. Alain Prost recorded six wins in the French GP.

NO DISCERNIBLE PATTERN

The 1982 World Championship in which 11 drivers won grands prix also produced the longest run of different winning drivers. Riccardo Patrese's surprise win in the sixth round in Monaco triggered a sequence of wins for different drivers that ran through to Keke Rosberg's win in the 14th round in the Swiss GP. There's never been another year like it.

TOP 10 DRIVERS WITH MOST GRAND PRIX WINS

	Driver	Wins
1	**Michael Schumacher**	91
2	Alain Prost	51
3	Ayrton Senna	41
4	Nigel Mansell	31
5	Jackie Stewart	27
6	Fernando Alonso	26
7	Jim Clark	25
=	Niki Lauda	25
9	Juan Manuel Fangio	24
10	Nelson Piquet	23

Left **Top 10 drivers with most grand prix wins:** Michael Schumacher got used to lifting the winner's trophy, doing so 91 times in all. *Above* **No discernible pattern:** With his victory at Monaco in 1982, Riccardo Patrese started a historic run of nine grands prix with a different winner each time.

THE LAP THAT COUNTS

Jochen Rindt was an expert at leading the final lap rather than the first one, and he pulled off the trick to the greatest effect at Monaco in 1970 when he hunted down Jack Brabham and pressured him into a mistake at the first corner of the final lap. Poor Brabham was pipped in another last-lap changeover later that year at Brands Hatch, when again Rindt demoted him as he coasted to the finish line, out of fuel.

A WONDERFUL YEAR'S WORK

Six wins in any World Championship campaign is an impressive and seldom achieved tally. However, World Championships were considerably shorter in the early 1950s and Alberto Ascari's six wins in his first title-winning year for Ferrari, 1952, came from just seven grands prix, giving him a winning rate of 86 per cent – the best ever. Michael Schumacher's 13 wins from 18 races in 2004 represented a 72 per cent return.

FIRST IMPRESSIONS

Jacques Villeneuve and Lewis Hamilton share the record for the most grand prix wins in their maiden season of F1. Their tally is four apiece, with Villeneuve scoring the first of these with Williams on his fourth outing, at the Nürburgring, and Hamilton taking his McLaren past the chequered flag first at his sixth attempt, in Canada. Juan Manuel Fangio and Giuseppe Farina both won three grands prix in 1950, the inaugural year of the F1 World Championship.

DOMINANT PAIRINGS

Michael Schumacher led home Rubens Barrichello on 19 occasions when they raced together at Ferrari. When he had a particular year's World Championship in the bag, Michael would ease off and let Rubens through to head home giving another Ferrari one-two. He did this five times, although one of these was a fumble when he tried to stage a dead heat at Indianapolis in 2002 and failed.

Above **First impressions:** Not only did Lewis Hamilton claim four wins in his rookie season, 2007, but he could have been champion. *Below* **When overtaking is essential:** John Watson had every reason to smile on the podium at Long Beach in 1983 after he'd driven his McLaren through the field from 22nd to first.

WINNING NATION

Great Britain's drivers have the greatest aggregate total of grand prix wins, with 19 of them sharing a table-topping 213 victories. The first of these wins was by Mike Hawthorn, when his Ferrari edged out Juan Manuel Fangio's Maserati to win the French GP at Reims in 1953 by a second. Germany rank as runners-up, almost solely due to seven-time world champion Michael Schumacher's tally of 91 wins. Only five of his compatriots have added to the haul.

COMETH THE HOUR, COMETH THE MAN

There are 22 drivers who have won just one solitary grand prix. How did it all go so right just the once then never again? In the case of Jean-Pierre Beltoise, a former French motorcycle racing champion who showed immense promise, he won in extremely wet conditions at Monaco in 1972. His BRM lacked the regular power of the other cars on the grid, but the rain negated this disadvantage and he never again had the equipment to add to that tally.

WHEN OVERTAKING IS ESSENTIAL

With overtaking becoming increasingly difficult, the possibility of a driver advancing from the rear of the grid is becoming less likely. Therefore, John Watson's record, set at the 1983 US West GP at Long Beach, California, of winning from 22nd on the grid is probably guaranteed its place in the history books for ever. He also holds the record for the third best charge, from 17th to 1st at Detroit in 1982.

A CLOSE SHAVE

A driver's first win is usually a time of celebration and often of relief at having "got the monkey off their back". For John Watson at the 1975 Austrian GP at the Österreichring, it was also a time to meet his side of a wager with his team boss Roger Penske. For winning, Watson had to shave off his beard, and he has never sported one since.

 ## HIT THE GROUND RUNNING

Nigel Mansell enjoyed the best start to a season when he and his Williams-Renault FW14B won the first five grands prix in 1992. It could have been the first six but for a wheel weight coming loose at Monaco and his subsequent charge just failed to overhaul Ayrton Senna's McLaren.

Below **No one shall pass:** Jim Clark claims the first of his 13 wins from pole for Lotus at Aintree in 1962. *Bottom* **By the skin of his teeth:** Peter Gethin noses his BRM past Ronnie Peterson's March (25) for the closest grand prix finish ever.

BY THE SKIN OF HIS TEETH

A last-lap lead change in the Italian GP at Monza in 1971 produced the closest finish in F1 history. Peter Gethin nosed his BRM to the front of a five-car pack after a slipstreaming dash out of the final corner, doing his best to gain the stewards' confidence that he'd secured victory by punching the air ostentatiously as he crossed the line. His margin of victory was 0.01 seconds over March's Ronnie Peterson, with the first five covered by just 0.61 seconds.

 ## ...AND RELAX

You've beaten the conditions – foul weather, the track criss-crossed with streams – and you've certainly beaten the odds. In fact, you've just scored your first grand prix win. It's time to celebrate, punch the air with delight and… lose control, wiping the nose off your car. Welcome to the wild world of March's Vittorio Brambilla at the 1975 Austrian GP. It also proved to be the last victory for the man nicknamed the "Monza Gorilla".

NO ONE SHALL PASS

Ayrton Senna started from pole position 65 times and he made the most of them as he holds the record for leading the most grands prix from start to finish. He did this 19 times, with Jim Clark next on this list with 13, ahead of Michael Schumacher and Jackie Stewart on 11.

TOP 10 COUNTRIES WITH MOST GRAND PRIX WINS

1	Great Britain	213
2	Germany	113
3	Brazil	101
4	France	79
5	Finland	44
6	Italy	43
7	Austria	41
8	Argentina	38
9	Australia	32
10	Spain	26

STARTING WITH A BANG

Two drivers hold the almost unbelievable record of winning a grand prix on their World Championship debut. Giuseppe Farina achieved this in 1950, in the first ever World Championship (he went on to win the title), but the more significant achievement was by Giancarlo Baghetti. Having been promoted through the Ferrari ranks in their search for a young Italian driver, in 1961 he won two non-championship races and then won a slipstreamer by 0.1 secs from Dan Gurney on his World Championship debut in the French GP at Reims. He never won again. Since then, only Jacques Villeneuve has come close to the same achievement, finishing as runner-up in Australia in 1996.

⫸ TAKING THEIR TIME

In 2009 Mark Webber usurped Rubens Barrichello to become the holder of the record for the most grands prix contested before scoring a win. He had 130 races under his belt before he and his Red Bull triumphed at the Nürburgring. Barrichello's 2009 teammate, Jenson Button (113 starts before winning), ranks fourth in this list behind Jarno Trulli (119).

⫸ WHO'D HAVE THOUGHT IT?

Throughout F1 history there have been wins that have surprised everyone. Jo Bonnier's victory in the 1959 Dutch GP is a good example as no one thought that a BRM would ever win. Vittorio Brambilla's win in Austria in 1975 came as a shock as no one expected that the wild Italian would be the one to stay on the track in the wet. However, Giancarlo Baghetti's win on his World Championship debut in France in 1961 was the most surprising as he had to work his way forward from 13th to do it, and it required his teammates to retire to aid his progress.

⫸ WINNING BY A COUNTRY MILE

Jackie Stewart was always an exponent of "winning at the lowest speed possible". Risks weren't something he considered worthwhile but the policy paid off as he won 27 grands prix and three World Championships. Stewart also holds the record for the largest winning margin in F1 history–two laps. At the 1969 Spanish GP at Montjuich Park he won by 4.711 miles. Damon Hill also won by two laps in the 1995 Australian GP at Adelaide, but his winning margin was 4.698 miles.

Above **Taking their time:** Victory at last for Mark Webber at the Nürburgring in 2009 after 130 previous attempts *Below* **Starting with a bang:** Ferrari's Giancarlo Baghetti holds off Dan Gurney to win on his debut in the 1961 French GP at Reims.

SMALLEST WINNING MARGIN

Margin	Winner	Runner-up	GP	Year
0.010 sec	Peter Gethin	Ronnie Peterson	Italian	1971
0.011 sec	Rubens Barrichello	Michael Schumacher	US	2002
0.014 sec	Ayrton Senna	Nigel Mansell	Spanish	1986
0.050 sec	Elio de Angelis	Keke Rosberg	Austrian	1982
0.080 sec	Jackie Stewart	Jochen Rindt	Italian	1969
0.100 sec	Juan Manuel Fangio	Karl Kling	French	1954
0.100 sec	Giancarlo Baghetti	Dan Gurney	French	1961
0.174 sec	Michael Schumacher	Rubens Barrichello	Canadian	2000
0.182 sec*	Michael Schumacher	Rubens Barrichello	Austrian	2002
0.200 sec*	Stirling Moss	Juan Manuel Fangio	British	1955

* The win was donated to a teammate due to team orders or benevolence

Below **Winning by a country mile:** On a day of mistakes and unusual attrition, Damon Hill won the 1995 Australian GP by two laps. *Right* **Beat the clock:** Stirling Moss was in a class of his own in his Vanwall in the 1958 Portuguese GP, winning by more than five minutes.

BEAT THE CLOCK

In terms of time, rather than laps, Stirling Moss holds the record for the greatest margin of victory. He took the chequered flag with his Vanwall 5 mins and 12.75 secs clear of Mike Hawthorn in the Portuguese GP at Oporto in 1958. Hawthorn half spun on the final lap and Moss, not wanting to embarrass his title rival by lapping him, slowed to let him rejoin, as he himself ambled around his slowing-down lap.

⋙ TAKING ON SCHUEY'S MANTLE

When Sebastian Vettel scored his first victory at the 2008 Italian GP for Scuderia Toro Rosso, he became the first German driver other than a Schumacher (Ralf six, Michael 91) to win a grand prix since McLaren's Jochen Mass was first to the finish in the crash-shortened Spanish GP of 1975 at Montjuich Park.

⋙ A LITTLE HELP FROM YOUR FRIENDS

Shared wins were allowed until 1957, when a team's lead driver might realize that something was wrong with his car and commandeer one of his teammates' cars to complete the race. The points would be split between them. This happened three times for wins, and many more times for lower placings. Juan Manuel Fangio took over Luigi Fagioli's Alfa Romeo to win the 1951 French GP and did the same to Ferrari teammate Luigi Musso in Argentina in 1956.

⋙ LA BELLE FRANCE

Michael Schumacher seemed to have an affinity with the French GP, as he won the race on eight occasions. This is the most times that any driver has won any nation's grand prix. His first success in France came in 1994 at Magny-Cours and his last at the same circuit in 2006.

⋙ HE CERTAINLY TRIED

The unwanted record for the most grands prix without a win belongs to Andrea de Cesaris, who entered 214 races (208 starts) between 1980 and 1994. His best results were two second-place finishes in 1983.

⋙ THEY ARE ALL MINE

Fernando Alonso is the most famous Spanish Formula One racer, as he should be with two World Championships and several near misses. However, he alone carries their flag, as none of his compatriots have won a grand prix and his tally of 26 wins boosted Spain to 10th in the chart of winners by nation.

⋙ A HAT-TRICK OF HAT-TRICKS

A grand slam is when a driver starts from pole, leads every lap and sets the fastest lap en route to victory. Twenty drivers have achieved this, but three stand out for managing it three times in a single season: Alberto Ascari, Jim Clark and Nigel Mansell, and all did it in a world-championship-winning campaign. Ascari did it for Ferrari, in 1952, at Rouen-les-Essarts, the Nürburgring and Zandvoort. Clark was next in 1963, at Zandvoort, Reims and Mexico City. Mansell matched them at Kyalami, Catalunya and Silverstone for Williams in 1992.

POLE POSITIONS

 ## THE PERFECT SCORE

Winning from pole position and also setting the race's fastest lap is just a dream for all but a few. The driver who achieved this most recently was Sebastian Vettel for Red Bull Racing in the 2009 British GP. However, the ultimate is to achieve the grand slam – pole position, fastest lap and lead every lap. Fernando Alonso was the last driver to achieve this, when he drove an exemplary race for Ferrari in the 2010 Singapore GP. Jim Clark achieved the grand slam a record eight times.

 ## AS EASY AS ONE, TWO, THREE

Achieving pole position, setting the race's fastest lap and then winning the race shows a certain style, and guess who has achieved this clean sweep the most times? Yes, Michael Schumacher, on 22 occasions. Jim Clark is next, on 11, meaning that Clark achieved this feat close to one in every six grands prix he entered.

Above **Turn up, take pole:** Juan Manuel Fangio, shown here in 1950, achieved the greatest pole to race average, taking 29 from 51. *Below* **Lucky seven:** Ayrton Senna leads from pole for the last time at Imola, in 1994.

 ## TURN UP, TAKE POLE

With World Championships in the 1950s having fewer rounds it's hard for drivers from that decade to be at the top of any list, but Juan Manuel Fangio still ranks sixth in the all-time list of pole positions achieved. Fangio also has by far the best pole to race average. His 29 pole positions, from a total of 51 races started, equates to a 57 per cent ratio, with Jim Clark in second place on 46 per cent.

 ## HE WAS THE MAN

Michael Schumacher tops the list for the most pole positions achieved, but his pole to race ratio is nowhere near as good as Ayrton Senna's. The great Brazilian was really the man when it came to a pure, focused, banzai lap. The 1988 Monaco GP is a perfect example; Senna was on pole by 1.4 secs. His tally of 65 poles, just three fewer than Schumacher, gave him a 40 per cent hit rate compared to the German's 27 per cent.

 ## TOP 10 DRIVERS WITH MOST POLE POSITIONS

1	Michael Schumacher	68
2	Ayrton Senna	65
3	Jim Clark	33
=	Alain Prost	33
5	Nigel Mansell	32
6	Juan Manuel Fangio	29
7	Mika Hakkinen	26
8	Niki Lauda	24
=	Nelson Piquet	24
10	Fernando Alonso	20
=	Damon Hill	20

 ## NIGEL MANSELL'S GOLDEN YEAR

Armed with the dominant Renault-powered Williams FW14B, Nigel Mansell took pole after pole after pole in 1992. In all he claimed pole at 14 of the season's 16 grands prix, missing out only at the Canadian GP, where he lined up behind Ayrton Senna, and the Hungarian GP, where he started second behind teammate Patrese. Senna achieved 13 poles from 16 in both 1988 and 1989, as did Alain Prost in 1993.

LUCKY SEVEN

Ayrton Senna clearly loved Imola as he qualified on pole position there for seven years in a row between 1985 and 1991, three times for Lotus and four for McLaren. He put his Williams on pole there in 1994, in the race that was to be his last.

 ## DESIGNED TO FLY

Red Bull Racing technical chief Adrian Newey has long been called a design genius, and he must have done something right in shaping the Red Bull RB6 as the team's drivers Sebastian Vettel and Mark Webber claimed 15 of 2010's 19 pole positions. And you can't manage that without a car that handles…

 Left **Four in a row:** Stirling Moss (*right*) started from pole for the 1957 British GP and shared victory with Tony Brooks. *Below* **Starting from the front:** Michael Schumacher sets off from his 68th pole, at Magny-Cours in 2006. *Bottom* **A shooting star:** Sebastian Vettel scored the fourth of his five pole positions at Silverstone in 2009.

POLE AT THE FIRST ATTEMPT

The record books show that Mario Andretti (1968 US GP), Carlos Reutemann (1972 Argentinian GP) and Jacques Villeneuve (1996 Australian GP) all claimed pole on their first World Championship outing, but it was actually Andretti's second appearance for Lotus. He'd qualified 11th for the Italian GP but wasn't allowed to start as he'd raced in an IndyCar event at Indiana State Fairgrounds within 24 hours.

STARTING FROM THE FRONT

Michael Schumacher edges out Ayrton Senna at the top of the all-time number of pole positions table by three, but his advantage is greater when front-row starting positions are considered. Schumacher qualified first or second 115 times, 28 more than Senna. Alain Prost is one behind the Brazilian.

IT'S SENNA AGAIN

Ayrton Senna emphasized his outstanding ability to qualify faster than anyone else when he claimed pole position for a record eight grands prix in a row in his McLaren. The run started at the 1988 Spanish GP and continued through to the 1989 US GP at Phoenix.

FOUR IN A ROW

British fans had every reason to expect a home driver to be on pole at the British GP in the 1950s and 1960s. Stirling Moss was on pole for four straight years, 1955–58, as the race alternated between Aintree and Silverstone. Then Jim Clark matched that feat between 1962–65, at Aintree, twice at Silverstone and Brands Hatch. The Scottish Lotus driver didn't manage pole in 1966, but was at the front of the grid in 1967.

A FRENCH AFFAIR

Jim Clark qualified his Lotus on pole position for the French GP four years straight from 1962–65 (matching his achievement at the British GP). He achieved this on three markedly different circuits – Rouen-les-Essarts (twice), Reims and Clermont-Ferrand.

THERE'S NO PLACE LIKE HOME

Ayrton Senna seemed fated never to win his home grand prix, although he finally managed it on his eighth attempt in 1991. But setting pole in Brazil came to him far more easily and he holds the record for the most number of times that a driver has qualified on pole for his home race. He did so six times, in 1986, from 1988 to 1991 inclusive and in 1994. The first three came at Rio de Janeiro's Jacarepagua circuit and the others at Interlagos in his home city of São Paulo.

A SHOOTING STAR

||||||||||||||||||||||||||||||||||||||||||||||

Sebastian Vettel holds the record for being the youngest pole-sitter, when he secured his place at the front of the grid at the 2008 Italian GP at the age of 21 years and 73 days. The previous holder of this record was Fernando Alonso, who outqualified the rest of the pack at the 2003 Malaysian GP at the age of 21 years and 236 days.

FASTEST LAPS

FASTER, FASTER

Michael Schumacher's all-round excellence is shown by the fact that he doesn't just top the record tables in race wins, pole positions, laps led and points scored, he also occupies first place for the most fastest laps set too, a career total of 75. He holds the record by some margin, as the second-placed driver on the list, Alain Prost, achieved the feat 41 times.

HITTING DOUBLE FIGURES

Michael Schumacher and Kimi Räikkönen both gave Ferrari a return of 10 fastest laps in a single season, with the German achieving this impressive tally in 2004 and the Finn doing the same in 2008, both from 18 starts. Räikkönen also claimed 10 fastest laps for McLaren in 2005, although this percentage is slightly lower because there were 19 grands prix that season.

Below **Ascari's dominance:** Alberto Ascari drove his Ferrari to the fastest lap in every grand prix he contested in 1952. *Above* **Faster, faster:** Renault's Alain Prost, leading early in the Dutch Grand Prix at Zandvoort in 1982, achieved fastest laps for Renault, McLaren, Ferrari and Williams.

TOP 10 FASTEST LAPS BY DRIVER NATIONALITY

1	Great Britain	191
2	Germany	106
3	France	86
4	Brazil	84
5	Finland	65
6	Italy	51
7	Austria	49
8	Argentina	37
9	Australia	31
10	USA	25

ASCARI'S DOMINANCE

Alberto Ascari's near total dominance of the 1952 World Championship left him with a tally of six fastest laps from seven rounds as he raced to the title for Ferrari. The Indianapolis 500 was also a round of the World Championship then, but he, like other F1 drivers, gave it a miss. So, his tally was even better than the six from eight that some record books show.

LOVING THE SMOOTH

David Coulthard demonstrated an affinity for the smooth surface and twisting nature of Magny-Cours as he set the fastest lap of the race there five years in succession for McLaren between 1998 and 2002, albeit coming away as the winner on just one of those occasions, in 2000.

NO ONE'S AN EXPERT

The Jarama circuit outside Madrid hosted nine Spanish GPs between 1968 and 1991, but not one driver was able to take the fastest lap more than once. A record nine different drivers set fastest lap times, starting with Matra's Jean-Pierre Beltoise in 1968 and ending with Williams's reigning world champion Alan Jones in 1981. Rival Spanish circuit Jerez ended up with a similar record, with seven drivers setting fastest laps there on F1's seven visits.

WAS IT REALLY?

Every now and again a fastest lap is set by a driver that no one had expected to be so fast. This often happens when a driver with nothing to lose pits for fresh tyres. The most notorious example was Masahiro Hasemi setting the fastest lap on his F1 debut in the 1976 Japanese GP. There were mitigating circumstances in that he knew Fuji Speedway well and it was F1's first visit. Furthermore, it was incredibly wet and his Kojima chassis was on Dunlop wets that were superior to the Goodyears used by the regulars, but still…

AN HONOUR, BUT…

Kimi Räikkönen's 10 fastest laps in 2008 – six of them in succession – reflected well on his ability, but this was at a time of refuelling pit stops and it actually showed his ambition to impress rather than his Ferrari's speed over a race distance, and he ended the year third overall despite his 55.55 per cent strike rate. Jim Clark hit an identical figure for Lotus in 1962, also without becoming world champion.

START AS THEY MEAN TO GO ON

After the inaugural season of 1950, just three drivers have set a fastest lap on their F1 debut. Masahiro Hasemi's amazing 1976 Japanese GP was the first, and it was followed by Jacques Villeneuve in the 1996 opener in Australia. Only Nico Roseberg, at Bahrain in 2006, has achieved a debut fastest lap since then.

NATIONAL PRIDE

Michael Schumacher is way out in front in the all-time list of drivers who have set the most fastest laps, but as none of his compatriots has even reached double figures it's not surprising that British drivers push the Germans into second place in the overall nationality list of fastest laps. The British have a combined tally of 185 fastest laps to Germany's 103, with French drivers third on 86.

KEEPING IT ALL GOING

Alberto Ascari set six fastest laps in seven rounds in 1952 – he missed the first race, in Switzerland, so he could compete in the Indianapolis 500 (but didn't set the fastest lap there) – and kept his run going into the 1953 campaign, adding a seventh consecutive fastest lap at the season-opening Argentinian GP. His run was broken by his Ferrari teammate Luigi Villoresi at the Dutch GP.

TOP 10 DRIVERS WHO HAVE SET MOST FASTEST LAPS

1	**Michael Schumacher**	75
2	Alain Prost	41
3	Kimi Räikkönen	35
4	Nigel Mansell	30
5	Jim Clark	28
6	Mika Hakkinen	25
7	Niki Lauda	24
8	Juan Manuel Fangio	23
=	Nelson Piquet	23
10	Gerhard Berger	21

Above **Top 10 drivers who have set most fastest laps:** Michael Schumacher set the first of his 75 fastest laps for Benetton in the 1992 Belgian GP. *Below* **An honour, but…:** Ferrari's Kimi Räikkönen set the most fastest laps in 2008, but ended the year third overall.

POINTS

QUICK NICK, BUT NO WINS

||||||||||||||||||||||||||||||||||||

Nick Heidfeld has twice come close to scoring his first grand prix win, most recently in the wet/dry 2009 Malaysian GP, but he has never ascended to the top step of the podium despite notching up a career tally of 225 points by the end of 2010. Martin Brundle is next on the all-time list of points scored without taking a win, with a tally of 98, thus emphasizing Heidfeld's perseverance.

ALMOST 10 SCORE SCORES

Michael Schumacher had the most remarkable career, almost all of which was spent in competitive cars, and proof of this is not just in his number of wins but in the fact that he was in the points in almost every race, starting with his second outing in 1991, when he moved from Jordan to Benetton. He went on to score in 202 of his 269 starts, achieving an average of 5.38 points per start, pipping Juan Manuel Fangio's 5.34.

KEEP ON SCORING

Yet another of Michael Schumacher's records is that of consecutive point-scoring drives. His best run is scoring points in 24 grands prix in a row, from the 2001 Hungarian GP to the 2003 Malaysian GP, during which time he won two drivers' titles and scored 191 points, which is a handful more than Stirling Moss managed in his entire F1 career.

ONCE AND ONCE ONLY

Scoring their first World Championship point is a breakthrough moment for any Formula 1 driver. However, 21 have taken that first point, either for fastest lap in the 1950s, or for sixth place from 1960–2002, then eighth from 2003–09 and for 10th from 2010, and yet never scored again. Lella Lombardi would have joined them, but her point for sixth in the 1975 Spanish GP was halved as the race was stopped before 60 per cent of the planned distance had been covered.

FROM CHAMPION TO SHORT RATIONS

America's first F1 world champion, Phil Hill, had a rapid fall from grace after his 1961 World Championship with Ferrari. Just over a year after winning the title he made a terrible mistake and followed some of Ferrari's staff to ATS, a new Italian team that proved to be a disaster. So, shortly after he peaked, he plummeted and ended up with a career tally of 98 points, the fewest for a world champion.

Right **From champion to short rations:** Phil Hill raced a red car in 1963, but it was an ATS not a Ferrari. *Below* **Quick Nick, but no wins:** Sauber's Nick Heidfeld scored 225 points in his 11-year Formula One career, but eight second places, including at Malaysia in 2009, were his best-ever finishes.

TOP 10 DRIVERS WITH MOST GRAND PRIX POINTS

1	Michael Schumacher	1,441
2	Fernando Alonso	829
3	**Alain Prost**	798.5
4	Rubens Barrichello	654
5	Ayrton Senna	614
6	Kimi Räikkönen	579
7	Jenson Button	541
8	David Coulthard	535
9	Lewis Hamilton	496
10	Nelson Piquet	489.5

Figures are gross, i.e. including scores that were later dropped

 POINTS FOR ALL

Even though points were allocated to only the first six finishers back in 1989, a record 29 different drivers made it on to the scoreboard that year: from world champion Alain Prost on 76, down to Philippe Alliot, Olivier Grouillard, Luis Perez Sala and Gabriele Tarquini on one point apiece. It was an incredible year, as 39 cars turned up for most races and a system of pre-qualifying had to be used to clear out the slowest before qualifying.

 ADD THEM TOGETHER

Since British drivers hold the highest cumulative tally of wins, it comes as no surprise that British drivers also hold the record for the most combined points scored. Up to the end of 2009, British drivers had scored 4,703.28 points, with Germany second on 2,560.5, Brazil third on 2,463 and France fourth on 2,326.47. Perhaps most impressive is Finland's tally of 1,306.5 points, despite having ever had only six drivers compete in F1.

 SHARED BY MANY

A total of 281 drivers have scored points in the World Championship since 1950 (plus 33 others who scored in the nominally included Indianapolis 500), split between 33 nationalities, with Great Britain producing the most point-scoring drivers – 59. The Italians have a total of 45 drivers in the points, the French 39 and the Germans 20.

 JUST WHAT'S THE POINT?

Prior to the start of the 2009 season, Luca Badoer held an unwanted record: after 49 races he had not scored a single point. He hoped to put a stop to the record getting any worse when he stood in at Ferrari for the injured Felipe Massa midway through the season. Unfortunately he didn't score, and he has extended that record to 51 races without a point. The closest he has come to a points finish was in the 1999 European GP, when he had to retire his Minardi while in fourth place with just 12 laps to go.

 SCORING A CENTURY FIRST TIME OUT

One hundred points is an impressive points tally for any driver in a World Championship campaign. However, Lewis Hamilton surpassed this figure in his maiden F1 season, amassing a superb 109 points for McLaren. No other rookie has ever scored as many.

 GIVEN A HELPING HAND

The change of the World Championship points system to boost a win from 10 points in 2009 to 25 in 2010, with points being awarded all the way down to the 10th place finisher, had a major effect on the table for the all-time top 10 points scorers, with Fernando Alonso vaulting from sixth to second and Jenson Button and Lewis Hamilton moving onto the table for the first time.

 **GAPING CHASM**

The biggest points gap between a world champion and the runner-up was the 67-point advantage that Michael Schumacher had over his Ferrari teammate, Rubens Barrichello, in 2002.

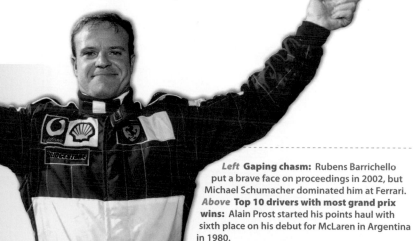

Left **Gaping chasm:** Rubens Barrichello put a brave face on proceedings in 2002, but Michael Schumacher dominated him at Ferrari. *Above* **Top 10 drivers with most grand prix wins:** Alain Prost started his points haul with sixth place on his debut for McLaren in Argentina in 1980.

CAREER DURATION

OLD FATHER TIME

Graham Hill held the record for the longest F1 career in terms of the number of years between his first race – the 1958 Monaco GP – and his last, in Brazil in 1975. Hill's F1 career span was 16 years and 253 days. However, Rubens Barrichello broke that record when he raced for Williams in 2010. The Brazilian had completed 17 years and 245 days as an active F1 driver by the end of the 2010 season.

EVER YOUNGER

Rubens Barrichello is very much the World Championship's old-timer now, when he embarks on his 19th F1 campaign in 2011 (he'll be 39 in May). However, he will still only be the same age that Graham Hill was when he completed his 10th season. Then again, Hill didn't pass his

Below **Old father time:** Graham Hill raced in Formula One for just short of 17 years. *Bottom* **Silver-haired flier:** Luigi Fagioli was still with Alfa Romeo 18 years after joining it when he raced to his final win in 1951.

driving test to drive on the road until he was 24 and actually did extremely well to get to F1 by the time he was 29.

NEVER GIVE UP!

Some drivers just never want to give up. Witness the haste with which the 40-year-old Michael Schumacher jumped at the chance to stand in for the injured Felipe Massa midway through 2009, three years after retiring, then he made his return in 2010. This is nothing compared to Jan Lammers, who returned to F1 in 1992 at the age of 36 after a break of 10 years and 114 days. He is still racing.

LOOKING DOWN FROM ABOVE

All drivers get a kick out of standing on the podium after a race, having finished first, second or third. The thrill is still as great as ever for Rubens Barrichello, who holds the record for the longest spell between his first podium place – at the 1994 Pacific GP – and his most recent appearance at the 2009 Italian GP. His record spans 15 years and 149 days.

SILVER-HAIRED FLIER

Racer Luigi Fagioli showed that staying power is rewarded. Fagioli raced for Alfa Romeo in 1933, and was still with the team in 1951 when he took his one win in the World Championship, 22 days past his 53rd birthday, making him the oldest person to win an F1 race. The victory came in strange circumstances as he was pulled out of his car when he pitted and was forced to hand it over to team leader Juan Manuel Fangio whose car was having mechanical difficulties. Fangio went on to win, but Fagioli was so unhappy, despite being credited with the win (shared with Fangio), that he quit.

TRIED AND TESTED

Michael Schumacher clearly believed in sticking with a winning formula, as his stay with Ferrari was the longest of any driver with one team in F1 history. He turned out for the team in 179 grands prix in 11 seasons between 1996 and 2006. And Schumacher's total would have been higher still, except for the fact that he missed six races in 1999 after breaking a leg in the British GP at Silverstone.

BLINK AND YOU MISSED IT

Marco Apicella was a decent driver, so it's odd that the Italian's spell in F1 remains the shortest on record. He had one crack at F1, with the Jordan team after Thierry Boutsen had been dropped, in his home race at Monza in 1993. He qualified 23rd out of 26 and, unfortunately, was unable to avoid the melee into the first chicane on the opening lap. His distance covered as an F1 racer was around ½ mile.

EXCELLENCE OVER A DECADE AND MORE

Michael Schumacher holds the record for the most years between his first grand prix victory and his last – 14 years and 32 days. This was between the 1992 Belgian GP at Spa-Francorchamps for Benetton and the 2006 Chinese GP at Shanghai for Ferrari.

F1: IT'S A CAREER

Graham Hill and Rubens Barrichello are the faces of longevity on the driving front, but their career spans are short next to the number of years put in by those out of the cockpit. Bernie Ecclestone has clocked up 54 years – from his first appearance as a driver-manager to his role as F1's ringmaster.

PAYBACK TIME

Alex Wurz's lengthy period as a test driver was rewarded when he subbed for McLaren in the 2005 San Marino GP at Imola. He was standing in for the injured Juan Pablo Montoya, and he came away with third place. This gave him the record for the longest period of time between podium places, at 7 years and 313 days. However, he didn't get to enjoy his moment in the sun this time as he was promoted to third after the podium ceremony had taken place because Jenson Button was subsequently disqualified.

A PREGNANT PAUSE

Riccardo Patrese scored six wins in his lengthy F1 career, but perhaps the most remarkable thing about them is the gap between his second win, for Brabham in the season-closing 1983 South African GP, and his third win in the 1990 San Marino GP at Imola for Williams, a record 6 years and 210 days later.

Left **Payback time:** Alex Wurz spent years as a test driver before returning to racing in 2005 and finishing third at Imola. *Above* **A pregnant pause:** The 1983 South African GP was Riccardo Patrese's second win, but it would be more than six years before he claimed a third victory.

TOP 10 LONGEST SERVERS

1	Bernie Ecclestone (1957–)	54 years
2	Tyler Alxander (1966–2009)	44 years
=	Ron Dennis (1966–2009)	44 years
4	Herbie Blash (1968–)	43 years
5	Frank Williams (1969–)	42 years
6	Jo Ramirez (1961–2001)	41 years
=	Giampaolo Dallara (1970–)	41 years
8	Max Mosley (1970–2009)	40 years
9	Eric Broadley (1960–1997)	38 years
=	Luca di Montezemolo (1973–)	38 years

YOUNGEST AND OLDEST

YOUNG AND KEEN

The youngest driver to compete in F1 is the Spaniard Jaime Alguersuari, who lowered the mark at the 2009 Hungarian GP driving for Toro Rosso at 19 years and 125 days. He beat Mike Thackwell's long-standing record of competing at the age of 19 years and 182 days at the 1980 Canadian GP. However, Thackwell's record was not universally recognized as he was involved in a first-lap crash and the race restarted without him.

AFTER YOU, YOUNG SIR

The youngest driver to lead a grand prix is Sebastian Vettel, who led the 2007 Japanese GP during a pit-stop sequence when racing for Toro Rosso. He was just 20 years and 89 days old. Later in the race he showed the impetuousness of youth when he took out Red Bull's Mark Webber when circulating behind the safety car, which put an end to the race for both drivers.

RACING IS ONE THING...

Some drivers get the lucky break and make it to F1 while still in their teens, but the next step up to getting a drive that offers the chance to win a grand prix is quite another thing. So Sebastian Vettel's record for being the youngest winner at just 21 years and 73 days is a remarkable one. His victory came in the 2008 Italian GP while driving for Toro Rosso.

Left **Young and keen:** Mike Thackwell was F1's youngest starter for almost 30 years but he never got the credit.
Right **From fresh-faced to veteran:** Sebastian Vettel beat Lewis Hamilton's record in 2010 to become the youngest ever F1 World Champion.

A WEALTH OF EXPERIENCE

Luigi Fagioli was just short of 37 when he scored his second to last grand prix win, for Mercedes at Monaco in 1935. So, it must have been for his experience that he was added to Alfa Romeo's line-up at the start of the first World Championship in 1950, in which he ranked third overall. In his one race in 1951, at the French GP, he was forced out of his car mid-race as team leader Juan Manuel Fangio's car had mechanical difficulties. They shared the win. Luigi was aged 53 years and 22 days. Giuseppe Farina was next oldest when he won in Germany in 1953, at 46 years and 276 days.

DELIVERING UNDER PRESSURE

Qualifying has always been an exacting element of a grand prix meeting, and it takes many drivers years to learn how to squeeze the maximum from themselves and their cars without pushing just that little bit too hard. The mercurial Sebastian Vettel is the youngest ever pole-sitter, being just 21 years and 72 days when he took first place on the grid at the 2008 Italian GP. Ferrari's Giuseppe Farina is the oldest pole-sitter, aged 47 years and 79 days at the 1954 Argentinian GP.

FROM FRESH-FACED TO VETERAN

The inaugural winner of the World Championship in 1950, Giuseppe Farina, was a couple of months short of his 44th birthday. Juan Manuel Fangio topped that, taking his final title in 1957 at 46 years and 41 days, making him the oldest ever World Championship winner. At the other end of the scale, in 2006, Fernando Alonso – at 24 years and 58 days – broke Emerson Fittipaldi's record from 1972 to become the youngest champion. Two years later Lewis Hamilton won the title aged 23 years and 300 days, but his record fell to Sebastian Vettel, aged 23 years and 134 days, in 2010.

10 YOUNGEST DRIVERS IN F1

	Name	Team	GP	Year	Age
1	Jaime Alguersuari	Toro Rosso	Hungarian	2009	19 years 125 days
2	Mike Thackwell	Tyrrell	Canadian	1980	19 years 182 days
3	Ricardo Rodriguez	Ferrari	Italian	1961	19 years 208 days
4	Fernando Alonso	Minardi	Australian	2001	19 years 218 days
5	Esteban Tuero	Minardi	Australian	1998	19 years 320 days
6	Chris Amon	Lola	Belgian	1963	19 years 324 days
7	Sebastian Vettel	BMW Sauber	US	2007	19 years 348 days
8	Jenson Button	Williams	Australian	2000	20 years 52 days
=	Eddie Cheever	Theodore	South African	1978	20 years 52 days
10	Tarso Marques	Minardi	Brazilian	1996	20 years 72 days

IF YOU'RE GOOD ENOUGH, YOU'RE READY

Nico Rosberg delighted his world champion father Keke on his grand prix debut for Williams at the 2006 Bahrain GP. He set the fastest lap and became the youngest driver ever to achieve this, at just 20 years and 258 days, beating Fernando Alonso's previous record by more than a year. The great Juan Manuel Fangio is the oldest, aged 46 years and 209 days, when he was swiftest in a Maserati in the 1958 Argentinian GP.

STILL A TEENAGER

Sebastian Vettel was still telling friends what he would like for his 20th birthday when he became the youngest driver ever to score a World Championship point at 19 years and 348 days. His achievement for BMW Sauber in the 2007 US GP came when he was 83 days younger than Jenson Button, the previous record holder. Philippe Etancelin is the oldest, at 53 years and 249 days, when he finished fifth in his Lago Talbot in the 1950 Italian GP.

10 OLDEST DRIVERS IN F1

	Name	Team	GP	Year	Age
1	Eitel Cantoni	Maserati	Italian	1952	55 years 337 days
2	Louis Chiron	Lancia	Monaco	1955	55 years 292 days
3	Philippe Etancelin	Maserati	French	1952	55 years 190 days
4	Arthur Legat	Veritas	Belgian	1953	54 years 232 days
5	Luigi Fagioli	Alfa Romeo	French	1951	53 years 21 days
6	Adolf Brudes	Veritas	German	1952	52 years 292 days
7	Hans Stuck	AFM	Italian	1953	52 years 260 days
8	Bill Aston	Aston	German	1952	52 years 127 days
9	Clemente Biondetti	Ferrari	Italian	1950	52 years 15 days
10	Louis Rosier	Maserati	German	1956	50 years 273 days

DON'T THEY ALL LOOK YOUNG?

The youngest, most fresh-faced trio to appear on the podium was at the 2008 Italian GP when Sebastian Vettel, Heikki Kovalainen and Robert Kubica finished first, second and third respectively. The trio had an average age of just 23 years and 350 days.

Above **Don't they all look young?:** Sebastian Vettel heads to his first win and the youngest ever podium grouping at Monza in 2008. *Below* **From another century:** Being aged 50 didn't appear to slow Louis Chiron as he raced to third place in his native Monaco in 1950. Alberto Ascari, behind, would go on to finish second.

FROM ANOTHER CENTURY

Apart from Luigi Fagioli, Louis Chiron is the only other driver over 50 to step up on to the podium. He was aged 50 years and 289 days when he finished third for Maserati in his hometown of Monaco in 1950. Both drivers were born in the 19th century.

RACE STARTS

CHOPPING AND CHANGING

Jo Bonnier and Johnny Claes share the record for driving for the most teams in a World Championship season – four. Claes turned out for Gordini, Ecurie Belge, HWM and Vickomtesse de Walckiers in 1952. Bonnier raced for his own team, Giorgio Scarlatti's, Scuderia Centro Sud and BRM in 1958.

Above **The wrong motto:** Jacques Villeneuve had a torrid time in BAR's much-trumpeted maiden season in 1999. *Below* **F1's centurions:** Rubens Barrichello rounds the La Source hairpin at Spa in 2010 during his 300th grand prix.

I'VE BEEN HERE BEFORE

Seven-time world champion Michael Schumacher has led no fewer than 141 grands prix for a minimum of one lap; this is far more than any other driver in F1 history. Ayrton Senna is next on the list, albeit way behind on 86 races led, and this is two more than the 84 achieved by his arch-rival, and sometime teammate, Alain Prost.

THE WRONG MOTTO

BAR was asking for trouble when the team was launched with the motto "A tradition of excellence". Firstly, it had no tradition. Secondly, its lead driver Jacques Villeneuve's run of retirements in the first 11 grands prix of the team's maiden season in 1999 set a record that is anything but excellent.

A FLYING START

Two drivers, Tiago Monteiro and Heikki Kovalainen, share the record for the most consecutive races finished from the first race of their F1 careers – 16 grands prix. Monteiro achieved it driving for Jordan in 2005, and Kovalainen repeated the feat as a member of the Renault team two years later.

F1'S CENTURIONS

The first driver to contest 100 grands prix was Jack Brabham, driving for his own team, at the 1968 Dutch GP. The first to break the 200 grands prix barrier was Williams racer Ricardo Patrese, at the British GP in 1990. In 2010 Brazil's Rubens Barrichello duly became the first driver to contest 300 grands prix, achieving it at the Belgian GP.

MAKING IT TO THE END

Nick Heidfeld's record run of 33 consecutive finishes includes all 18 grands prix in the 2008 season. However, he is matched in making 18 finishes in a single year by Portuguese driver Tiago Monteiro. Monteiro achieved this tally for Jordan in his rookie season in 2005, failing to finish only once, at the Brazilian GP, the 17th of that year's 19 races.

STARTING AND FINISHING

Nick Heidfeld is often considered unremarkable as he has tended to operate under the radar, starting neither at the front nor the back of the grid, but usually in with the pack. The German, however, does own one remarkable record. From the 2007 Chinese GP until the 2009 Singapore GP, Heidfeld achieved 33 consecutive finishes. Heidfeld's exceptional run came to an end when his BMW Sauber was hit by Adrian Sutil and he was forced to retire.

A NATIONAL SPORT

British drivers have the most appearances in grands prix. In total, 143 have qualified and raced. The next most prodigious country in getting its drivers on to an F1 grid is Italy, with 84 drivers, then France with 67 and 47 from the USA.

MANY AND FEW

In 1952 a mind-boggling total of 75 drivers contested the seven grands prix that season. In 2008, just 22 drivers went head-to-head in 18 grands prix.

FIRST ON THE START LINE

British drivers have between them racked up a table-topping 3,393 grand prix starts since the World Championship began at Silverstone in 1950. Italy's drivers are next on the all-time starts list with 2,884.

36 AND RISING

By the end of the 2010 Formula 1 World Championship, drivers from 36 nations have taken part since its inception in 1950. Over those 61 seasons, there have been drivers from all of the world's continents, apart from Antarctica.

PODIUMS, BUT NO WINS

Despite starting 174 F1 races across 11 seasons, from 2000 to 2010, Nick Heidfeld has still to claim a grand prix victory. He did clock up another second place at the Malaysian GP in 2009 to bring his tally of podiums to 12, without taking a win. The German driver also equalled the record for podiums without a win, set by Stefan Johansson between 1985 and 1989.

Above **Making it to the end:** Tiago Monteiro claims third at Indy in a remarkable maiden season. *Below* **Podiums, but no wins:** Nick Heidfeld's record run of 33 finishes in a row ended at Singapore in 2009. *Bottom* **Top 10 drivers with most GP starts:** Rubens Barrichello passed Riccardo Patrese's record in 2008.

TOP 10 DRIVERS WITH MOST GP STARTS

1	**Rubens Barrichello**	306
2	Michael Schumacher	269
3	Riccardo Patrese	256
4	David Coulthard	247
5	Jarno Trulli	238
6	Giancarlo Fisichella	231
7	Gerhard Berger	210
8	Andrea de Cesaris	208
9	Nelson Piquet	204
10	Jean Alesi	201

 ## CLOSE, BUT NO CIGAR

Gabriele Tarquini holds the unenviable record of the most grand prix appearances that didn't result in a start. Forty times he turned up then failed to qualify. This was the price he paid for driving for uncompetitive teams such as Coloni and AGS in the late 1980s, when 39 cars fought for 26 grid spots and a pre-qualifying session was necessary to decide which were even worthy of a chance to qualify. Luckily, he qualified on 38 other occasions.

 ## HIGHEST WIN RATE

Juan Manuel Fangio won 24 times from 51 starts to give him a record win rate of 0.471. Second on the list is Alberto Ascari, who dominated for Ferrari in the early 1950s and ended up with a rate of 0.419 after winning 13 of his 31 races. Michael Schumacher's tally of 91 wins is spread across 268 grands prix, a strike rate of 0.338. Jim Clark ranks fourth and would certainly have ranked higher but for his Lotus often suffering from mechanical problems.

 ## BANG, SPLUTTER, PHUT!

So promising early in his career, it all started to go wrong for Ivan Capelli when he retired from the 1990 Italian GP. He retired his Leyton House from the next 15 grands prix, making this the longest run of retirements in F1 history.

 ## NOT FOR WANT OF TRYING

Italian driver Andrea de Cesaris holds the record for the most grands prix contested without a win. In all, his F1 career stretched from 1980 (with Alfa Romeo) to 1994 (with Sauber), yet he did not produce one win from his 208 starts. His best results were a pair of second-place finishes in 1983.

 ## WHAT'S A CHEQUERED FLAG?

From his 208 starts, Andrea de Cesaris failed to reach the finish of the race 137 times. There were certainly numerous mechanical failures when he raced for Alfa Romeo in the early 1980s, but he was equally responsible as there were many crashes too. Compatriot Riccardo Patrese clocked up 130 retirements from his 256 starts, but at least he scored six wins.

 ## WELL, HE TRIED...

Claudio Langes seldom sported a smile in the paddock and his one and only campaign in F1, in 1990, gave him every reason to look forlorn. The Italian had

Above **Bang, splutter, phut!:** Ivan Capelli and Leyton House turned retiring into an art form, as evidenced by the shower of sparks at Monaco in 1990. *Below* **How not to do it:** Andrea de Cesaris retired his Brabham from all 16 grands prix in 1987.

stepped up from F3000 to drive for the EuroBrun Racing team. But the car was not up to scratch and he failed to pre-qualify for all 14 races he entered. And that was the end of his F1 career.

 ## NEW SEASON, NEW TEAM

Chris Amon is described as the best driver never to win a grand prix. One look at his F1 career shows that he wasn't worried about changing teams to chase his dream, as he raced for 12: Reg Parnell Racing, Ian Raby Racing, Cooper, his own team, Ferrari, March, Matra, Tecno, Tyrrell, BRM, Ensign and Walter Wolf Racing. In total he drove 13 different makes of car. Andrea de Cesaris, Stefan Johansson, Stirling Moss and Maurice Trintignant raced 10.

HOW NOT TO DO IT

Andrea de Cesaris retired from all 16 grands prix in 1987 while racing for Brabham; a record for F1's hall of shame. He was actually running third in Monaco, but was stationary when the chequered flag fell, his car having run out of fuel; and he was in eighth place in the Adelaide season finale, but spun off with four laps to go.

THE RISKIEST LAP

All the efforts exerted to develop a car through practice and then to qualify it as far up the grid as possible can come to naught on the opening lap, when the cars are racing at their closest. Take the 1978 Italian GP, the worst ever example of wastage, as 10 cars were eliminated before they had reached the first corner. Sadly, Lotus ace Ronnie Peterson died of his injuries.

TRY, TRY AND TRY AGAIN

While Nick Heidfeld of Germany holds the record for the most starts without a win by a driver (174), Arrows hold the team record. Founded by Jackie Oliver in 1978, the British-based team took part in 383 grands prix without achieving a victory. Arrows ran out of money and bowed out of F1 with five races remaining in the 2002 season.

TOP 10 TEAMS WITH MOST STARTS

1	Ferrari	812
2	McLaren	685
3	Williams	604
4	Lotus	509
5	Toro Rosso (née Minardi)	430
6	Tyrrell	418
7	Prost (née Ligier)	409
8	Brabham	394
9	Arrows	383
10	Force India (née Jordan – Midland – Spyker)	339

MICHAEL LOVES FERRARI

Michael Schumacher made Ferrari a team to fear again in 1996 when he shook it by the scruff of its neck with the Scuderia CEO Jean Todt. Their success triggered the longest stay any driver has had with a team in F1 history and stretched to 201 starts before Schumacher retired at the end of 2006. It would have been six more had he not broken a leg at the 1999 British GP. David Coulthard has the next longest stay, racing 150 times for McLaren.

Below **Michael loves Ferrari:** Jean Todt (left) and Michael Schumacher returned Ferrari to the top. *Below* **That's how to do it!:** Jody Scheckter gave Wolf a dream start by winning the 1977 season-opener in Argentina.

THAT'S HOW TO DO IT!

Jody Scheckter was enticed by Canadian industrialist Walter Wolf to join his new team, Wolf, for 1977. The move paid off immediately as Scheckter won the first race of the season in Argentina and went on to win two more. No team has made such an instant impact since. (Some might suggest Brawn GP in 2009, but this team was developed from Honda Racing, and didn't start from scratch.)

MISCELLANEOUS DRIVER RECORDS

THE DARKEST DAYS

Death was a regular feature of F1 in the early years, with driver safety scarcely considered in the 1950s. Six drivers died at the wheel in both 1957 and 1958, with five being killed in other events and one in F1 testing in 1957. In 1958, Luigi Musso died in the French GP, Peter Collins in the German GP and Stuart Lewis-Evans from burns received in the Moroccan GP, with three others being killed in non-F1 events.

Above **The darkest days:** Stuart Lewis-Evans sustained fatal burns in the 1958 Moroccan GP, as one of three to die in grands prix that year. *Below* **You don't have to be male:** Lella Lombardi is the only female driver to have scored a point in F1.

TOP 10 DRIVERS WITH MOST LAPS IN LEAD

1	Michael Schumacher	5,108
2	Ayrton Senna	2,931
3	Alain Prost	2,683
4	Nigel Mansell	2,058
5	Jim Clark	1,940
6	Jackie Stewart	1,918
7	Nelson Piquet	1,633
8	Niki Lauda	1,590
9	Mika Hakkinen	1,490
10	Damon Hill	1,363

THE MOST COSMOPOLITAN YEAR

The 1970s proved to be the decade when the most different nations had drivers competing in F1, with 18 countries being represented in 1978. They were: Argentina, Australia, Austria, Brazil, Canada, Finland, France, Germany, Great Britain, Holland, Ireland, Italy, Mexico, South Africa, Spain, Sweden, Switzerland and the USA.

NOT AHEAD WHEN IT COUNTED

Neither Jean Behra nor Chris Amon ever won a grand prix, but they both led races seven times. Nick Heidfeld equalled their record tally, but his situation is perhaps more easily explained as racing in the 21st century is peppered with pit stops and different race strategies mean that a driver can have a moment of glory before dropping out of the reckoning.

SAD DAY IN MEXICO

Ricardo Rodriguez was the driver who was going to put Mexico on the map. He raced cars from an incredibly early age, starting at 14 after he gave up racing motorbikes. Rodriguez was immediately quick and Ferrari gave him his F1 break in 1961 and kept him on for 1962, but he was killed in a non-championship F1 race in Mexico on 1 November 1962, aged 20. He is the youngest driver to die in an F1 car.

LET'S ALL TAKE TURNS

In the days before tyre and fuel pit stops, a driver leading the race really was leading the race, not just leading for a short period until the "two-stoppers" made their next pit call. In the light of this the 1971 Italian GP stands out as it holds the record for the number of race leaders on merit – eight. They were Clay Regazzoni, Ronnie Peterson, Jackie Stewart, François Cevert, Mike Hailwood, Jo Siffert, Chris Amon and winner, Peter Gethin.

YOU DON'T HAVE TO BE MALE

Only five female racers have entered World Championship grands prix, and only Lella Lombardi and Maria-Teresa de Filippis managed to qualify. Giovanna Amati, Divina Galica and Desire Wilson failed to make it on to the starting grid. Lombardi scored too, finishing sixth for March in the 1975 Spanish GP at Montjuich Park. The race was stopped after 29 laps (out of 75) because of a major accident.

SHOWING WHO'S BOSS

Michael Schumacher's 2004 world title-winning campaign was one of dominance as he outscored his closest rival, teammate Rubens Barrichello, by 34 points. Such was his speed in his Ferrari that Schumacher led 16 of the year's 18 grands prix, totalling 683 laps (2,085 miles) in front, which equates to 61 per cent of all the laps. Nigel Mansell's swagger to the 1992 title came close, as he led 693 laps (2,043 miles).

TOP 10 DRIVERS WITH MOST MILES IN LEAD

1	Michael Schumacher	14,992
2	Ayrton Senna	8,345
3	Alain Prost	7,751
4	Jim Clark	6,282
5	Nigel Mansell	5,905
6	Juan Manuel Fangio	5,789
7	Jackie Stewart	5,692
8	Nelson Piquet	4,820
9	Mika Hakkinen	4,475
10	Niki Lauda	4,386

CHOPPING AND CHANGING

The most lead changes in a grand prix came in one of the cut and thrust races at Monza, where drivers slipstreamed the car in front down the long straights then dived out to overtake. The record isn't from the classic 1971 encounter in which the lead changed 25 times, but the race in 1965 in which the lead changed a staggering 41 times.

NO BROTHERLY LOVE

Quite a few brothers have competed in F1 at the same time, such as the Fittipaldis, the Scheckters, the Villeneuves and the less well-known Whiteheads. However, the Schumachers are the best known, with Michael taking 91 wins and Ralf six. Michael never cut Ralf any slack on track and was once accused of "trying to kill" him when he edged Ralf towards the wall.

FEW FLAGS TO WAVE

The lowest number of different driver nationalities competing in a season was in 1954, 1966, 1999 and 2008, when just 10 were represented. This is less surprising in the latter years, as despite the fact that the sport is global, drivers tended to stay with their teams throughout the season rather than changing.

THE LONG AND WINDING ROAD

Fernando Alonso's first world title season of 2005 comprised 19 grands prix, covering a total distance of 3,592 miles. Alonso and his Renault covered 3,312 of them. In 2010, when there were also 19 grands prix, representing 3,601 miles in all, Alonso broke his record for distance covered,

Above **No brotherly love:** There was a clear fraternal order between Michael and Ralf Schumacher. *Below* **Chopping and changing:** Monza's long straights offered plenty of chances to slipstream, and it led to a record 41 lead changes in the 1965 Italian Grand Prix. John Surtees is shown leading for Ferrari.

managing 3,564 in his Ferrari. But for a crash in the Belgian GP, it would have been further still.

HE LOOKS A LITTLE FAMILIAR

From the early 1990s to the mid-2000s, it felt odd if there wasn't one particular face grinning down from the podium – Michael Schumacher's. He was usually second or third if he didn't win and so made 154 podium appearances in his 250 starts. He was on the podium at all the races in 2002, completing a record run of 19 podium

appearances that began at Indianapolis in 2001.

FAMILY MATTERS

There are many familiar family names in F1. Brothers and fathers and sons have competed in F1, with Graham and Damon Hill the only father and son to have both become world champions. Other world champions – Mario Andretti, Jack Brabham, Nelson Piquet and Keke Rosberg – have had sons who have competed in F1, as did grand-prix winner Gilles Villeneuve. There have also been uncles and nephews and even brothers-in-law.

CONSTRUCTORS

Alfa Romeo, Maserati, Vanwall, Cooper, BRM, Lotus, Tyrrell, Brabham, Benetton and Honda have all shone then disappeared. McLaren, Williams and Red Bull Racing are still in there competing. Yet, however the Formula One landscape changes, as it does continually, Ferrari continues to win grands prix and attracts unswerving support. It is the only team to have been racing since Formula One began.

Note: The Renault statistics listed are based on the team that evolved from Benetton in 2002, plus stats from Renault's first spell in Formula One between 1977 and 1985. The figures for Benetton include those of Toleman; stats for Red Bull include Stewart and Jaguar Racing teams; Force India's stats include Jordan and Midland Spyker; Scuderia Toro Rosso figures include Minardi; and Brawn GP's those of BAR and Honda Racing.

Below **Stalking horses:** Fernando Alonso passes Felipe Massa on the first lap of the 2010 season-opening Bahrain GP. The Spaniard took the chequered flag ahead of his Brazilian teammate to give Ferrari yet another 1-2.

TEAM WINS

FERRARI – TITLES AND MORE TITLES

The team with the most constructors' titles to its name is Ferrari. It has 16, compared with Williams's nine and McLaren's eight. Ferrari would have had a couple more, but the Constructors' Cup wasn't awarded until 1958, therefore its dominant seasons in 1952 and 1953 don't count.

McLAREN'S FIRST XI

McLaren holds the record for the most successive grand prix wins, with a run of 11 in the first 11 races of the 1988 season. Ayrton Senna and Alain Prost dominated, but they tripped up when Ferrari came good at the place that mattered most to them, Monza, with Gerhard Berger winning the Italian GP. McLaren closed the season by winning the final four races.

THE RISE AND FALL

Ferrari's position at the top of the all-time grand prix wins list is assured thanks to its longevity, but it hasn't been the most successful team in each of the six decades in which it has raced. Take the 1960s: Lotus led the way in technical innovation and scored 36 wins. Ferrari was second, but with a tally of only 13, just one ahead of both Brabham and BRM.

DECADE BY DECADE

If you add up team grand prix wins and look at them decade by decade the 1950s belonged to Ferrari with 29 wins, the 1960s to Lotus with 36 wins, the 1970s to Ferrari with 37 wins, the 1980s to McLaren with 56 wins, the 1990s to Williams with 61 wins and the 2000s to Ferrari with a huge 85 wins. Almost all of the 85 were achieved by Michael Schumacher as he raced to five drivers' titles.

HOME ADVANTAGE

Ferrari has scored the most wins at its home grand prix, its drivers winning the Italian GP 17 times since Alberto Ascari's win at Monza in 1951 and Fernando Alonso's in 2010. Ferrari has also won Italy's second race, the San Marino GP, eight times.

Below **McLaren's First XI:** Ayrton Senna's win in the 1988 Belgian GP made it 11 wins in a row for McLaren. *Bottom* **Clean sweeps are as rare as hens' teeth:** Nino Farina (10) leads Alfa Romeo teammate Juan Manuel Fangio (18) in the 1950 Italian Grand Prix, a race the former won to claim the first World Championship.

CLEAN SWEEPS ARE AS RARE AS HENS' TEETH

Only two teams have achieved 100 per cent win rates across a season. Alfa Romeo was the first to achieve this, winning all six grands prix in the first World Championship in 1950. Two years later Ferrari matched its national rivals, who quit after 1951, and won seven from seven. The closest any team has come since is when McLaren won 15 from 16 in 1988.

MOST WINS IN ONE SEASON

No. of wins	Team	Years
15	Ferrari	2002
=	Ferrari	2004
=	McLaren	1988
12	McLaren	1984
=	Williams	1996
11	Benetton	1995
10	Ferrari	2000
=	McLaren	2005
=	McLaren	1989
=	**Williams**	1992
=	Williams	1993

TOP 10 TEAMS WITH MOST GRAND PRIX WINS

1	Ferrari	215
2	**McLaren**	169
3	Williams	113
4	Lotus	79
5	Brabham	35
=	Renault	35
7	Benetton	27
8	Tyrrell	23
9	BRM	17
10	Cooper	16

A HUNGRY WOLF

Walter Wolf had backed Williams in 1976, but he wanted his own team and set one up for the following year. What an impact his team made when the 1977 World Championship opened in Argentina. After front-row starters James Hunt and John Watson faltered, Jody Scheckter came through to take the only maiden team win in F1 history.

THE JOY OF SIX

It's debatable whether Brawn GP can be viewed as a new team in 2009, as it was effectively a continuation of Honda Racing after the Japanese manufacturer quit at the end of 2008. Even if it was more of a new team

name rather than a new team, its six wins were the best haul from a team in its first season.

WINNING FOR YOUR COUNTRY

Looking at stats in terms of the nationality of the team, or the country out of which it operated, there can be no denying that Britain is the home of F1, with an "arc of excellence" around London from Cambridgeshire to Surrey. The majority of F1 teams have long been based in Britain, even if the owners are not British. As a result of this, British-based teams had won 557 of the 839 grands prix held by the end of 2010, with Italy next, almost entirely thanks to Ferrari, on 235 wins. French teams are third, having claimed 24 victories.

PERSEVERANCE PAYS OFF

Scuderia Toro Rosso holds the record for the most races contested by a team before scoring its first win. It started life in 1985 as Minardi and never looked likely to score points on a regular basis let alone have its drivers mount the podium or take a win. It took a change of ownership in 2007 and an injection of money into its coffers to turn its fortunes around. Young flyer Sebastian Vettel did the rest, winning in the wet in the Italian GP at Monza in 2008, the team's first victory out of 372 starts.

MANY WINS, NO PRIZE

As the Constructors' Championship was not contested until 1958, Alfa Romeo goes down in the history books as the marque with the most grand prix wins without a title. It dominated the 1950 and 1951 seasons, taking 10 wins. Mercedes-Benz, with five of its nine wins coming in 1955, and Maserati, four of its nine in 1957, were also denied official recognition. In the post-Constructors' Cup era, Ligier, who ran from 1976 to 1996, also scored nine wins, three of which came in 1979, its best season, is third overall.

Above **Most wins in one season:** Riccardo Patrese leads Nigel Mansell in Brazil in 1992, when Williams won 10 races. *Top* **Top 10 teams with most grand prix wins:** Lewis Hamilton claimed McLaren's 164th win in Singapore in 2009. *Below* **The *Tifosi's* favourite:** Michael Schumacher did a lot of celebrating with Ferrari, including in 2003, after he had taken his sixth title.

THE TIFOSI'S FAVOURITE

Michael Schumacher was admired rather than liked by the *Tifosi* when he joined Ferrari in 1996, but they soon warmed to him when he and the team started winning on a regular basis. He is by far the most successful Ferrari driver, having won 72 times for the Scuderia. The next most successful is Niki Lauda on 15, just ahead of another Ferrari double champion, Alberto Ascari, who took 13 wins.

TEAM POLE POSITIONS

FOR THE TIFOSI

It almost feels like a birthright that a Ferrari should take pole position in the Italian GP and the team has achieved this on 19 occasions, rising to the challenge even in years when its form has been patchy elsewhere. After Ferrari's qualifying glories at Monza, the next most pole positions set by a team at an individual circuit is shared by a group of three: Ferrari at the Nürburgring; McLaren at Hockenheim and Monaco; and Williams at Silverstone.

CHARGING UP THE ORDER

Red Bull Racing's flurry of pole positions in 2010, its title breakthrough campaign, with 10 claimed by Sebastian Vettel and five by Mark Webber, not only moved the Milton Keynes-based team into the top 10 in the all-time poles table, but moved it up to seventh ahead of Benetton.

DISCOVERING OLD FORM

When Nico Hulkenberg claimed a surprise pole position in wet conditions for the 2010 Brazilian GP at Interlagos, the German rookie gave the Williams team its first pole in five and a half years. Nick Heidfeld had done the honours for the British team at the 2005 European GP at the Nürburgring.

ALL BUT PERFECT

The record for the most poles in a year is shared by McLaren, Williams and Red Bull. McLaren grabbed 15 poles from 16 races in 1988 and 1989, courtesy of Ayrton Senna and Alain Prost, while Williams did it in 1992 (Nigel Mansell claiming 14 and Riccardo Patrese one) and 1993 (Prost 13, Damon Hill two). Red Bull's Sebastian Vettel (10) and Mark Webber (five) took pole in 15 out of 19 grands prix in 2010.

McLAREN'S YEAR OF YEARS

McLaren had it all in 1988: its MP4/4 chassis was supreme; its Honda engine mighty; and in Alain Prost and Ayrton Senna it had the two best drivers. Between them, Prost and Senna took pole at every race except one, when Gerhard Berger took pole for Ferrari at the British GP. McLaren's record for the year was 15 poles from 16 grands prix, with Senna taking 13. McLaren repeated the feat in 1989 and Williams matched it in 1992 and 1993.

FROM ZERO TO HERO

A number of teams have taken their first win without having previously achieved a pole position, including debutants Alfa Romeo in 1950, Mercedes in 1954 and Wolf in 1977, plus others who'd been racing a while, such as Cooper, Honda, Matra, McLaren and Porsche. Some teams, including BRM, Ferrari, Lotus, Toro Rosso, Vanwall and Williams, hit form and claimed their first pole and first win at the same race.

Below **McLaren's year of years:** Ayrton Senna lines up on pole with Alain Prost second on the grid at Monaco in 1988 after McLaren had dominated qualifying yet again. *Opposite* **And, at last...:** Alan Jones gave the Shadow team its one and only grand prix victory, at the Osterreichring in 1977.

A DEAD HEAT

When Lewis Hamilton claimed pole position and then raced to victory at the 2010 Canadian GP, he moved McLaren one ahead of Ferrari at the top of the table for teams with the most pole position/win doubles. It was McLaren's 37th race victory from pole position. Lotus remain ranked third in this category, largely due to the efforts of Ayrton Senna in 1986 when his car was fast but fragile.

INCREDIBLE TREBLE

Taking pole then winning is an achievement, but even more prestigious than that is adding the fastest lap to make it a treble. Ferrari has achieved this an incredible 82 times, with Michael Schumacher the main driving force. Williams is next up on 50, edging McLaren out by one. Lotus is ranked fourth on 26, with Renault fifth on 11.

Above **The more the merrier:** Both Brawn (top at the Australian GP) and Force India (above at the Belgian GP) claimed their first pole positions in 2009.

AND, AT LAST...

The most pole positions achieved by a team before its first victory is just three. Shadow was on pole three times in 1975 through Jean-Pierre Jarier (twice) and Tom Pryce. However, the first win, in fact the team's only win, came two years later when Alan Jones raced from 14th to first on a damp track in the Austrian GP.

TOP 10 TEAM POLES

1	Ferrari	205
2	McLaren	146
3	Williams	125
4	Lotus	107
5	Renault	51
6	Brabham	39
7	Red Bull Racing	21
8	Benetton	16
9	Tyrrell	14
10	Alfa Romeo	12

THE MORE THE MERRIER

The record for the greatest number of different teams to achieve pole position in one season is six. The ever-increasing number of rounds favours teams competing in recent years over those who raced in the early 1950s when there were sometimes only seven races in a season, in addition to the fact that there were only a handful of competitive teams in the early years. So the record was first set in 1972, but then matched in 1976, 1981, 1985, 2005 and in 2009.

In 2009 Brawn and Red Bull led the way in terms of the number of poles achieved, ahead of McLaren, Force India, Renault and Toyota.

TEAM FASTEST LAPS

SPEED OVER RESULTS

Ferrari has set the most fastest laps of any team at any circuit, with 16 at Monaco, but it would gladly swap that record for McLaren's table-topping figure of 15 wins around the street circuit. McLaren's drivers, it seems, have kept the cooler heads and delivered what every team boss wants most, especially in front of friends and sponsors on the yachts in the harbour.

FERRARI LEADS THE WAY

Ferrari has been competing in the World Championship since it began in 1950 and has been competitive in the vast majority of seasons since. So it's no surprise that Ferrari tops the table as the team that has set or equalled the most fastest laps at 50 of the 68 circuits used up to the end of 2010. McLaren is the next most successful in its spread of fastest laps, being top or equal top at 46 circuits.

ALMOST IDENTICAL

Being in pole position is thought to have more bearing on whether a team wins than if it sets the fastest lap, but the correlation between the two can't be ignored. British or British-based teams had started from pole 542 times by the end of 2010 and set the fastest lap on 538 occasions. Italian teams have 254 fastest laps, with French teams next best on 31.

A BRITISH BONANZA

Italian teams started F1 with a bang, with Alfa Romeo, Ferrari or Maserati setting the fastest lap at each of the first 30 grands prix. However, this is no longer the record for the most successive fastest laps set by teams from one country. It was finally bettered between 1991 and 1995 when the British teams of Williams, McLaren, Benetton and Jordan set fastest laps for an incredible 62 races in a row.

WHO'S FASTEST?

Since the 1960s most of the F1 teams have been British or based in Britain, so it's not surprising that their combined tally of 519 fastest laps exceeds the best that Italy (largely Ferrari) and other countries have managed. Italy's combined attack includes Ferrari, Alfa Romeo, Maserati and Lancia, with a total of 253.

FERRARI FLIES

Michael Schumacher was peerless in 2004, setting 10 fastest laps from 18 rounds. But Ferrari's number-two driver, Rubens Barrichello, was also able to reel off fastest laps in his F2004, helping the Italian team to a record 14 fastest laps in a season. This is one more than its 2008 line-up of Felipe Massa (3) and Kimi Räikkönen (10) managed.

Right **Who's fastest?:** Jenson Button celebrates after winning the 2009 Malaysian GP for Brawn, and he also set the fastest lap. *Bottom* **Renault's glory days:** René Arnoux set fastest lap for Renault at Dijon-Prenois, with teammate Jean-Pierre Jabouille taking its first win in the same race.

RENAULT'S GLORY DAYS

Renault struggled when it arrived in the World Championship midway through 1977. The team had F1's first turbocharged engine, and while power wasn't a problem, reliability was. However, within two years the team's yellow and black cars were flying. Jean-Pierre Jabouille took the marque's first win at Dijon-Prenois and René Arnoux set the race's fastest lap. Renault again bagged the fastest lap on its return visit to the circuit in 1981.

TOP 10 TEAMS WITH THE MOST FASTEST LAPS

1	Ferrari	223
2	McLaren	143
3	Williams	130
4	Lotus	71
5	Brabham	40
6	Benetton	35
7	Renault	29
8	Tyrrell	20
9	BRM	15
=	Maserati	15

A YEAR OF VARIETY

The 1975 World Championship offered the greatest number of teams that set fastest laps across the 14 grands prix in the season. Eight teams got in on the act: Ferrari (six fastest laps), McLaren (two), Brabham, Hesketh, March, Parnelli, Shadow and Tyrrell (all with one).

STRONG ON THE DAY

A host of teams have had drivers who have been experts at qualifying – such as Ayrton Senna, who took 65 poles from his 161 starts – but unless the car is resilient enough to last the race this speed does not necessarily translate into a race win. Across the first 61 years of F1, Ferrari holds the record for the most wins/fastest lap doubles, at 52. McLaren is the next most successful team, with 35, and Williams is in third place, having achieved it on 22 occasions.

Below **Favouring America:** Graham Hill added to Lotus's collection of fastest laps in the United States GP in 1967. *Bottom* **Red racers:** Rubens Barrichello controlled the 2004 Italian GP, also bagging another Monza fastest lap for Ferrari.

FAVOURING AMERICA

With a need to sell road-going sports cars as well as its range of racing cars, Lotus boss Colin Chapman was always delighted that his F1 cars seemed to shine in North America. The team has the most or equal most fastest laps at Detroit, Riverside and, most importantly, Watkins Glen in New York State.

RED RACERS

An ample supply of horsepower has been a feature of Ferrari's engines over the years, and this is evident in the stats for which team has set the most fastest laps at an individual circuit. The Italian team tops the table with 18 at its home circuit of Monza, where the long, long straights require plenty of grunt.

TEAM POINTS

RAKING THEM IN

The change of the World Championship points system – awarding points from first place to 10th from 2010, with 25 for a win whereas it had previously been 10 – meant that Red Bull Racing achieved a new record tally when Seabstian Vettel raced to the title and teammate Mark Webber backed him up by being ranked third for a joint tally of 498 points. This worked out at an average of 26.21 points at each of the campaign's 19 grands prix.

ONE AND TWO

F1's most successful teams aren't always at the top, but they all have periods when they manage to have the best chassis, the best engine, the best tyres and the best drivers at the same time; then the one-two finishes flow. McLaren exemplified this when Ayrton Senna and Alain Prost dominated in 1988 and they scored 10 one-twos that year alone, with Senna in front in seven of them.

POINTS ALL THE WAY

Several teams have scored points in every grand prix of the year. This was easier to do in the 1950s when there were fewer teams and fewer grands prix. The most recent team to achieve this was Brawn GP, which managed to score in each of the 17 races in 2009 – its only season under that branding – and then McLaren in 2010, when either Lewis Hamilton or Jenson Button, or both, proved effective in all of the grands prix.

MAXIMUM POINTS HAULS

The best way for a team to rack up points is obviously to have its cars finish first and second, and Ferrari is the most successful team at this, having achieved it 76 times, starting all the way back at the Italian GP in 1951. McLaren, the next most successful team in taking one-two results, with 44, didn't score its first one until 17 years later in Belgium when Denny Hulme led home team owner Bruce McLaren.

TOP 10 TEAMS WITH MOST POINTS

1	Ferrari	4,473.5
2	McLaren	3,816.5
3	Williams	2,675
4	Lotus	1,352
5	Renault	1,309
6	Benetton	877.5
7	Brabham	854
8	Red Bull (née Stewart)	842.5
9	Mercedes (née BAR– (Honda–Brawn)	710
10	Tyrrell	617

BY THE THOUSANDS

British and British-based teams lead the way in points accrued, with their combined tally being 13,263.5 at the end of 2009. Italian teams rank second, on 4,264.5 points, with French teams on 777 and Swiss-based Sauber and BMW Sauber accumulating 503 points between them.

Above Points all the way: Brawn GP had a remarkable debut year in 2009, with either Jenson Button (shown winning in Bahrain) or Rubens Barrichello scoring in every round. **Below Perseverance pays off:** Benetton team boss Flavio Briatore and Michael Schumacher had plenty to smile about in 1995.

COMING GOOD IN THE END

Benetton scored the most points before landing its first constructors' title. This came in 1995, by which time it had scored 663.5 points across 15 campaigns since starting life as the Toleman team back in 1981. Ironically, the team later became Renault in 2002 after being taken over by the French manufacturer, which had actually started its bid for a title back in 1977.

SCORING AT HOME

Not only because of its speed and success, but also its longevity, Ferrari is the team that has scored the most points at its home race. From 1958, the first year of the Constructors' Cup, to 2009, Ferrari collected 314 points from the Italian GP at Monza. Ferrari's record in Italy's second race, the San Marino GP that ran from 1981 to 2006, is not as strong, although it did record eight victories.

LOOKING DOWN FROM ABOVE

Ferrari holds the record for the most consecutive top-three finishes which, largely thanks to the might of Michael Schumacher, resulted in podium finishes at an incredible 53 straight grands prix between the 1999 Malaysian GP and the final grand prix of 2002 in Japan. The team kept the stream of points flowing into 2003, but only for the next two grands prix. Disaster struck in the third race of the season at Interlagos when Ferrari went home empty handed as both Michael Schumacher (crashed) and Rubens Barrichello (fuel shortage) retired. It bounced back to finish first and third next time out.

CLOSEST TO PERFECTION

The scoring system has changed four times since the World Championship began in 1950* but, even taking this into account, Alfa Romeo achieved the highest points average ever in that inaugural season, as its drivers finished first and second in every race, except two. This gave the Italian marque a points score of 90.476 per cent of the maximum. In recent years, McLaren's 1988 tally is the best, with an 82.917 per cent hit rate, edging out Ferrari in 2002 (81.250 per cent) and 2004 (80.864 per cent).

Points from 1950–57 counted only towards the drivers' tally, but have been added here for comparative purposes.

SO LITTLE REWARD

You could never criticize Minardi for its effort, but a lack of finance left it struggling to be competitive. The team's record of 38 points from 340 starts is poor, equal to a return of 0.112 points per race. Still, that is impressive compared to both the Zakspeed, which accumulated just two points in 53 starts (0.0377), and Osella, five points from 132 (0.0379). Needless to say, none of the teams managed a single podium finish.

TOP 10 TEAMS WITH MOST ONE-TWO FINISHES

1	Ferrari	78
2	McLaren	47
3	Williams	32
4	Brabham	8
=	Tyrrell	8
6	Lotus	7
=	Red Bull Racing	7
8	BRM	5
=	Mercedes	5
10	Alfa Romeo	4
=	Brawn	4

Below **Something for almost everyone:** Lola – this is Philippe Alliot at Monaco – was one of 16 teams to score points in 1989. *Bottom* **Looking down from above:** Michael Schumacher and race winner Eddie Irvine started Ferrari's run of podium finishes at Sepang in 1999.

SOMETHING FOR ALMOST EVERYONE

In 1989 16 different teams scored points in the World Championship, the most ever. This statistic is even more remarkable when you note that points were awarded down to only sixth rather than eighth place, as was the situation from 2003. The scoring teams were, in points order:
McLaren, Williams, Ferrari, Benetton, Tyrrell, Lotus, Arrows, Dallara, Brabham, Onyx, Minardi, March, Rial, Ligier, AGS and Lola. Only the Coloni, EuroBrun, Osella and Zakspeed teams failed to score.

TEAM TITLES

FORZA FERRARI

Ferrari's head start in the 1950s and its incredibly strong run of success from 2000 onwards – with Michael Schumacher leading the way – ensure that the Italian team has more constructors' titles than any other, with sixteen to Williams's nine and McLaren's eight. Had the constructors' title been awarded before 1958, it would be closer to 20.

GLORY IS HARD TO COME BY

British or British-based teams rule in terms of race wins, with 557 to Italy's 235. In fact, such is the centralization of expertise that teams based in only six countries have won a grand prix. France's Renault (in its first iteration), Ligier and Matra help the country rank third on 33, while Mercedes won 10 for

Germany. At the foot of the table on one win apiece are the Netherlands, home of the Honda team from 1964–66, and Switzerland, with BMW Sauber's one and only win coming at Montreal in 2008.

FERRARI'S FLOP

There's no doubt that the worst follow-up season by a champion team was that of the inaugural constructors' champions, Vanwall, as it scaled down its involvement to almost nothing due to patron Tony Vandervell's ill health. However, of those who returned to defend their titles, Ferrari has had the worst time, scoring just eight points in 1980. As there was no driver change, 1979 world champion Jody Scheckter and Gilles Villeneuve staying on, the blame fell on the car.

CROWNS FOR COUNTRIES

British or British-based teams hold sway in terms of the most constructors' titles won, with their combined forces achieving 37 titles, largely thanks to Williams and McLaren, to Italy's 16. France, the country that hosted the first road races starting in 1894, and the first grand prix in 1906, has three titles (one from Matra and two from Renault), but its claims to titles are debatable as in each case the teams were run out of Great Britain.

TAKE THAT

Ferrari had its most dominant seasons when Michael Schumacher was leading the driver line-up. In 2004, he and Rubens Barrichello guided the team to a winning margin of 143 points in the Constructors' Championship over BAR's

Jenson Button and Takuma Sato. McLaren's Ayrton Senna and Alain Prost achieved the second-largest title-winning margin, when their 15 wins from 16 starts in 1988 meant that the team was 134 points clear of Ferrari.

GETTING BY, JUST

The team that has won the Constructors' Championship with the fewest grand prix wins is Ferrari, with just three wins proving sufficient both in 1964 and in 1982. The latter of these two championships was won in the most extraordinary year for the drivers' title. Keke Rosberg (Williams) was crowned world champion with just one win to his name, in the 14th of the year's 16 grands prix.

A SIGN OF EXCELLENCE

To wrap up the constructors' title before the final round is always the sign of a team in control and 11 teams have managed it since the Constructors' Championship began in 1958. They are: Benetton, Brabham (two), Brawn, Cooper (two), Ferrari (nine), Lotus (five), McLaren (four), Red Bull Racing, Tyrrell, Vanwall and Williams (eight).

Below **Squeaking home:** Lorenzo Bandini celebrates his only win, in Austria in 1964, to help Ferrari win the title by just three points. *Bottom* **A sign of excellence:** Tyrrell, with Jackie Stewart leading François Cevert to a one-two in Germany, wrapped up the title early in 1973.

SQUEAKING HOME

The narrowest title-winning margin is just three points, which was the result back in 1964 when Ferrari edged out BRM thanks to John Surtees and Lorenzo Bandini getting the better of the British team's Graham Hill and Richie Ginther. However, that season was contested across only 10 rounds, making Ferrari's victory over McLaren by four points after 16 grands prix in 1999 statistically closer.

≫ COME IN NUMBER 14

Demonstrating a clear shuffling of the pack, three constructors have landed their first constructors' title since 2005. First it was Renault (formed from the team that ran as Benetton for years), duly repeating the feat the following year. Then in 2009 it was Brawn GP (formerly BAR and Honda Racing). Most recently, in 2010, Red Bull Racing (formerly Stewart Grand Prix then Jaguar Racing) became the 14th constructor to be crowned.

≫ NEVER AT HOME

Despite the Italian GP taking place towards the end of the F1 racing calendar, not once has the *Tifosi* seen Ferrari claim the constructors' title on home ground, even in the years of Michael Schumacher's dominance. However, in two of those years – 2002 and 2004 – Ferrari had already won the title before heading for Monza, wrapping it up several rounds earlier at the Hungarian GP.

Above **Never at home:** Michael Schumacher gave Ferrari a home win at Monza in 2000, but not the constructors' title. *Below* **Come in number 14:** Mark Webber, leading Sebastian Vettel at Monaco in 2010, helped Red Bull Racing to its first title. *Bottom* **Economies of scale:** Jack Brabham won the Monaco GP to help Cooper be crowned after just 25 starts.

MOST CONSTRUCTORS' TITLES

1	Ferrari	16
2	Williams	9
3	McLaren	8
4	Lotus	7
5	Brabham	2
=	Cooper	2
=	Renault	2
8	Benetton	1
=	Brawn GP	1
=	BRM	1
=	Matra	1
=	Red Bull Racing	1
=	Tyrrell	1
=	**Vanwall**	1

ECONOMIES OF SCALE

The teams that won the constructors' titles in the early years have the best record in terms of having the fewest race starts to their name before landing the title. The first constructors' champions, Vanwall, had made a total of just 27 starts when it took the 1958 title, only to be trumped by Cooper in 1959, who became champions with just 25 starts.

PARTICIPATION

I'LL START, SO I'LL FINISH

|||||||||||||||||||||||||||||||||||

Someone always retires, well, except in three of the 820 grands prix held between 1950 and the end of 2009. At the 1961 Dutch GP, all 15 starters finished. Then every car on the starting grid finished the 2005 US GP, but that was just six, as the other 14 had pulled off after the formation lap protesting over tyre safety. However, all 20 starters finished at Monza later that year, showing just how much car reliability has improved.

YOUR NAME ON THE NOSE

Winning is wonderful, and a handful of drivers have sought to do it in a car bearing their name. Most successful by far is Jack Brabham, who won seven grands prix in 1966 and landed both the drivers' and constructors' titles. His former teammate Bruce McLaren founded a successful dynasty, although it flourished mainly after his death in 1970.

WHY MOVE WHEN YOU'RE WINNING?

Michael Schumacher turned Ferrari back into a winning machine and so saw no reason to move elsewhere. He landed 72 of his 91 grand prix wins and five of his seven world titles while driving for the Italian team, before retiring from racing after a record 162 grands prix for the team from Maranello. David Coulthard is the next most long-staying driver, clocking up 150 races for McLaren.

ONE-YEAR WONDERS

Many a bid to graduate to F1 failed before getting even to the starting grid, but a good number of teams and self-run drivers failed to advance to a second season after running out of money or even the death of their driver. Others required a name change to achieve the budget they

Above **Your name on the nose:** Bruce McLaren founded his eponymous team, but was killed before it really thrived. *Below* **I'll start, so I'll finish:** All 15 cars that started the 1961 Dutch GP reached the finish, with Wolfgang von Trips (3) beating pole-sitting Ferrari teammate Phil Hill.

TEAMS THAT HAVE LED MOST MILES

1	Ferrari	42,888
2	McLaren	29,331
3	Williams	21,622
4	Lotus	16,263
5	Tyrrell	4,186

required to carry on racing. Thus far, more than 200 teams have not made it into a second year.

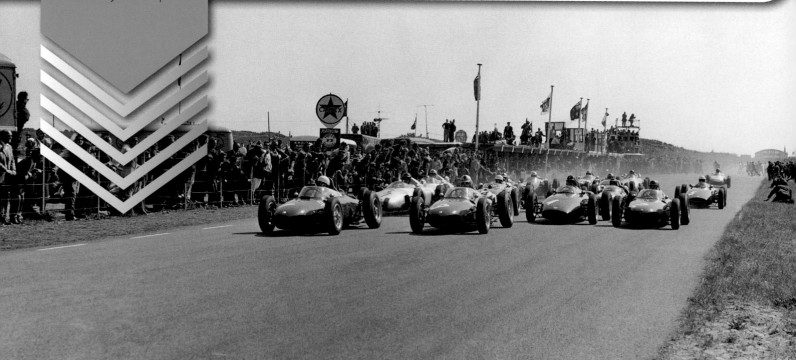

TEAMS THAT HAVE LED MOST LAPS

1	Ferrari	13,247
2	McLaren	9,966
3	Williams	7,497
4	Lotus	5,498
5	Brabham	2,717

WHICH MICHAEL SCHUMACHER?

The crash-strewn 1996 Monaco GP was confusing enough, but it was all the more puzzling to those spectators who weren't listening to the commentary as there appeared to be two Michael Schumachers in the race, one driving for Ferrari, the other for McLaren. This was because David Coulthard's own helmet was misting up in the rain, so he borrowed one of Michael's spares.

TO FINISH FIRST, FIRST YOU HAVE TO FINISH

The 1996 Monaco GP was an odd one. The Minardis took each other out before the first corner; Michael Schumacher took himself out further around the lap; and Rubens Barrichello spun out in his Jordan before the lap was over. At the end of it all, Olivier Panis scored his

one and only win, for Ligier, and there were just four classified finishers, only three of which were still running at flag-fall. No race has come close to being as destructive.

WHO ARE YOU THIS YEAR?

Race fans like their favoured teams to have a clear identity Jordan fitted that bill well. From its formation for 1991, it looked young and sassy. But, like many other teams before it, financial shortfalls meant that it changed owner and, soon after, changed its name to Midland F1 then Spyker before becoming Force India in 2008. Minardi was distinctive as the "other Italian team" from 1985 until it became Scuderia Toro Rosso in 2007.

POINTS, BUT NO PRIZES

The Arrows team is no more, but at least it will never extend its record of being the team with the most grand prix starts without winning a grand prix – 382. It came close twice. Riccardo Patrese was leading until 15 laps before the end of the team's third race, in South Africa in 1978, before the engine failed and Damon Hill led the 1997 Hungarian GP until a lap before the finish when Jacques Villeneuve swept past to win and Hill came second.

KEEP IT SHORT

Which is the most successful team if you pit wins against starts? Answer: it is neither Ferrari (0.265) nor McLaren (0.246), but Mercedes, when it raced in F1 first time around for a season and a half in 1954–55. It had a strike rate of 0.75 – nine wins in 12 starts. Add in the 2010 rebirth, however, and that falls to 0.290. Had Alfa Romeo not returned in 1979, its 1950–51 strike rate would have been 0.769: instead it's 0.091 (10 wins in 110 starts).

Above **Points, but no prizes:** At the 1997 Hungarian GP, Damon Hill led for all but the most important lap, the last one. *Right* **Keep it short:** Alfa Romeo's 1951 line-up of Juan Manuel Fangio, Giuseppe Farina, Felice Bonetto and Toulo de Graffenried. *Right* **Sticking together:** David Coulthard and Mika Hakkinen, on the podium in Melbourne in 1998, raced together 99 times.

STICKING TOGETHER

David Coulthard and Mika Hakkinen raced together more times than any other teammates in the history of F1, totalling 99 grands prix as a duo. They had a six-year stretch together at McLaren between 1996 and 2001 before Hakkinen took what he'd planned to be a sabbatical, which by mid-2002 had become full retirement from F1.

TEAM PRINCIPALS

PASSION HIDDEN BEHIND DARK GLASSES

Enzo Ferrari was drawn to the sport by a desire to compete. In the 1930s, he was put in charge of Alfa Romeo's racing activities. Fired in 1939, Enzo started building his own cars after the Second World War. His team's first World Championship win came at the 1951 British GP and the legend grew from there. Enzo was famously unemotional about his cars, which were broken up after they were superseded. He remained enigmatic in the extreme, and by the end of his career would no longer watch races at the track.

A SHARP BRAIN AND A STERN LOOK

Alfred Neubauer was the man who made the Mercedes team tick during its one-and-a-half-year stint in F1 in the mid-1950s. He joined Mercedes as a racing driver in 1923, but he quit after a teammate was killed at the 1924 Italian GP and turned to team management. He guided the "Silver Arrows" through its glory years of the late 1920s and 1930s. Portly, never without a jacket and tie, and usually with a serious expression, he was still at the helm after the Second World War and he encouraged the team back into racing in 1954 when it set new standards.

A RESTLESS, DRIVEN GENIUS

Colin Chapman probably shaped F1 more than any other team principal through his restless quest to find an engineering advantage. In 1962 his Lotus team was the first to use a monocoque chassis, and Jim Clark started to win. He made ground effects work for the 1978 season and Mario Andretti duly did the same. He tried to introduce a double chassis, but it was banned, infuriating this effervescent character. He died of a heart attack in 1988, leaving memories of a man dressed in black hurling his cap in the air when his drivers won.

TIMBER MERCHANT TURNED CHAMPION CHIEF

Ken Tyrrell was a racing driver, financed by his family's timber business. Following the end of his driving career he ran the Cooper Formula Junior team in 1960, and advanced, with Jackie Stewart, to F2 in 1965. They switched to a Matra chassis for F2 and Ken moved into F1 with his own team in 1968, running a Matra-Ford for Stewart. They won races and improved to win the 1969 title. The first Tyrrell car appeared in 1970, and Stewart won titles in 1971 and 1973, but the team struggled financially after sponsor Elf quit, being taken over by BAR in 1998. Ken died of cancer in 2001.

MID-ENGINES TO MINIS

John Cooper's father Charles got him interested in racing and they started building small chassis powered by motorbike engines after the Second World War. Stirling Moss gave Cooper its first F1 win in 1958 and Jack Brabham claimed the next two drivers' and constructors' titles for the team before Lotus stole its thunder. John took over the running of the team in 1964 after his father died, but was then injured in a car crash and decided to sell the company, moving on to create the high-performance Mini Cooper. John died in 2000.

Top **A sharp brain and a stern look:** Alfred Neubauer checks on Moss and Fangio's progress at the 1955 British GP. *Above* **Passion hidden behind dark glasses:** Enzo Ferrari watches over one of Ferrari's mechanics working at the 1966 Italian GP. *Right* **Mid-engines to Minis:** Jack Brabham and John Cooper formed a great partnership.

A DRIVEN MAN

Guy Ligier's first love was rugby and he was a top-class player, but he had an even greater drive to become rich, and he achieved this by building up a successful construction firm. This financed forays into motorcycle racing before Guy tried cars, moving into sports cars before driving in F1 in 1966. His best result was sixth in Germany in 1967. After retiring from driving he turned to building racing sports cars and, in 1976, an F1 car. The team won nine times. Guy sold up in 1992.

CAPTAIN AMERICA

Roger Penske started racing when at university and was competitive enough to enter the US GP in 1961 and 1962, ranking eighth at his first attempt. However, his skills as a businessman soon became more apparent as he built up a chain of car dealerships that is now the second largest in the USA. He also set up a team and ran Mark Donohue to success in TransAm in 1968 before branching into single-seaters. This was mainly in IndyCars, but he tried F1 from 1974–77 and took one win, with John Watson, at the Österreichring in 1976.

FRANCE'S FIXER

Gerard Larrousse came to prominence in rallying, then turned to racing in 1966 and made his name by finishing second in the 1969 Le Mans 24 Hours. He went on to win this race in 1973 and 1974 for Matra. He then set up an F2 team and Jean-Pierre Jabouille won the 1976 crown, after which Gerard became Renault's competitions manager, managing its entry into F1 in 1977. After Renault closed in 1985, he set up his own F1 team for 1987, running Lola chassis. The team's best result was a third place in Japan in 1990 but it folded at the end of 1994.

Left **McLaren's meticulous man:** Ron Dennis looks proud rather than happy after Senna and Prost gave McLaren a one-two at Monaco in 1989. *Below* **A technical and tactical brain:** Ross Brawn hugs Jenson Button after he'd won on the team's debut in Australia in 2009.

McLAREN'S METICULOUS MAN

Ron Dennis started as a race mechanic with Cooper. He moved to Brabham in 1968, before starting a team, Rondel, with Neil Trundle in 1972. They were successful in F2 and built an F1 car that they had to sell when their sponsor pulled out. Back in F2, Ron gained management experience and, with backing from Marlboro, he returned to F1 in 1981, taking over McLaren. Through his legendary attention to detail he turned it into the second most successful team in F1 history. In 2009 he took a step back from F1 to concentrate on the rest of the McLaren Group business.

A TECHNICAL AND TACTICAL BRAIN

Ross Brawn joined March from the atomic industry. From there, he moved to Williams and learnt to be an aerodynamicist. After spells at Beatrice and Arrows, he designed Jaguar's sports cars but returned to F1 and Benetton. Ross started working with Michael Schumacher at Benetton, displaying both tactical and technical skills. The pair moved to Ferrari and won five more titles before Ross took a sabbatical. He came back with Honda, which became Brawn GP for 2009. The team with his name won the drivers' and constructors' titles in 2009 before being renamed as Mercedes GP for 2010.

ONE BIG TEDDY BEAR

||||||||||||||||||||||||||||||||||||||

Lord Hesketh made quite a splash in F1 in the mid-1970s when he rolled in with a plain white car daubed with patriotic red and blue stripes and a teddy bear on the nose. There was no sponsorship to be seen. "The Good Lord", as driver James Hunt called him, was bankrolling his foray into F1 from his considerable inheritance.

They raced a March in 1974, but soon built their own car and had their day of days when Hunt won the Dutch GP at Zandvoort in 1975. Then Hesketh sold the team and moved into politics, leaving F1 all the poorer without his flamboyance.

DRIVEN BY PATRIOTIC FERVOUR

A racer first and foremost, up to F3 level, Frank Williams never had the money to go any higher and turned to running cars for others, most notably for Piers Courage in 1969 and 1970, until Courage died at the Dutch GP. Some lean years followed as Frank fought on in F1, always short of money. In 1977 he formed Williams Grand Prix Engineering with Patrick Head. It developed into F1's third most successful team, winning nine constructors' titles, despite the setback of Frank being paralysed in a car crash in 1986.

FROM RACER TO PRESIDENT

Max Mosley has spent his life being referred to as the son of fascist politician Sir Oswald Mosley, precluding any dreams of a political career. Instead, Max tried racing, reaching F2 before becoming one of the founder members of March in 1969. He quit March in 1977 and moved into helping the teams form a united front through the Formula One Constructors' Association (FOCA), working with Bernie Ecclestone. He then became president of the Fédération Internationale de l'Automobile (FIA) in 1986 and held the position until late 2009 when he stood down and was replaced by the newly elected Jean Todt.

Above **Driven by patriotic fervour:** Frank Williams and partner Patrick Head watch the action at the 1980 British GP. *Below* **One big teddy bear:** Racing was always fun when Lord Hesketh (left with James Hunt and "Bubbles" Horsley) was around.

AN INDUSTRIALIST DEMANDING SUCCESS

Sir Alfred Owen inherited the family's industrial empire on his father's death. He was only 21, but continued its expansion across the globe. Disappointed by the BRM team's floundering attempts to put Britain on the map in F1, he bought it in 1952, running it under the Owen Racing Organisation banner. After a weak 1961 campaign he demanded success in 1962 or he would close the team. It responded and won the constructors' and drivers' title, but he tired of its form after that and gave the team to his sister, to be run by her husband, Louis Stanley.

THE ULTIMATE ENTREPRENEUR

Bernie Ecclestone made his first fortune selling motorbike parts. A club-level car racer, Bernie was busier away from the tracks, establishing a multi-pronged business empire. He bought the Connaught F1 team in 1958 and even tried to qualify a car himself at Monaco. His attempt was unsuccessful so he settled for driver management. After the death of charge Jochen Rindt in 1970, he bought Brabham in 1972 and ran that until he sold it in 1987. But it's

FLAMBOYANT BUT FLAWED

Flavio Briatore had no love of racing, but became involved through the Benetton family after he'd headed up their clothing chain's push into the USA. He was asked to be commercial director of their team in 1988 and brought in Tom Walkinshaw to help run it. Signing Michael Schumacher was the key to success and titles followed in 1994 (drivers') and 1995 (drivers' and constructors'). He has since been involved with supplying teams with Renault engines and then ran Renault's F1 return until he was banned from the sport in 2009 for his role in "Singaporegate", the race-fixing scandal that arose as a result of the 2008 Singapore GP.

his role as the F1 rights holder through his Formula One Management company that has given him both power and considerable wealth.

LOOKING FOR THE DEAL

Eddie Jordan is one of motor sport's great wheeler-dealers. He raced, up to F2 level, but turned to running cars for others, with Eddie Jordan Racing becoming a key player in British F3 in the 1980s. The team stepped up to F3000 and took Jean Alesi to the 1989 title. However, F1 was the dream of this fast-talking Irishman and Jordan's team made an instant impact on its arrival in 1991. Eddie had to keep doing deals to sustain the team, revelled in its first win in 1998 and then sold the team in 2005. He is now a TV pundit.

A MODEL PROFESSIONAL

Jackie Stewart achieved far more in F1 than winning 27 grands prix and three World Championships. He pushed for driver safety when it was far from fashionable to do so,

his efforts no doubt saving many lives. He also sought a more professional level than his contemporaries and, after a spell commentating for American TV, returned to F1 as a team owner in 1997, in conjunction with older son Paul. Stewart GP won once, at the Nürburgring in 1999, but was sold on to Ford, who rebranded it as Jaguar Racing and it later became Red Bull Racing.

THE FACE OF FERRARI

Aristocrat Luca di Montezemolo was a rally driver, but quit to pursue a business career, as every Agnelli family member was expected to do. His family firm – Fiat – snapped up Ferrari in 1969 and he became Enzo Ferrari's right-hand man in 1973. By 1974, he was running Ferrari's F1 team and titles followed quickly from 1975. By 1977, he was in charge of the entire Fiat group. He ran Italy's hosting of the 1990 FIFA World Cup before taking over Ferrari in 1991 and, recently, he became head of the teams' governing body, Formula One Teams' Association (FOTA).

Left **An industrialist demanding success:** Vanwall's Tony Vandervell and BRM's Alfred Owen check on their cars' progress. *Right* **Ferrari's fierce little Napoleon:** Jean Todt used his nervous energy and piercing brain to achieve great success with Ferrari.

FERRARI'S FIERCE LITTLE NAPOLEON

Jean Todt was a successful rally co-driver through the 1970s before being given his break in management in 1982 when he was asked to set up Peugeot Talbot Sport. Wins and world titles soon followed through Ari Vatanen, before Peugeot sought success in sports car racing, and got it in 1992. After Peugeot declined to enter F1, Todt joined Ferrari in 1993 and stabilized the team, making it more clinical in its approach. The team won its first constructors' title under Todt's leadership in 1999 and then, in conjunction with Michael Schumacher, won title after title from 2000 until 2004. Todt became FIA president in 2009, replacing Max Mosley.

TYRE MANUFACTURERS

MADE TO LAST

||||||||||||||||||||||||||||||||||||

Goodyear is the tyre company with the longest association with F1. Its involvement began in 1959 and ended at the conclusion of the 1998 season, in which time its tyres had been used in just short of 500 grands prix. Bridgestone edged past Michelin (215 grands prix) in 2009, to become the second most used tyre, at 244 races by the end of 2010, both having passed Pirelli, which ended its involvement in F1 in 1991 after 200 starts.

 ## GOODYEAR'S BREAKTHROUGH

F1's most successful tyre supplier, Goodyear, had no clue what lay ahead when it did a deal with Honda in 1965 and driver Richie Ginther guided the combination to its first win in the last round of the World Championship in Mexico City. No one then would have predicted that this famous American tyre manufacturer would go on to become F1's leading supplier, achieving a further 367 wins.

 ## NO TREAD REQUIRED

The tyres used in the World Championship have changed in many ways since 1950, but few changes have been as greats as the arrival of slick tyres in 1971, when tread was dispensed with by Firestone and Goodyear in their quest to provide extra grip. These reigned supreme until 1998 when, to slow the cars, grooved tyres became obligatory. It wasn't until 2009 that slick tyres returned.

Above **Goodyear's breakthrough:** Richie Ginther and Honda set Goodyear on the road to become the most successful F1 tyre supplier by winning in Mexico in 1965. *Below* **Made to last:** Bridgestone moved past Michelin in 2009 to become F1's second most prolific tyre company.

 ## YET ANOTHER GOOD YEAR

Cars fitted with Goodyear tyres have started more grands prix than those fitted with any other tyre brand by a factor of two. Goodyear-shod cars have claimed 24 titles between 1966 and 1997, which is also more than twice the tally of its closest rival, Bridgestone, which has 10 titles.

TYRE MANUFACTURER WITH MOST POLE POSITIONS

1	Goodyear	358
2	Bridgestone	168
3	Michelin	111
4	Dunlop	76
5	Firestone	49
6	Pirelli	46
7	Englebert	12
8	Continental	8

SOME MORE NEW TYRES PLEASE

The record number of pit stops made in a single grand prix is an almost unbelievable 75, for the 22 cars contesting the European GP at the Nürburgring in 2007. With weather conditions changing almost by the lap, the teams just didn't know what sort of tyres to fit. Fernando Alonso guessed best and won for McLaren after making four pit visits, which was two fewer than three of his rivals.

THEY SHOOT, THEY SCORE

By sheer weight of numbers, Goodyear scored more World Championship points than any other tyre manufacturer, its tally standing at 9,474.5 when it packed up its tyre trucks for the final time after the 1998 Japanese GP, two races after Michael Schumacher gave the American company its final F1 win at Monza. That tally represents just over 19 points for each grand prix that it attended. Don't forget, this would have been higher still had the current 10-8-6-5-4-3-2-1 system been in operation in those years when usually only the top six scored.

Above **They shoot, they score.** The tyre manufacturers have their own paddock area, such as Goodyear's.
Top **Some more new tyres please:** Fernando Alonso kept his pit crew on its toes by pitting four times to change tyres in the 2007 European GP.

 ### FORMULA FARCE

The 2005 US GP at Indianapolis remains the biggest farce in F1 history. Following tyre failure on Ralf Schumacher's Toyota as it went through Turn 13, the only high-speed banked turn on an F1 circuit, during Friday practice, Michelin declared that it couldn't guarantee the safety of the identical tyres that it was supplying for BAR, McLaren, Red Bull, Renault, Sauber and Williams. So, the 14 cars on Michelin tyres peeled into the pits after the formation lap and refused to start, leaving just the six cars with Bridgestone tyres to race.

 ### IN THE BLACK CORNER

The most tyre manufacturers to go head-to-head in a World Championship season is six. This happened in 1958 when Avon, Continental, Dunlop, Englebert, Firestone and Pirelli all sought glory. Dunlop took the most wins.

THERE'S A PATTERN

If you look at the records for the number of starts, pole positions, fastest laps and wins, the order is the same in each. Goodyear is top, usually by a factor of roughly two and a half, which equates to its

proportional number of starts, followed by Bridgestone and Michelin. Pirelli has the fourth most starts, but Dunlop was more successful by ranking fourth for wins, poles and fastest laps, with Firestone demoting Pirelli to sixth in poles and fastest laps.

 ### A CHANGING OF THE GUARD

Tyre manufacturers have come and gone through Formula 1's long history and Bridgestone's spell closed at the end of the 2010 season, with Pirelli returning for 2011 after 20 years away. As it is now the World Championship's sole tyre

supplier, the Italian company is guaranteed to boost its tally of wins from 44 to 64.

TYRE MANUFACTURER WITH MOST WINS

1	Goodyear	368
2	Bridgestone	175
3	Michelin	102
4	Dunlop	83
5	Pirelli	44
6	Firestone	38
7	Continental	10
8	Englebert	8

ENGINE MANUFACTURERS

STRAIGHT EIGHT OR IN A VEE?

When F1 began in 1950, the dominant Alfa Romeos were powered by supercharged straight-eight engines, with their rivals using straight-six or even four-cylinder engines. Since then the V8 engine has been most successful, with 314 grand prix wins, and the more recently popular V10 next on 240.

GO, GO, GO!

Believe it or not, F1 cars are not the quickest racing cars in the acceleration stakes, as their exposed wheels make them less aerodynamically efficient than larger-engined competition sports-prototype cars with their enclosing bodywork. However, they still

hit 100mph from a standstill in around four seconds and keep on accelerating to 200mph and beyond.

MORE THAN JUST A BADGE

Some road cars bore the legend "turbo" on their boot lids, but the engine performance wasn't vastly different. Not so in F1, after Renault's pioneering years in the late 1970s. As more and more horsepower was produced by these engines, the arbitrary 1.5-litre equivalency allowed against the 3.0-litre normally aspirated engines

soon gave the turbo teams a big advantage and they won race after race.

THE MOST BANGS FOR YOUR BUCK

F1 technical regulations have changed constantly since the World Championship began in 1950 and the most recent engines are not the most powerful. That honour goes to the turbocharged engines when their boost was wound up for qualifying for a burst of one lap. The BMW turbo used by Benetton racers Gerhard Berger and Teo Fabi in 1986

is estimated to have pushed out 1400bhp, rather than the 900bhp without the boost cranked up.

STOP NOW!

The acceleration capability of a contemporary F1 car is phenomenal, therefore the braking performance has to be sensational too. It's hard to equate it to a normal road car's braking, but imagine travelling at 200mph as a tight corner approaches. An F1 car can slow to 50mph in just three seconds, which equates to 109 yards.

TOP 10 ENGINE MANUFACTURERS WITH MOST STARTS

1	Ferrari	812
2	Ford	587
3	Renault	461
4	Honda	340
5	Mercedes	301
6	BMW	269
7	Alfa Romeo	222
8	BRM	189
9	Mugen Honda	147
10	Hart	128

Above **Straight eight or in a vee?:** The dominant Alfa Romeos needed long noses in 1950 to accommodate their lengthy straight-eight engines. *Below* **Spinners can be winners:** Williams racer Ralf Schumacher enjoyed an incredible 19,200rpm from his BMW engine in 2003.

SPINNERS CAN BE WINNERS

BMW took peak revolutions per minute to a new level in 2003 when its V10-format P83 engines revved up to 19,200rpm and pushed out more than 900bhp in the back of Juan Pablo Montoya's and Ralf Schumacher's Williams. Within two years, engine capacity was cut back from 3.0 litres to 2.4 to reduce performance in the name of driver safety.

FERRARI LEADS THE WAY

Ferrari's engines have claimed the most wins (215), set the most pole positions (205), fastest laps (223) and scored the most championship points (4,473.5) up to the end of the 2010 World Championship.

THE PACE OF CHANGE

As there couldn't possibly be a more testing arena for technical development than F1, it's not surprising that there have been developments almost every year since the World Championship began. The most visible ones have been to the car, but the engines have changed greatly too (see below).

1950 Cars allowed 4500cc normally aspirated or 1500cc supercharged engines.
1952 Engine capacity restricted to 2000cc or 500cc supercharged engines as F2 rules adopted.
1954 Capacity boosted to 2500cc or 750cc supercharged engines.
1958 Use of commercial fuel made mandatory.
1961 Supercharged engines banned and engine size reduced to 1500–1300cc.
1966 Engine capacity enlarged to 3000cc.
1972 Maximum of 12 cylinders imposed.
1987 Engine capacity enlarged to 3500cc.
1989 Turbocharged engines banned.
1995 Reduction of maximum engine capacity to 3000cc.
2006 Engines restricted to eight cylinders and 2400cc.

TOP 10 ENGINE MANUFACTURERS WITH MOST WINS

1	Ferrari	215
2	Ford	176
3	Renault	130
4	Mercedes	80
5	Honda	72
6	Coventry Climax	40
7	Porsche	26
8	BMW	20
9	BRM	18
10	Alfa Romeo	12

FERRARI POWERS TOP DRIVERS

Ferrari's prancing horses have powered drivers to the most World Championship titles – 15 in all, between Alberto Ascari in 1952 and Kimi Räikkönen's title in 2007. Ford is next on 13, from 1968 to 1994, with the first 12 of those up to 1982 won with the most successful F1 engine ever: the Ford Cosworth DFV.

Below **The heartbeat of America:** Ferrari's Luigi Musso races towards the first win for a V8, in Buenos Aires in 1956.
Bottom **Ferrari powers top drivers:** Kimi Räikkönen was the most recent Ferrari world champion, when he pipped Lewis Hamilton and Fernando Alonso in 2007.

THE HEARTBEAT OF AMERICA

The V8 engine is still the heartbeat of America, ticking over through the suburbs in Fords and Chevrolets. However, the first winning V8 in F1 was fitted to Luigi Musso's Lancia Ferrari in the 1956 Argentinian GP. That said, the Ford Motor Company put its name to F1's most successful V8 of all, the Cosworth DFV.

TRACKS

The names of the great grand prix circuits flow off the tongue mellifluously: Monaco, Monza, Spa-Francorchamps, Silverstone and Suzuka. They are temples to high speed and their toughest corners a real challenge to the drivers. Most have been changed out of all recognition in the name of safety, but they all retain the soul that marks them out from the bright new facilities that have yet to earn their spurs.

Below **Brave new world:** *Lucas di Grassi has little time to admire the architectural merits of the bridge over Abu Dhabi's Yas Marina Circuit as he flashes past in his Virgin VR-01 in 2010.*

TRACK LENGTHS

 GOING ROUND AND ROUND

The greatest number of laps in a grand prix was the 110 laps covered by the winning entrants in the US GP at Watkins Glen between 1963 and 1965. This equated to a race distance of 258.5 miles. In 1966, maximum race distances were cut back to 248.5 miles.

 NOT THE BEST OF STARTS

The Monaco street circuit had been hosting races since 1929, but its World Championship debut in 1950 was a near disaster as there was an accident at Tabac at the end of the opening lap after Giuseppe Farina lost control and triggered a shunt that eliminated nine cars. The wreckage was spread across the track, but Juan Manuel Fangio was able to thread his way through and race clear to score his first win for Alfa Romeo.

 WILL IT BE OVER SOON?

Grands prix up to 1957 were run to a target time of three hours, although some went on for even longer. The 1954 German GP held at the 14.167-mile-long Nürburgring Nordschleife holds the record as the longest grand prix in terms of time. It took race winner Juan Manuel Fangio 3 hrs 45 mins 45.8 secs to cover the allotted 22 laps, and he was rewarded with victory by 1 min 36.5 secs.

 JUST FOUR LEFT RUNNING

It seems inconceivable, but two grands prix since 1950 have finished with just four cars still running. Less hard to imagine is that both of these were at Monaco, where the walls can bite. The first occasion was in 1966 when Jackie Stewart won for BRM, albeit with two further finishers not being classified as they were so far behind. The second was 30 years later when Olivier Panis won a wet/dry race for Ligier as others crashed out.

WORST LINE INTO FIRST CORNER

Irish driver Derek Daly will always be remembered for getting his approach to the first corner, Ste Devote, horribly

THE CRUELLEST CUT

Once it ran for a full 14.189 miles through the Eifel Forest, the second longest circuit ever in the World Championship, but although the Nürburgring still hosts the German GP on alternate years, its Nordschleife lay-out was dropped by F1 after 1976 and when it next hosted a World Championship round in 1985, it had been hacked back to just 2.822 miles, leaving the forest loop to club racers.

Above **The cruellest cut:** A gaggle of midfielders climb the sloping approach to Shell Kurve at the Nürburgring in 1996 with the Dunlop Kehre in the background.
Below **Hungaroring:** The circuit's endless twists – this is Turn 2 – keep speeds in check.

TRACKS WITH SHORTEST LAP LENGTHS

1	Monaco	1.954 miles
2	Zeltweg (Austria)	1.988 miles
3	Long Beach (USA)	2.020 miles
4	Dijon-Prenois (France)	2.044 miles
5	Jarama (Spain)	2.058 miles

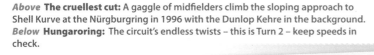

HUNGARORING

Grand prix years: 1986 onwards

No. of grands prix held: 25

Lap length: From 2.494 miles to 2.466 miles to 2.722 miles

Fastest qualifying lap: 1 min 18. 773 secs, Sebastian Vettel (Red Bull), 2010

Fastest race lap: 1 min 19.071 secs, Michael Schumacher (Ferrari), 2004

Driver with most wins: Michael Schumacher – four (1994, 1998, 2001, 2004)

wrong at the start of the 1980 Monaco GP. His Tyrrell clipped Bruno Giacomelli's Alfa Romeo under braking, vaulted clean over it and landed on top of the car in front, that of his teammate Jean-Pierre Jarier. None of the drivers was seriously hurt.

OVER ALMOST BEFORE IT STARTED

||||||||||||||||||||||||||||||||||||||||

Heavy rain made the Adelaide street circuit almost undriveable at the 1991 Australian GP and it had to be called to a permanent halt after just 24 mins 34.899 secs, with 14 laps (32.858 miles) covered. McLaren's pole-starter Ayrton Senna was the winner from Nigel Mansell's Williams, with Gerhard Berger third in the second McLaren.

 ### ARE YOU GOING VERY FAR SIR?

Discounting the 500-mile Indianapolis 500 that was nominally a round of the World Championship from 1950–60, the longest grand prix in terms of distance was the 1951 French GP at Reims, with its 77 laps equating to 373.912 miles. It's no surprise that Juan Manuel Fangio's Alfa Romeo started to fail, forcing him to take over the sister car that started the race in the hands of Luigi Fagioli. Fangio's winning time was 3 hrs 22 mins 11 secs.

 ### GOING ON AND ON

Almost every F1 fan will tell you that the Nürburgring Nordschleife is the longest ever circuit used by F1, at over 14 miles. But the longest is actually the Pescara circuit on Italy's Adriatic coast, which held a grand prix in 1957. The 15.894-mile lap ran uphill, through villages and over level crossings before returning for a blast along the seafront. Stirling Moss beat Juan Manuel Fangio by more than three minutes.

TRACKS WITH LONGEST LAP LENGTHS

1	**Pescara (Italy)**	15.894 miles
2	Nürburgring (Germany)	14.189 miles
3	Spa-Francorchamps (Belgium)	8.774 miles
4	Monza (Italy)	6.214 miles
5	Sebring (USA)	5.200 miles

 ### OVER IN A FLASH

Because the Monza circuit produces such a high average speed, it is usually the shortest race on the F1 calendar in terms of duration. Whereas most modern-day grands prix take around 1 hr 30–40 mins, drivers know that, in the Italian GP, if they don't clash and the safety car doesn't have to be involved they can have their afternoon's work completed in just 1 hr 15 mins.

- - - - - - - - - - - - - - - - - - - -

Above **Tracks with longest lap lengths.** Masten Gregory points his Maserati around Pescara's 15.894-mile lap in 1957. *Below* **Over almost before it started:** Ayrton Senna blinds the field with his spray as he leads the soon-to-be-stopped 1991 Australian GP.

LOCATIONS

BANKING ON SUCCESS

Racing on banked oval circuits is the domain of American IndyCar racing, but the World Championship has also taken to the banking, at least in sections of five circuits. These are Monza (using the banked section as part of the lap most years between 1955 and 1961), Avus, Interlagos (Turn 1 on the old layout until 1979), Mexico City (the lightly banked Peraltada) and Indianapolis (using the full oval when the Indy 500 was a World Championship round from 1950–60, then just a section combined with an infield loop from 2000–07).

Above **Banking on success:** Few drivers liked the steep banking at Avus, but Tony Brooks mastered it for Ferrari in 1959. *Below* **How not to finish the first lap:** Cars scatter in all directions at Silverstone in 1973 after Jody Scheckter spun in front of them at the end of the opening lap.

ITALY LEADS THE WAY

As a result of being among the founding group of countries that held grands prix in the World Championship's inaugural year (1950) and having hosted two grands prix per year (the Italian and San Marino) for several decades, Italy has hosted more grands prix than any other nation. It leads the way after 2010 with 88, Germany is second with 71 (its tally boosted by hosting the additional European GP for many years), Great Britain is third on 64 and France fourth on 59.

WORTH A GAMBLE

Two F1 former circuits have horse racing connections – Aintree, and Adelaide's street circuit which wrapped around the Victoria Park Racecourse. The Las Vegas, Montreal and Monaco circuits all passed a casino.

HOW NOT TO FINISH THE FIRST LAP

Jody Scheckter was looking to impress when he made his fourth grand prix appearance for McLaren at the 1973 British GP. Starting sixth, he was up to fourth when he ran wide out of Woodcote at the end of the first lap, went on to the grass, then took out a third of the field as he scattered the cars behind. Only 19 of 28 starters were able to take the restart 90 minutes later.

COVERING THE GLOBE

The World Championship is a much more accurate term in the 21st century than it was in the 1950s. Back then, almost all grands prix were held in Europe. Now, with the recent addition of races in the Middle East, Korea and India, with Russia slated to join the circus in 2014, European races now are almost the exception rather than the rule.

 ## DOES ANYONE WANT TO FINISH?

A heavy burst of rain that hit the far side of the circuit led to carnage in the 1975 British GP, when car after car aquaplaned off into the catch fencing at Stowe and Club to bring the race to a premature halt. Race leader Emerson Fittipaldi managed to pussyfoot his McLaren through the corners, but Carlos Pace and Jody Scheckter, who were classified second and third, did not, along with 10 others.

 ## MIND THE WATER!

A crash at every twist and turn around the streets of Monaco is a possibility. However, there is also the additional danger of crashing into the harbour, which the 1952 and 1953 world champion Alberto Ascari did in 1955. He emerged unscathed, but unbelievably experienced the reverse side of fortune four days later when he turned up at Monza to test a sports car, crashed and was killed.

 ## A CHANGE OF TACK

Several circuits that hosted grands prix have disappeared under urban sprawl. Riverside, in California – home to the 1960 US GP – is now under a housing development. The upper reaches of Kyalami (South Africa) are now a part of an industrial estate, while the far end of the Zandvoort circuit in the Netherlands is a complex of holiday chalets in the sand dunes.

 ## EUROPE LEADS THE WAY

Europe has hosted grands prix at 37 circuits. They are: A1-Ring, Aintree, Anderstorp, Avus, Brands Hatch, Bremgarten, Catalunya, Clermont-Ferrand, Dijon-Prenois, Donington Park, Estoril, Hockenheim, Hungaroring, Imola, Jarama, Jerez, Le Mans Bugatti, Magny-Cours, Monaco, Monsanto, Montjuich Park, Monza, Nivelles, Nürburgring, Österreichring, Paul Ricard, Pedralbes, Pescara, Porto, Reims, Rouen-les Essarts, Silverstone, Spa-Francorchamps, Valencia, Zandvoort, Zeltweg and Zolder.

NUMBER OF F1 CIRCUITS BY CONTINENT

1	Europe	37
2	North America	13
3	Asia	10
4	Africa	3
=	South America	3
6	Australasia	2

 ## ALL THE FUN OF THE FAIR

Suzuka is the only circuit built in an amusement park, although the Le Mans Bugatti circuit had a famous funfair on its flanks when it was used for the only time by F1 in 1967. The Yas Marina GP circuit in Abu Dhabi, which made its championship debut in 2009, has the Ferrari World theme park right alongside it.

 ## HOTSPOT LOCATIONS

Three F1 circuits have volcanic connections: Fuji Speedway in Japan is situated on the side slopes of Mount Fuji; France's Clermont-Ferrand is built among volcanic outcrops; and the Mexico City circuit is actually located in a volcanic basin, along with the rest of the city.

Above **Covering the globe:** The Korean International Circuit at Yeongam, Korea, hosted its first Formula One GP in 2010. *Below* **Suzuka:** The Casio Triangle.

SUZUKA

Grand prix years: 1987-2006, 2009 onwards

No. of grands prix held: 22

Lap length: From 3.641 miles to 3.644 miles to current 3.609 miles

Fastest qualifying lap: 1 min 29.599 secs, Felipe Massa (Ferrari), 2006

Fastest race lap: 1 min 31.540 secs, Kimi Raikkonen (McLaren), 2005

Driver with most wins: Michael Schumacher – six (1995, 1997, 2000, 2001, 2002, 2004)

LAP RECORDS

RED-HOT RUBENS

Qualifying inevitably produces the fastest laps of a grand prix meeting. These laps are often set with special rubber or next to no fuel on board, and the fastest ever of these was set at Monza by the Brazilian Rubens Barrichello in his Ferrari as he secured pole for the 2004 Italian GP in front of the *Tifosi*. His pole time was 1 min 20.089 secs, equating to 161.802mph.

FAST, FASTER, FASTEST

Monza and Spa-Francorchamps used to vie for the fastest average race-winning speed – a mind-boggling 150mph. Then chicanes were inserted. But the cars kept getting faster and faster and the winning average speed for Michael Schumacher's Ferrari in the 2003 Italian GP at Monza was 153.842mph. The fastest Spa average dates back to 1970 on the old circuit, when Pedro Rodriguez lapped his BRM in a race-winning average of 149.942mph.

MONZA, THE FASTEST OF THEM ALL

The home of the Italian GP, Monza, remains the circuit with the highest race lap speed recorded – 159.909mph set in 2004. Those circuits ranked behind Monza in terms of lap speed are: Silverstone, Spa-Francorchamps, the Österreichring, Hockenheim, Avus, Suzuka, A1-Ring, Reims and Melbourne. Of these,

only Monza, Suzuka and Melbourne have a similar track configuration to when these fastest laps were set.

GET A MOVE ON

Not all circuits produce average lap speeds that are double what you'd normally travel at in the fast lane of a motorway. The tight confines of Monaco limit drivers to average speeds in double rather than treble figures, as do many of the other street circuits used, notably in the USA. However, the slowest fastest lap in a grand prix was set by Juan Manuel Fangio at Monaco in 1950, at 64.085mph. Detroit's track is second on this list.

A DOUBLE DISASTER

The 1960 Belgian GP at Spa-Francorchamps had already bared its teeth before the race; Stirling Moss broke his legs in practice and Mike Taylor received considerable injuries in another crash. Worse was to follow in the race as first Chris Bristow crashed to his death while dicing with Willy Mairesse at Burnenville, then five laps later Alan Stacey was hit in the face by a bird and was killed by the resulting crash.

Below **Get a move on:** A narrow track littered with hairpins slows drivers at Monaco, as shown by Juan Manuel Fangio in 1950 as he recorded the slowest ever fastest lap. *Bottom* **Red-hot Rubens:** Barrichello has the pedal to the metal as he streaks around Monza for a record lap of 161.802mph.

A MEDAL FOR BRAVERY

Gilles Villeneuve famously spun at almost every corner in practice at his first grand prix, at Silverstone in 1977. This was his way of finding the maximum. Always wanting to run right on the ragged edge, he put on a masterclass of driving in the wet in practice at the 1979 US GP when he went out and lapped all but 10 secs faster than anyone else. As it was only practice it counted for nothing, but it certainly laid down a marker.

MIND THE WALLS

Street circuits are almost invariably a bit "point-and-squirt", with tight turns surrounded by walls or barriers rather than fast, open sweeps. However, the Valencia circuit, which has hosted the European GP since 2008, breaks the mould with a more open layout and has an appreciable straight. This resulted in a lap record of 122.837mph, set by Toyota racer Timo Glock in 2009.

ALMOST ALL STRAIGHTS

The Avus circuit in Berlin had a remarkably simple layout. It was an up-and-down dual carriageway, with a corner at its southern end that made its shape look like a hairclip and at the northern end there was a high, banked corner. These were its only features. As a result, lap speeds were high, with Tony Brooks's winning average speed for Ferrari being 143.342mph all the way back in 1959.

LOOKING FOR SPEED

When the Silverstone circuit was reshaped for 2010 and beyond, as part of its modernization project, there was talk that its average lap speed would soar. However, such headlines had to be forgotten when the new Arena infield section failed to boost average lap speeds. Indeed, Fernando Alonso's fastest race lap equated to 145.011mph, falling short of the 146.059mph lap average that Michael Schumacher set in his Ferrari in 2004.

Above **Fastest of the fast:** Keke Rosberg took his Williams to a new level when he took pole for the 1985 British GP with a lap at 160.925mph. *Below* **Barcelona:** The downhill run past the pits.

ENTERING NEW TERRITORY

||||||||||||||||||||||||||||||||

Official fastest laps are recorded during the race only and are exceeded almost always by single, flying laps in qualifying, when the tyres are fresh and the fuel load often optimum. For 19 years, the fastest ever lap in qualifying was set by Keke Rosberg when he lapped Silverstone in his Williams at 160.925mph in 1985. Rubens Barrichello driving a Ferrari at Monza in 2004 beat it by just under 1mph.

TOP 10 CIRCUITS WITH FASTEST LAP RECORDS

	Circuit	Avg. speed
1	Monza	159.909mph
2	Silverstone	153.053mph
3	Spa-Francorchamps	152.049mph
4	Österreichring	150.509mph
5	Hockenheim	150.059mph
6	Avus	149.129mph
7	Suzuka	141.904mph
8	A1-Ring	141.606mph
9	Reims	141.424mph
10	Melbourne	141.009mph

BARCELONA

Grand prix years: 1991 onwards

No. of grands prix held: 20

Lap length: From 2.950 miles to 2.875 miles to current 2.892 miles

Fastest qualifying lap: 1 min 19.995 secs, Mark Webber (Red Bull), 2010

Fastest race lap: 1 min 21.670 secs, Kimi Raikkonen (Ferrari), 2008

Driver with most wins: Michael Schumacher – six (1995, 1996, 2001, 2002, 2003, 2004)

VICTORY ROLLS

 ### HOME SWEET HOME

If you are going to set the record for the most wins in a particular country's grand prix by drivers from a particular nation, then you may as well do it at home. This is what British drivers have managed, winning the British GP 21 times, first with Stirling Moss at Aintree for Mercedes in 1955 and most recently with Lewis Hamilton's wet-track masterclass for McLaren in 2008.

 ### ALL BUT A FEW

British teams have won more races than teams based in other countries, in every country that the World Championship has visited since 1950 bar two. These are Switzerland, where Ferrari has won three of the five grands prix held, and Korea where it has won the only one.

Below **Buenos Aires:** The pit straight and run to Turn 1 seen from the air.
Right **Ferrari's Monza magic:** The *Tifosi* celebrates a Ferrari one-two at Monza in 2004.

 ### THAT SPECIAL RELATIONSHIP

British drivers grew to love their forays across the Atlantic to the US GP not only because they spoke the same language and the largest winner's cheque of the year was up for grabs, but because they enjoyed remarkable success. There was a run of nine straight US wins for British drivers between Stirling Moss's triumph in 1960 and Jackie Stewart's in 1968.

 ### STREETS AHEAD

British teams experienced significant success in Monaco in the 1950s, 60s and 70s. Sure, there was extra work for the mechanics as they repaired the damage from brushes with the barriers and worn gearboxes had to be changed, but the drivers tended to come up trumps, winning there 16 times in a row from Maurice Trintignant's win in Rob Walker's Cooper in 1958 to Ronnie Peterson's victory for Lotus in 1974.

 ### GIMME FIVE

Ferrari and McLaren have claimed five wins in succession in a particular grand prix. The British team achieved this first, winning the Belgian GP at Spa-Francorchamps each year from 1987 to 1991, with a win for Alain Prost followed by four for Ayrton Senna. Ferrari took its sequence in the Japanese GP at Suzuka between 2000 and 2004, with four going to Michael Schumacher, and one to Rubens Barrichello in 2003.

 ### FERRARI'S MONZA MAGIC

The Italian GP is one of the originals and it is here above all other venues that Ferrari wants to win, right in front of its fans (the *Tifosi*). The team, whose scarlet cars bear the famous prancing horse emblem, has done just that on 18 occasions, from Alberto Ascari's victory in 1951 to Fernando Alonso's in 2010.

 ### HIGH FIVE

Ayrton Senna rose to the challenge of the Monte Carlo street circuit like no other driver and won there five times in a row for McLaren from 1989 to 1993. He also won there for Lotus in 1987. He led the first 66 laps in 1988 before crashing out with 12 laps to go, and if things had turned out differently that day his run at Monaco would have been a predominant seven. Jim Clark (twice), Juan Manuel Fangio and Michael Schumacher (twice) have all won a particular grand prix four times in a row.

BUENOS AIRES

Grand prix years: 1953-1958, 1960, 1972-1975, 1995-1998

No. of grands prix held: 20

Lap length: From 2.431 miles to 3.708 miles to 2.646 miles

Fastest qualifying lap: 1 min 24.473 secs, Jacques Villeneuve (Williams), 1997

Fastest race lap: 1 min 27.981 secs, Gerhard Berger (Benetton), 1997

Driver with most wins: Juan Manuel Fangio – four (1954, 1955, 1967, 1957)

TOP 10 TEAMS WITH MOST WINS AT ONE CIRCUIT

1	18	Ferrari	Monza
2	15	McLaren	Monaco
3	14	Ferrari	Nürburgring
4	12	Ferrari	Silverstone
=	12	Ferrari	Spa-Francorchamps
=	12	McLaren	Silverstone
7	10	Ferrari	Hockenheim
=	10	Ferrari	Montreal
9	9	McLaren	Hungaroring
=	9	Williams	Hockenheim

⫸ BEATING THE ELEMENTS

Jackie Stewart's first Nürburgring win in 1968 came not only in torrential rain but also in fog and so it is regarded as one of the greatest wins ever. Not only did the Scot win around the mighty Nordschleife by just over 4 mins in his Matra, with Graham Hill's Lotus finishing second, but he achieved all this nursing an injured wrist.

Above **The most dangerous place to race:** Niki Lauda was lucky to survive this fiery crash in 1976. *Right* **Achieving across the board:** Michael Schumacher celebrates his first win, at Spa in 1992. *Below* **Rolling the dice:** Ayrton Senna's run to victory for Lotus at Monaco in 1987 was followed by five more for McLaren.

THE MOST DANGEROUS PLACE TO RACE

The Nürburgring Nordschleife had the reputation as the sport's most deadly circuit, as it claimed the lives of seven F1 drivers: Onofre Marimon in practice in 1954, Erwin Bauer in a sports car race in 1958, Peter Collins in the 1958 grand prix, Carel Godin de Beaufort in practice in 1964, John Taylor in 1966, Georges Berger in an endurance race in 1967 and Gerhard Mitter in practice in 1969. Niki Lauda was almost added to that list in 1976.

⫸ ACHIEVING ACROSS THE BOARD

Michael Schumacher, the setter of so many records, proved his versatility by winning at 22 circuits. They were, in the order he conquered them. Spa-Francorchamps, Estoril, Interlagos, TI Circuit, Imola, Monaco, Montreal, Magny-Cours, the Hungaroring, Jerez, Barcelona, Hockenheim, the Nürburgring, Suzuka, Monza, Buenos Aires, Silverstone, Melbourne, Indianapolis, Sepang, the A1-Ring and Bahrain.

ROLLING THE DICE

Monaco is famed both for its grand prix and its casino, and the all-enclosing barriers mean that there's more than a little luck involved in winning there. However, McLaren, a team that is too organized to factor in luck, has clearly found the winning formula as it holds the record for the most consecutive wins at a circuit, six, and did so at Monaco of all places thanks to Alain Prost in 1988 then Ayrton Senna each year through to 1993.

NUMBER OF RACES HELD

 **BEFORE FANS HAD PROTECTION**

F1 spectators sometimes complain that they are kept back from the action, but there is a very good reason for this – their safety. In 1961 there was little protection for them and certainly no chain-link fencing. Had there been, then 14 fans at Monza probably wouldn't have died after Jim Clark and Wolfgang von Trips touched and von Trips's Ferrari was sent cart-wheeling into the crowd, killing the German aristocrat as well.

 BUSY, BUSY

The 2005 World Championship set a new record for comprising the most grands prix, at 19. However, this total was equalled in 2010 and the 2010 season was actually longer by three weeks as it stretched from the opening round in Bahrain on 14 March through until the Abu Dhabi finale on 14 November. Its duration was stretched by the summer break that now has to be built in to give the team personnel a well-earned rest.

 MORE AND EVER MORE

The trend for the number of grands prix in each World Championship is on the up, as 2010 had the equal most grands prix, 19, but spanned the longest period. In 2011, for the first time, there are 20 grands prix on the calendar. The average number of grand prix in the 1950s (excluding the Indianapolis 500) was 7.4, it was 9.9 in the 1960s, 14.4 in the 1970s, 15.6 in the 1980s, 16.2 in the 1990s and 17.4 in the 2000s.

 HONOUR OF OPENING THE SEASON

Argentina holds the record for hosting the most opening grands prix of the season, having done so on 15 occasions at its Buenos Aires circuit. Australia's Melbourne circuit is next with 13, and South Africa's Kyalami circuit is the third most popular place to kick off the action, having held the opening race eight times.

 SOMETHING ON THE SIDE

The World Championship was augmented by non-championship races in the early years, with the six championship grands prix in 1950 supported by 16 non-championship events in which the drivers raced for prize money. Juan Manuel Fangio won four of them.

 VARIETY APLENTY

The Long Beach street circuit in California has been used just eight times as a second US GP, but its tricky, bumpy course is one that no individual driver conquered as pole position went to a different driver each time, from Clay Regazzoni in 1976 to Patrick Tambay in 1983, both driving for Ferrari.

TOP 10 MOST-USED CIRCUITS

1	Monza	60
2	Monaco	57
3	Silverstone	44
4	Spa-Francorchamps	43
5	Nürburgring	38
6	Hockenheim	32
7	Montreal	31
8	Zandvoort	30
9	Interlagos	28
10	Imola	26

Above **Busy, busy:** Red Bull Racing's Sebastian Vettel needed the 19th race of 2010, at Abu Dhabi, to take the win and wrap up the drivers' title. *Below* **Doubling up:** Michael Schumacher is greeted by a fan after winning the 2006 San Marino GP at Imola.

DOUBLING UP

Italy is the country that has hosted the most grands prix since the World Championship began in 1950. It has outstripped Great Britain, Monaco and Belgium, all of which hosted races in 1950 and are still doing so in 2011, because it held a second race each year from 1981 to 2006 under the nominal title of the San Marino GP. By the end of 2010, Italy had hosted 87 grands prix, 16 ahead of Germany, which has hosted the European GP 12 times and the Luxembourg GP twice to boost its tally to 71.

A CLASH WITH TRAGIC CONSEQUENCES

||||||||||||||||||||||||||||||

Ronnie Peterson was a driver admired around the world for his spectacular style. Sadly, he was not to survive the 1978 Italian GP as his Lotus was caught up in a shunt as the cars accelerated away from the start, with 10 cars left battered and Peterson's on fire. Vittorio Brambilla was knocked out and Peterson had to be taken to hospital with leg injuries. He died during the night.

AND SO TO BED

Countries fight over who will hold the final grand prix of the year as this more often than not has the added drama of being the title battle decider. Brazil has hosted it most of late, but the USA edges Australia overall, 12 to 11, with Sebring, Riverside, Watkins Glen and the Caesar's Palace circuit in Las Vegas all having brought the curtain down on the season. Australia's closers were all held on the Adelaide street circuit.

Below **Kyalami:** The drop then climb from the start to Sunset bend. *Bottom* **A clash with tragic consequences:** The aftermath of the first-lap accident at Monza in 1978, with Ronnie Peterson's Lotus (6) on the left.

KYALAMI

Grand prix years: 1967-1980, 1982-1985, 1992-1993

No. of grands prix held: 20

Lap length: From 2.544 miles to 2.550 miles to 2.648 miles

Fastest qualifying lap: 1 min 15.486 secs, Nigel Mansell (Williams), 1992

Fastest race lap: 1 min 17.578 secs, Nigel Mansell (Williams), 1992

Driver with most wins: Niki Lauda – three (1976, 1977, 1984)

HIGHEST AND LOWEST SPEEDS

CIRCUIT BOUND

||||||||||||||||||||||||||||||||||||

David Coulthard was something of an expert at getting cars to fly in a low downforce setting when he raced for McLaren, as he proved when he recorded F1's fastest speed-trap figure of 224.8mph at Monza in 1999. This exceeded the previous record of 221.5mph that he'd set just a year earlier in practice for the German GP at Hockenheim. (This was when the Hockenheim layout had a long loop through the forest before it was cut back.)

TAKING IT TO EXTREMES

Honda Racing decided to show what its F1 car could do if it was given every opportunity to go for the max, not constrained by the limits of circuits. In 2006, test driver Alan van der Merwe drove its RA106 on the Bonneville salt flats and clocked a top speed of 246.908mph on an early morning run over the flying mile, making it the fastest F1 car ever, but falling just short of its 248.5mph target.

SURPRISE, SURPRISE

One glance at the tight layout of the Monte Carlo street circuit and it comes as no surprise that it's the slowest circuit used by F1. Its first World Championship grand prix in 1950 was won by Juan Manuel Fangio in his

Alfa Romeo, doing an average speed of just 61.331mph. There have been circuit modifications since, but not appreciable ones, yet the highest winning average rose to 96.655mph when Fernando Alonso won for McLaren in 2007.

Below **Stop at the red light:** The Toro Rosso of Sébastien Buemi was clocked at 195.421mph at Valenica in 2010.
Bottom **Circuit bound:** With wings angled as far back as possible on his McLaren, David Coulthard goes for broke at Monza in 1999.

STOP AT THE RED LIGHT

The highest speed recorded through a speed trap on a street circuit by an F1 car was at the third race on the Valencia circuit around the city's docks in 2010. Swiss driver Sébastien Buemi clocked 195.421mph at the end of the back straight just before Turn 12 in his Ferrari-powered Scuderia Toro Rosso.

STILL WAITING

Having spent his childhood in his family home overlooking Interlagos, Rubens Barrichello always dreamt that one day he would stand on top of the podium there as winner of the Brazilian GP. However, he seems to be "cursed" at his home race and, by the end of 2009, had a best result of only third, despite having led the race in 1999, 2000, 2002, 2003, 2004 and 2009.

TOP 10 HIGHEST SPEEDS IN 2010

1	Monza	215.429mph
2	Montreal	201.759mph
3	Istanbul	199.708mph
4	Yas Marina	198.901mph
5	Hockenheim	198.528mph
6	Shanghai	197.596mph
7	Bahrain	195.607mph
8	Valencia	195.421mph
9	Interlagos	195.110mph
10	Barcelona	193.992mph

All figures recorded at speed trap.

 ### FASTER IN THE WET

So slow were the grands prix around the streets of Monaco in the 1950s that the average speeds along the harbour front, up the hill to Casino Square and back down again were never faster than 70mph, and thus lower even than the average speed for race winner Ayrton Senna in the rain-hit 1991 Australian GP at Adelaide, a race that had to be called to a halt after 14 laps as cars were aquaplaning everywhere.

 ### MIKEY LIKES IT

Interlagos is a circuit that provides more than its share of race incidents, which is why it isn't one of those circuits where one driver has managed to produce a string of wins. Ayrton Senna managed to win only twice here, but Michael Schumacher kept out of trouble at the tricky first corner enough to win four times, in 1994, 1995, 2000 and 2002.

 ### FOR THE FANS

Interlagos has a proud boast of being a good track for Brazil's F1 stars, as both Emerson Fittipaldi and Carlos Pace won there during the circuit's first spell of hosting the Brazilian GP in the 1970s, sending the partisan crowd home happy. Ayrton Senna and Felipe Massa have won there since it took over the race again from Rio de Janeiro's Jacarepagua circuit in 1990, but Rubens Barrichello still has not managed a victory.

Above **Still waiting:** Rubens Barrichello has done everything but win at his home circuit, Interlagos, even after starting from pole position in 2009. *Below* **Melbourne:** Aerial shot of Albert Park with its attractive lakeside setting. *Right* **Show us the numbers:** The spectacular Yas Marina, Abu Dhabi, circuit might see drivers exceed 200mph on its long straight. Here, in 2009, Lewis Hamilton leads Sebastian Vettel.

 ### SHOW US THE NUMBERS

Arab petrolheads love performance cars and F1 too, but enticing them to watch it in the flesh has proved a problem, with Bahrain failing to draw in large crowds for its grand prix. Perhaps with this in mind, Abu Dhabi's incredible Yas Marina circuit was built with a straight that could produce speeds in excess of 200mph, the sort of figure that really impresses car nuts and hopefully encourages them to turn up rather than watch it on TV.

MELBOURNE

Grand prix years: 1996 onwards

No. of grands prix held: 15

Lap length: 3.295 miles

Fastest qualifying lap: 1 min 23.919 secs, Sebastian Vettel (Red Bull), 2010

Fastest race lap: 1 min 24.125 secs, Michael Schumacher (Ferrari), 2004

Driver with most wins: Michael Schumacher – four (2000, 2001, 2002, 2004)

PART 2

LEGENDARY DRIVERS

To top the all-time tables in Formula One a driver has to race for the right team at the right time. However, to appreciate the merits of the greatest drivers from the early decades of the World Championship, one has to consider that they contested fewer than half the number of races each year and, sadly, often failed to live long enough to gather as many scalps as today's best drivers. Dig a little deeper and it is clear that the brilliance of early champions Alberto Ascari, Jack Brabham and Jim Clark easily stands comparison with multiple-winners Ayrton Senna and Alain Prost, if not Michael Schumacher.

*Below **Championship contenders:** Ayrton Senna (Lotus-Renault), Alain Prost (McLaren-TAG Porsche), Nigel Mansell and Nelson Piquet (both Williams-Honda) prepare to do battle at the 1986 Portuguese GP at Estoril.*

MICHAEL SCHUMACHER

Michael Schumacher took a year from his F1 debut to taking his first grand prix win and the wins kept rolling in across the next decade and more, racing to seven world titles, so it's no surprise that he is the driver at the top of pretty much every list of F1 statistics. And now he's back for more.

Below **Winning for Ferrari:** When Michael Schumacher won the Japanese GP at Suzuka for Ferrari in 2000 his normal podium delight was taken to a new level as it gave him the first of his five world titles won for Ferrari.

FACT FILE

Name: Michael Schumacher
Nationality: German
Date of birth: 3/1/69
F1 career span: 1991-2006, 2010 on
Teams: Jordan 1991, Benetton 1991-1995, Ferrari 1996-2006, Mercedes 2010 on
Races contested: 269
Wins: 91
Poles: 68
Fastest laps: 75
Points: 1441
Championships: 1994, 1995, 2000, 2001, 2002, 2003, 2004

A HAPPY ANNIVERARY

Michael's first win came at his 18th start, on the anniversary of his debut, at the 1992 Belgian GP. After qualifying his Benetton third behind Nigel Mansell and Ayrton Senna, he enjoyed three slices of luck. Senna's gamble to start on slicks on a damp track backfired. Mansell's engine lost power. Finally, he slid off the circuit and rejoined behind team-mate Martin Brundle, noticed his tyres were blistering and changed his own at the optimum moment.

CAREER STATS

Year	Team	Races	Wins	Points	Ranking
1991	Jordan & Benetton	6	0	4	12th
1992	Benetton	16	1	53	3rd
1993	Benetton	16	1	52	4th
1994	Benetton	14	8	92	1st
1995	Benetton	17	9	102	1st
1996	Ferrari	16	3	59	3rd
1997	Ferrari	17	5	78	Not placed*
1998	Ferrari	16	6	86	2nd
1999	Ferrari	10	2	44	5th
2000	Ferrari	17	9	108	1st
2001	Ferrari	17	9	123	1st
2002	Ferrari	17	11	144	1st
2003	Ferrari	16	6	93	1st
2004	Ferrari	18	13	148	1st
2005	Ferrari	19	1	62	3rd
2006	Ferrari	18	7	121	2nd
2010	Mercedes	19	0	72	9th

* Removed from championship ranking for driving into Jacques Villeneuve in the final round at Jerez

 ### MAKING AN IMPRESSION

Michael Schumacher arrived with a bang when he gained his F1 break towards the end of 1991 when Jordan driver Bertrand Gachot was jailed for assaulting a taxi driver. He flew in practice for the Belgian GP then outpaced team-mate Andrea de Cesaris to qualify seventh. Sadly, he burnt out his clutch at the start and was out. By the next race, this hot property had been snapped up by Benetton, starting a title-winning relationship.

Right **Making an Impression:** Michael was on the pace on his F1 debut for Jordan in Belgium, but his race was a short one.
Below **A happy anniverary:** One year on from his debut at Spa-Francorchamps, now driving for Benetton, Michael raced to his first victory there in 1992.

CONTROVERSIAL CLINCHER

The 1994 World Championship was full of controversy for Benetton and Michael Schumacher. However, Michael kept winning and wrapped up the first of his seven titles at the final round, on the streets of Adelaide. He was being harried by Damon Hill, who needed to get by to become World Champion. Michael then glanced a wall, realized that his car was broken and simply drove across at Hill as he dived for the gap, taking him out.

 ## KART BLANCHE

Michael was given the flying start of which other aspiring racers can only dream. His father Rolf ran a kart circuit, so Michael spent all his spare time during his childhood in Kerpen behind the wheel.

 ## WHO NEEDS FULL POWER?

Perhaps Michael's greatest race performance came at the 1996 Spanish GP. This was in his first year with Ferrari, coming off the back of two consecutive title-winning seasons with Benetton, and the team was at a low ebb. However, Michael produced an extraordinary drive at a very wet Circuit de Catalunya. His Ferrari dropped onto only nine of its 10 cylinders at mid-distance, but he was still able to press on at scarcely abated speed for his first win for Ferrari.

 ## 13 IS UNLUCKY FOR OTHERS

Michael's illustrious career was never better than when taking the most recent of his seven world titles. This was in 2004 when he claimed his fifth title in succession for Ferrari with the remarkable tally of 13 wins from the season's 18 grands prix. No other driver has ever matched such an impressive tally. Having won the first five races and then clashed with Juan Pablo Montoya at Monaco, he duly won the next seven.

 ## MAKE IT TWO SCHUMACHERS

Racing alongside one's brother is a rare thing, but Michael and Ralf Schumacher were pitched together in F1 from 1997 to 2006. In this time, they established the most joint podium finishes for a pair of brothers, managing it 16 times. In that time, Ralf finished ahead of Michael just three times, in Canada in 2001, Malaysia in 2002 and France in 2003.

IN FRONT AT LAST

It was only the pace of the Williams drivers that kept Michael Schumacher from pole position in 1992 and 1993, but he finally claimed his first pole position in the 1994 Monaco GP, the fourth race of the season and the one after which that arch pole qualifier Ayrton Senna had died at the San Marino GP. Michael would go on to score 67 more before he took his sabbatical from F1 at the end of 2006.

Right **Seven in succession:** Michael celebrates scoring seven grand prix victories in a row to put him on the cusp of landing his seventh world title. *Above* **In front at last:** Monaco yielded the first pole of Michael's F1 career, for Benetton in 1994. He would go on to score 67 more.

SEVEN IN SUCCESSION

Michael and Ferrari were simply dominant in 2004 in a manner seldom seen in F1, save for Alberto Ascari in 1952/53, Jim Clark in 1963 and 1965 plus Nigel Mansell in 1992. If 2002 was a great season for Michael, then 2004 was even better and in it he achieved his greatest winning sequence, being first to the chequered flag at the European, Canadian, US, French, British, German and Hungarian GPs. He then wrapped up his seventh title next time out.

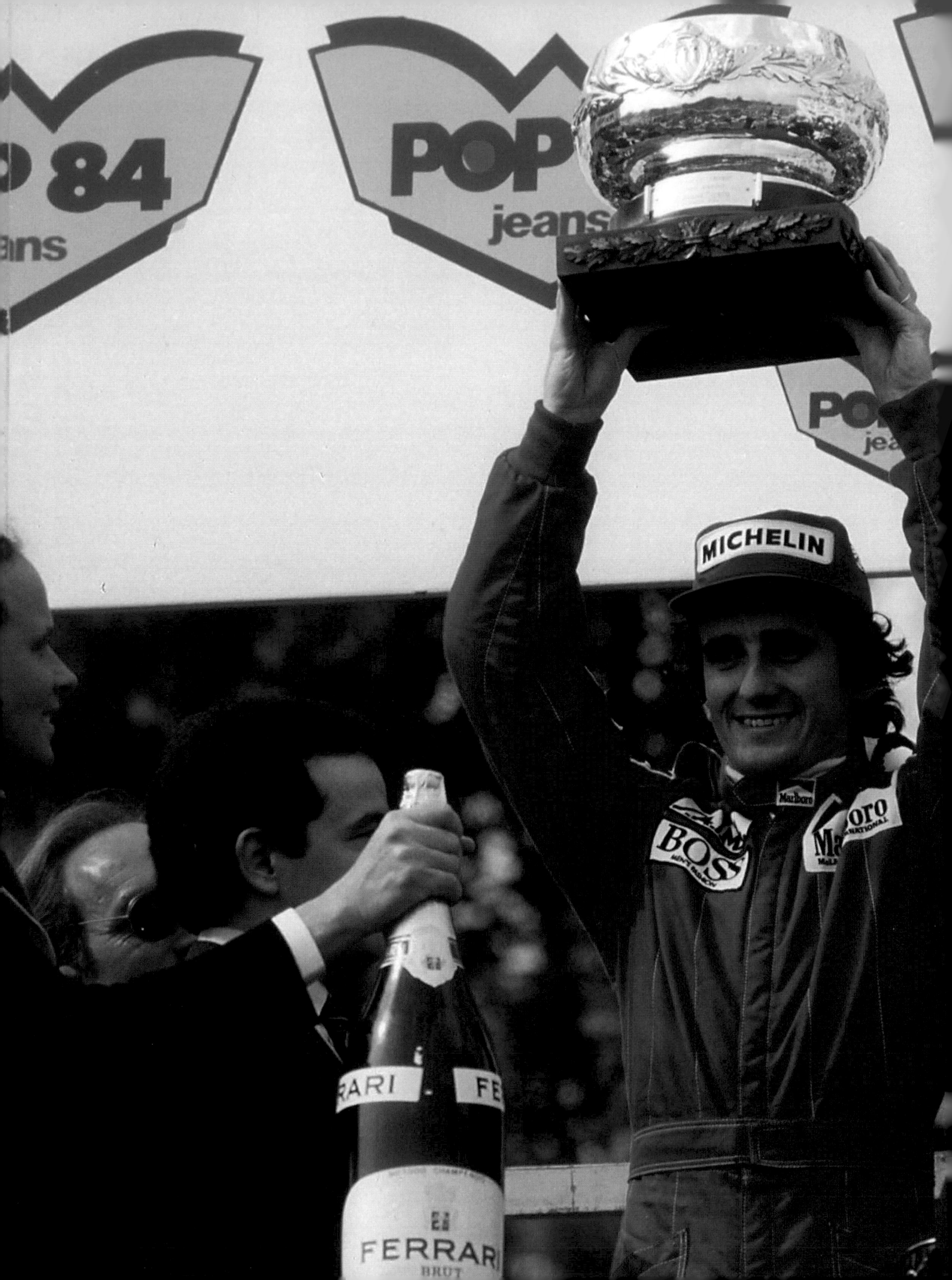
MICHELIN
FERRARI
BRUT

ALAIN PROST

Alain Prost was extremely fast but seldom looked it as he wasn't flamboyant. It was the way that he used his head to drive supremely tactical races that earned him the sobriquet "Le Professeur". This cerebral driving style guided him to his four world drivers' titles for McLaren and then Williams.

Below **Winning for McLaren:** *Alain joined McLaren at the start of the 1984 season and this celebration at Imola with Ferrari's Rene Arnoux marks his second win in just four outings.*

FACT FILE

Name: Alain Prost

Nationality: French

Date of birth: 24/2/55

F1 career span: 1980-1991 & 1993

Teams: McLaren 1980, Renault 1981-83, McLaren 1984 89, Ferrari 1990-91, Williams 1993

Races contested: 200

Wins: 51

Poles: 33

Fastest laps: 41

Points: 798.5

Championships: 1985, 1986, 1989, 1993

SOCCER GETS THE BOOT

Alain had other sporting pretensions before he settled on racing. He was a handy football player, good enough to be given trials, but after trying karting when he was on holiday aged 14 he made up his mind on the matter.

FIRST PAST 50

Alain now has only marginally more than half of Michael Schumacher's career tally of 91 wins, but he was once clear at the top of the list of winners. His victory in the 1993 British GP made him the first driver to score 50. Alain added one more to that tally at the next race at Hockenheim, but this proved to be his last as his Williams team-mate Damon Hill came on strong and won three of the remaining six grands prix.

CAREER STATS

Year	Team	Races	Wins	Points	Ranking
1980	McLaren	11	0	5	15th
1981	Renault	15	3	43	5th
1982	Renault	16	2	34	4th
1983	Renault	15	4	57	2nd
1984	McLaren	16	7	71.5	2nd
1985	McLaren	16	5	76	1st
1986	McLaren	16	4	74	1st
1987	McLaren	16	3	46	4th
1988	McLaren	16	7	95	2nd
1989	McLaren	16	4	81	1st
1990	Ferrari	16	5	73	2nd
1991	Ferrari	15	0	31	5th
1993	Williams	16	7	99	1st

STEPPING UP IN STYLE

Back in the days when outstanding Formula 3 drivers could leap direct to F1, Alain Prost demonstrated that the skills that landed him the 1979 European F3 crown were more than good enough for F1. On his debut in the 1980 Argentinian GP, Alain qualified his McLaren midgrid and advanced from there to sixth place. When he finished fifth next time out, Prost emphasized the talents that would land him four world titles.

FALLING AT THE LAST

Renault was so confident that Alain would clinch the title in 1983 that the manufacturer flew out plane loads of journalists to South Africa to cover the occasion. Alain held a two-point lead over Nelson Piquet but wasn't confident as he felt Brabham was still pushing on with its development. Piquet vaulted from second into the lead at the start and Alain could run only fourth, which wasn't going to be enough. When he felt his turbo start to fail, Alain quit the race.

Below **First Past 50:** Alain's victory for Williams at Silverstone in 1993 made him the first to top 50 grand prix wins.

Above **Fresh start:** Alain's win for Williams at Hockenheim in 1993 helped him to claim a fourth world title. *Left* **Close call:** Prost started 1984 with this win in Brazil, but would end the year half a point down.

⟫ THE CLOSEST MISS

After quitting Renault at the end of 1983, Alain had a fruitful year with McLaren in 1984, starting with victory first time out at the Brazilian GP (above). After adding wins at Imola, Hockenheim, Zandvoort and the Nürburgring, Alain went to the final round at Estoril just 3.5 points down on teammate Niki Lauda. Alain did all he could, passing Nelson Piquet for the lead. However, Lauda gained second place when Nigel Mansell spun out and that was enough to clinch the title by half a point.

⟫ SCORING TO THE VERY END

When Alain Prost brought his Williams home second behind Ayrton Senna in his final race, the 1993 Australian GP at Adelaide, he cemented his position as the scorer of the highest career tally of points. The French ace achieved 798.5 points, a total that Michael Schumacher passed in the final round of 2001. Michael went on to score 1,369 points before his retirement in 2006 and has continued to add to that tally since returning in 2010.

⟫ FINISHING THE JOB

Having been runner-up in 1983 and 1984, Alain was desperate to go one better in 1985, his second year with McLaren. And so he did, thanks to a good mid-season run of results. By the time he reached Brands Hatch for the European GP, Alain was in touching distance. An evasive move at the start of the race dropped him to 14th and it took a solid run to fourth to end the title bid of closest challenger Michele Alboreto whose Ferrari's turbo failed.

FRESH FROM A YEAR OUT

After quitting F1 in 1991 after two years with Ferrari, Alain came back from his year's sabbatical to prove his ability yet again, this time with Williams. The car was very much the class of the field in 1993. Alain claimed seven wins (equalling his record haul for a season as recorded in 1984 and 1988) to land his fourth title, wrapping it up with second place at the Portuguese GP at Estoril.

ALAIN'S ARRIVAL

Impressed by his maiden season with McLaren, Renault snapped Alain up for 1981. He was soon proving that he was the best French driver of his generation by claiming his first podium, coming third in the third round in Argentina. Alain went better still at his home grand prix at Dijon-Prenois (*right*) by not only setting his first fastest lap but going on to secure his first win, heading home John Watson in a race interrupted by a downpour.

NTARCT
Cha
É O SAB
YEAR
Grand Prix
BOSS
McLAREN INTERNATIONAL
ONAL
Shell
OMP
Senna

AYRTON SENNA

The late Ayrton Senna was a driver who polarized opinions. He was supremely fast but spoiled that, for some, by his "win at all costs" approach. No-one, though, could deny his presence. His career with McLaren was synonymous with winning but shortly after a move to Williams his life came to a sudden end.

*Below **There's no place like home:** Ayrton tried for seven years before he collected his first win on home soil in Brazil, winning at last at Interlagos for McLaren in 1991, the year of his third world title.*

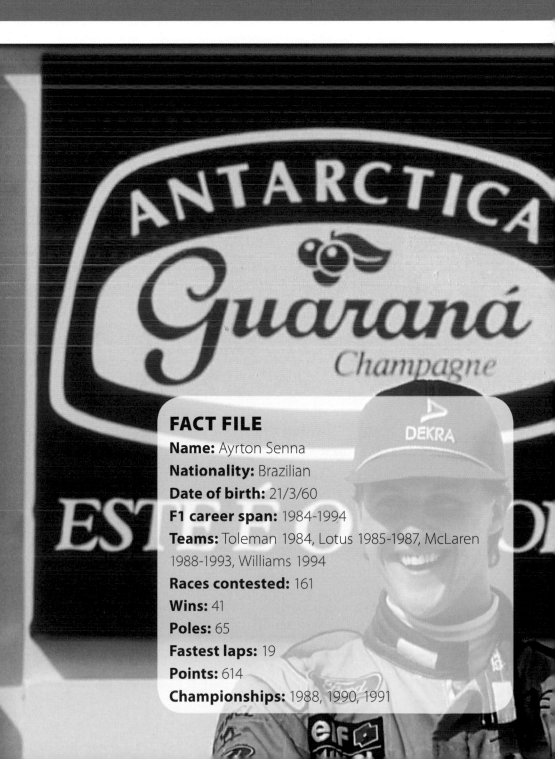

FACT FILE

Name: Ayrton Senna

Nationality: Brazilian

Date of birth: 21/3/60

F1 career span: 1984-1994

Teams: Toleman 1984, Lotus 1985-1987, McLaren 1988-1993, Williams 1994

Races contested: 161

Wins: 41

Poles: 65

Fastest laps: 19

Points: 614

Championships: 1988, 1990, 1991

IN A CLASS OF HIS OWN

Ayrton could be untouchable in qualifying, as you would imagine from someone who claimed 65 poles. His day of days in qualifying came at the 1989 Japanese GP, when he was fastest by 1.730 secs. His speed advantage was greatest at Monaco and he qualified on pole there by more than 1 sec in 1988 and 1989, which he also did at Detroit in 1985, Phoenix in 1989 and the Hungaroring in 1991.

Above **In a class of his own:** Ayrton dominated qualifying at Suzuka in 1989, but team-mate Alain Prost got a grippier start and led. *Below* **Wet weather masterpiece:** Ayrton was untouchable in the wet at Donington Park in 1993 and was soon lapping his rivals, including Riccardo Patrese and Fabrizio Barbazza.

A FALSE START

Anyone who had watched Ayrton Senna trounce his rivals in the junior single-seater formulae knew that he was special. However, when he made his break into F1 with Toleman in 1984, not much was expected as the team was midfield at best. Having qualified 17th out of 27 starters for his first grand prix, at home in Brazil, he climbed three places in the opening few laps before retiring with turbo failure.

THWARTED BY A RED FLAG

Having scored points on his second and third grand prix outings, Ayrton produced a stunning drive at his sixth attempt, at the 1984 Monaco GP. Conditions were extremely wet and very treacherous, but the Brazilian rookie was still able to reel in experienced race leader Alain Prost's McLaren. But, just as Ayrton latched onto Prost's tail, the race was red-flagged and brought to a premature conclusion by Clerk of the Course, Jacky Ickx.

WET WEATHER MASTERPIECE

Ayrton produced some mesmerizing performances among his 41 runs to grand prix victories, but his greatest race of all was the 1993 European GP at Donington Park. Conditions were wet and he lost a place at the start, falling to fifth. However, with a singular focus and outstanding car control, Ayrton picked off each and every one of the drivers ahead to take the lead before lap 1 was complete and then raced ever further clear.

AYRTON'S TREBLE BREAKTHROUGH

Joining Lotus for his second year in F1, after his rookie season with the Toleman team, was a great move for Ayrton Senna. He claimed his first pole position on his second outing at the 1985 Portuguese GP. Better than that, he was then able to set the fastest lap in the race around a very wet Estoril circuit and lead every lap through the deluge to record his first grand prix win.

Above **Ayrton's treble breakthrough:** The Estoril circuit was streaming with water at the 1985 Portuguese GP, but Ayrton was in control from start to finish. *Below* **A proud Brazilian:** Ayrton waves the flag for Brazil after victory at the 1988 Japanese GP was enough for him to become world champion.

CAREER STATS

Year	Team	Races	Wins	Points	Ranking
1984	Toleman	15	0	13	9th
1985	Lotus	16	2	38	4th
1986	Lotus	16	2	55	4th
1987	Lotus	16	2	57	3rd
1988	McLaren	16	8	94	1st
1989	McLaren	16	5	60	2nd
1990	McLaren	16	6	78	1st
1991	McLaren	16	6	96	1st
1992	McLaren	16	3	50	4th
1993	McLaren	16	5	73	2nd
1994	Williams	3	0	0	-

A NATION MOURNED

Such was the impact of Ayrton's death in the 1994 San Marino GP that Brazil declared three days of national mourning. It was estimated that a million people lined the streets of São Paulo for his funeral.

PICKING OFF THE POLES

Acknowledged as the supreme qualifier, Ayrton Senna notched up 65 pole positions, at an average that the more long-serving Michael Schumacher has never been able to match. Ayrton achieved the remarkable tally of 13 pole positions in a season twice. Once in 1988 and again in 1989 when he guided his McLaren to 13 poles, starting 1988 with six straight poles and rounding out 1989 with the same sequence.

TWO SETS OF FOUR

Ayrton Senna was far more than the king of the qualifying lap, as his world titles in 1988, 1989 and 1991 attest. Indeed, he claimed 41 wins to put him second in the rankings behind Alain Prost (later third when Michael Schumacher moved past both). His best winning sequence was four in a row, which he managed twice by winning the British, German, Hungarian and Belgian GPs in 1998 then the US, Brazilian, San Marino and Monaco GPs in 1991.

MIND OVER MATTER

Winning in a competitive car is one thing, but doing so in one that is not the pick of the pack deserves even more respect. In 1993, his final season with McLaren, Ayrton drove some of his greatest races. And, in the final race of the campaign, at Adelaide, he managed to manhandle his Ford-powered MP4/8 around faster than the dominant Williams-Renaults for his only pole of the year. He then outraced Prost for what proved to be the last of his 41 wins.

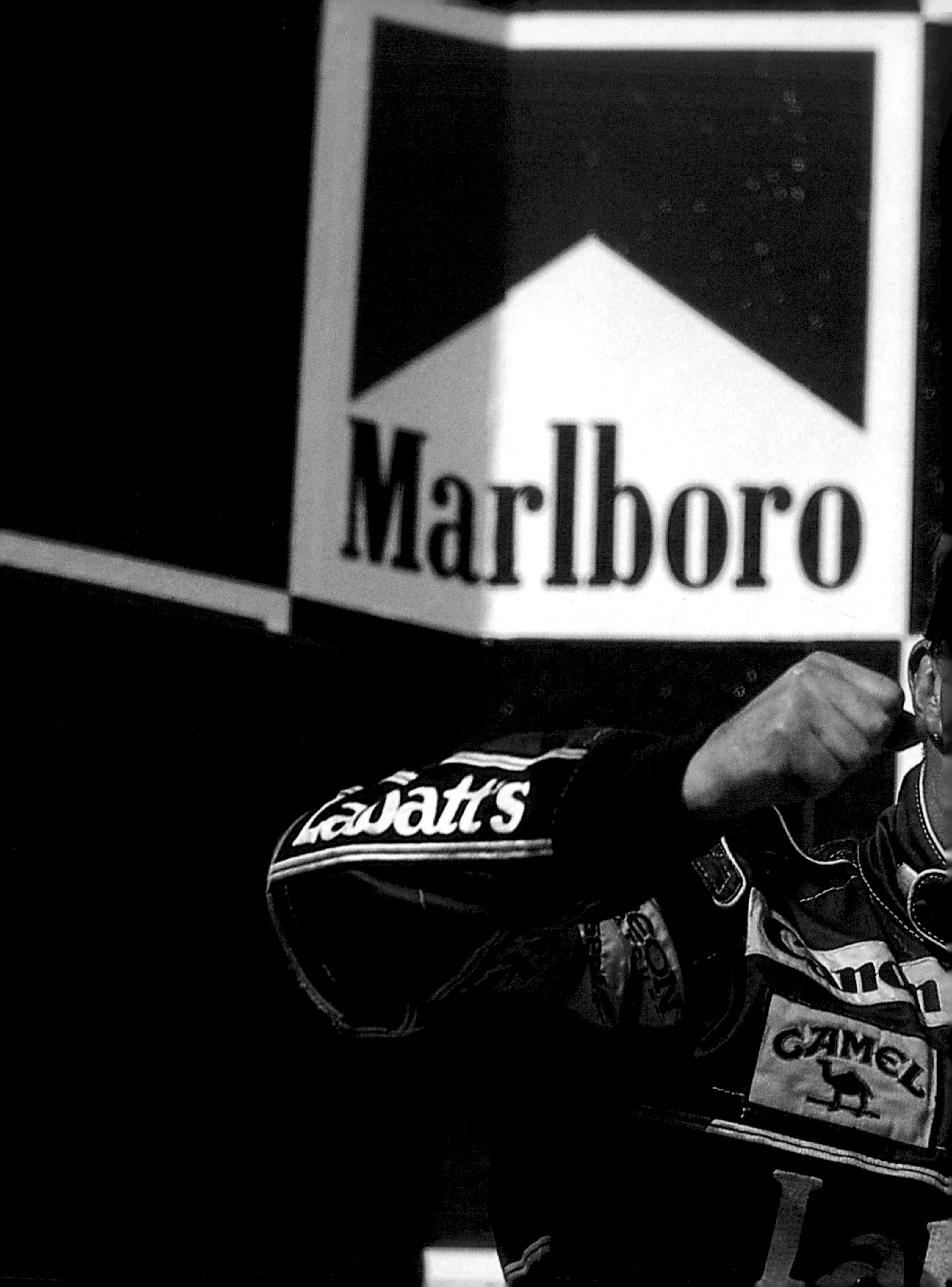
Marlboro
CAMEL

NIGEL MANSELL

Nigel Mansell never had a quiet race. They were all packed with drama, problems or performances of dogged brilliance. When all was right, he would wring every last drop of speed out of the car and out of himself in a flamboyant, entertaining style. Then, when his chance came in 1992, he grabbed it.

*Below **A British bulldog:** The passion that Nigel always put into his racing is shown on his face as he celebrates victory at Silverstone for Williams in his title-winning year: 1992.*

FACT FILE

Name: Nigel Mansell

Nationality: British

Date of birth: 8/8/53

F1 career span: 1980-1992, 1994 & 1995

Teams: Lotus 1980-1984, Williams 1985-1988, Ferrari 1989-1990, Williams 1991-1992 & 1994, McLaren 1995

Races contested: 187

Wins: 31

Poles: 32

Fastest laps: 30

Points: 482

Championships: 1992

CAREER STATS

Year	Team	Races	Wins	Points	Ranking
1980	Lotus	3	0	0	-
1981	Lotus	14	0	8	14th
1982	Lotus	13	0	7	14th
1983	Lotus	15	0	10	13th
1984	Lotus	16	0	13	9th
1985	Williams	16	2	31	6th
1986	Williams	16	5	72	2nd
1987	Williams	15	6	61	2nd
1988	Williams	14	0	12	9th
1989	Ferrari	15	2	38	4th
1990	Ferrari	16	1	37	5th
1991	Williams	16	5	72	2nd
1992	Williams	16	9	108	1st
1994	Williams	4	1	13	9th
1995	McLaren	2	0	0	-

LOOKING DOWN ON OTHERS

All aspiring racing drivers conjure images of themselves smiling down from the podium. Obviously, mounting the top step as a winner would be best, but Nigel would have been happy enough to claim his first podium finish. This came in the 1981 Belgian GP at Zolder when he brought his Lotus home behind Carlos Reutemann's Williams and Jacques Laffite's Ligier. For his first win, he'd have to wait another four years and more.

MOVING TO THE FRONT

To top timesheets or win grands prix, a driver needs a really competitive car. Nigel Mansell never really had that in his first few years of F1. However, by 1984, with Renault turbo power, he was on the pace and duly delivered his first pole position halfway through the season on the World Championship's one and only visit to the Dallas street circuit. This didn't result in his first win, though, as Nigel could finish no higher than sixth.

PLEASING THE HOME CROWD

There can be no better place to secure your first win than on home ground and Nigel did just that in the 1985 European GP at Brands Hatch. He qualified his Williams behind Ayrton Senna and Nelson Piquet but lost a place to Keke Rosberg at the start. Nigel moved into second when Rosberg spun while attacking Senna and Piquet hit him. Three laps later, Nigel took a lead he was never to lose when he passed Senna. With the monkey off his back, he won the following race at Kyalami.

Left **Looking down on others:** Nigel savours his first grand prix podium after finishing third in the 1981 Belgian GP. *Below* **Dogged determination:** Nigel was soaked with fuel, burning his back, but he kept going on his F1 debut for Lotus in the 1980 Austrian GP until his car's engine failed.

DOGGED DETERMINATION

Nigel Mansell had had to fight more than almost any of his rivals to get his break in F1 and, because of this, he was not going to give up when the going got tough. And it did on his F1 debut at the 1980 Austrian GP. Petrol leaked into the cockpit of Nigel's Lotus, causing him extreme pain. He soldiered on until the car's engine failed, earning Nigel increased respect from team boss Colin Chapman and first-degree burns to his back.

MAKING THE MOST OF IT

Having been so close to landing the world title in 1986, only to be robbed by a blow-out, Nigel must have felt that he deserved the crown, and his 1992 campaign finally produced it. That year's Williams FW14B was the pick of the pack and Nigel made the most of it, starting with a run of five straight wins, in the South African, Mexican, Brazilian, Spanish and San Marino GPs. This provided the largest part of his tally of nine wins that landed him the title with five rounds to spare.

LE MANS HOPES GO POP

Nigel's attempt to conquer the Le Mans 24 Hours with sons Leo and Greg in 2010 came to nought. Nigel was pitched into the barriers on only the fifth lap, due to a slow puncture.

A SEASON TO FORGET

The loss of the Honda engine cost Williams dear in 1988 when it had to replace them with Judd engines. Nigel Mansell dropped from second in the 1987 title race to ninth in 1988 – his worst ever year in terms of retirements, failing to finish in 12 of the 14 rounds, albeit four of these being due to driver error. Showing the thwarted promise, he came home second in each of the races he finished.

INSTANT AFFECTION

The *Tifosi* don't immediately warm to Ferrari's new signings, but Nigel Mansell gave them every reason to love him when he joined in 1989. How? By winning on his first outing. He did this at the Brazilian GP at Jacarepagua when he qualified sixth alongside team-mate Gerhard Berger. Nigel was up to third on the opening lap before working his way past Thierry Boutsen's failing Williams and then Alain Prost's McLaren. He would win just once more in 1989.

NO RESPECT FOR YOUTH

The best way to augment one's reputation after retiring is to pop back for a cameo performance and stick it to the young guns. Nigel Mansell achieved this in 1994 when the fourth of his stand-in outings for Williams resulted in victory. This happened at the Australian GP when third place turned into first place after Michael Schumacher collided with Damon Hill while fighting over the lead. It was Nigel's final F1 win.

Left **Instant affection:** Nigel showed how to win friends with the *Tifosi* by winning on his first outing, in Brazil. *Below* **Making the most of it:** Supplied with a pace-setting car by Williams in 1992, Nigel did the rest to record nine wins and land the title.

JACKIE STEWART

The immaculate Jackie Stewart was a driver who raced by the principle of wanting to win grands prix by the lowest speed possible. He had all the pace in the world but, in an age when cars were fragile and drivers died if they slipped up, he calculated his victories and earned himself three world titles.

Below **Emotions under control:** *Jackie seems lost in thought as he stands with the spoils of one of his 17 grand prix victories for the Tyrrell team.*

FACT FILE

Name: Jackie Stewart

Nationality: British

Date of birth: 11/6/39

F1 career span: 1965-1973

Teams: BRM 1965-1967, Matra 1968-1969, Tyrrell 1970-1973

Races contested: 99

Wins: 27

Poles: 17

Fastest laps: 15

Points: 360

Championships: 1969, 1971 & 1973

Below **A pair of threes:** Jackie savours victory in the 1969 Dutch GP in his Ken Tyrrell-run Matra.

A PAIR OF THREES

Jackie Stewart twice enjoyed a hat-trick of wins, taking three wins in a row at the Dutch, French and British GPs in his Ken Tyrrell-run Matra in 1969, his first title-winning year. In 1971 he achieved the feat again at the French, British and German GPs in his Elf-sponsored Tyrrell to claim the second of his three F1 titles.

STARTING IN THE POINTS

Jackie Stewart made his F1 debut in 1965 after strong seasons in F3 then F2. Driving for BRM, after turning down the chance to join fellow Scot Jim Clark at Lotus, Jackie qualified 11th out of 25 on his debut in the South African GP at East London. Jackie advanced to sixth place and claimed points first time out. This feat remains something of a rarity, even with points extended first to the top eight then the top 10 finishers.

KEEPING BUSY

Jackie, with numerous business interests, has never been one for a quiet retirement. The one that kept him busiest was starting Stewart GP with his eldest son Paul in 1997. They ran the team until 2000 when it was sold to Jaguar.

Below **Leaving his mark:** Jackie jumps his Tyrrell 006 over one of the Nürburgring's many brows en route to his 27th and last grand prix win.

LEAVING HIS MARK

Victory in the 1973 Dutch GP put Jackie clear as the driver with the most grand prix wins, exceeding the record held by fellow Scot Jim Clark. Then, at the Nürburgring, not only did Jackie head home Tyrrell teammate Francois Cevert for his 27th win, but this final win would leave him at the top of the list until Alain Prost passed this mark in 1987. The Frenchman would go on to win 51 times, a record bettered only by Michael Schumacher with 91.

IN FRONT AT THE FINISH

Having been in the points on his debut in the South African GP and scored his first podium finish next time out at Monaco, it seemed likely that Jackie Stewart would take his first win in his maiden season. And so he did at the 1965 Italian GP. Jackie started the race third on the grid and worked his way up to enjoy a typical Monza slipstreaming battle with BRM teammate Richie Ginther before taking the lead with two laps to go.

Left **On the podium:** Jackie races through Monaco's narrow streets in his BRM in 1965, heading for third place for his first podium finish.
Below **In front at the finish:** Having scored points on his F1 debut in South Africa, Jackie would claim his first victory in just his eighth race, at Monza in the 1965 Italian Grand Prix.

⫸ NO DRIP IN THE WET

The Nürburgring Nordschleife sorted the men from the boys. Add rain to that mix and the potential gap in performance was even greater. For the 1968 German GP, there was low cloud too and Jackie Stewart produced his greatest ever drive to jump from sixth on the grid to lead before the end of the first 14-mile lap. His Matra was then never headed again and he won by four minutes from Graham Hill's Lotus.

⫸ A DOUBLE VICTORY

To win an F1 drivers' title is a feather in any driver's cap, but to do so with a victory gives extra kudos, and this is what Jackie Stewart managed when he claimed the first of his three titles in 1969. He lined up his Matra third on the grid for the Italian GP behind Jochen Rindt's Lotus and Denny Hulme's McLaren, then jumped both and raced clear before holding off a slipstreaming pack to land his sixth win of the year and the title.

⫸ MISSING OUT ON A CENTURY

Jackie Stewart was a driver of immense precision and he would have liked the fact that the last race before he quit driving would have been his 100th. However, the death of his Tyrrell teammate Francois Cevert in practice for the 1973 United States GP at Watkins Glen led to the team withdrawing, and so Jackie remains eternally with 99 not 100 grands prix starts to his name.

Above **No drip in the wet:** Jackie splashes his Matra around the Nürburgring to score a famous win in 1968, crossing the finish line just over four minutes ahead of Graham Hill's second-placed Lotus.

CAREER STATS

Year	Team	Races	Wins	Points	Ranking
1965	BRM	10	1	34	3rd
1966	BRM	8	1	14	7th
1967	BRM	11	0	10	9th
1968	Matra	10	3	36	2nd
1969	Matra	11	6	63	1st
1970	Tyrrell	13	1	25	5th
1971	Tyrrell	11	6	62	1st
1972	Tyrrell	11	4	45	2nd
1973	Tyrrell	14	5	71	1st

JIM CLARK

Jim Clark was a driver who was so effortlessly quick in whatever type of car he drove that he appeared to be in a different class to even his closest rivals. In the years when his flying Lotus was strong enough for the job, he was crowned World Champion, but then a freak accident in an F2 race claimed his life.

Below **The first flying Scot:** *Jim is dwarfed by his garland after winning the 1965 German GP at the Nürburgring for Lotus in what proved to be his second title-winning campaign.*

FACT FILE

Name: Jim Clark
Nationality: British
Date of birth: 4/3/36
Date of death: 7/4/68
F1 career span: 1960-1968
Teams: Lotus 1960-1968
Races contested: 72
Wins: 25
Poles: 33
Fastest laps: 28
Points: 274
Championships: 1963 & 1965

Above **Conquering his fear:** Jim loathed Spa-Francorchamps, but still managed to win there on four occasions, including this run in 1964.

CONQUERING HIS FEAR

Spa-Francorchamps in the 1960s was a circuit to be feared. This wasn't surprising as it was ultra-fast with little to stop cars from flying off into the trees. Jim Clark loathed it after his first visit in 1958 saw Archie Scott-Brown killed, followed by teammate Alan Stacey and Chris Bristow in 1960. However, he managed to put the fear aside and win there each year from 1962 to 1965, with his 1962 victory the first of his 25 grand prix wins.

A FALSE START

Jim Clark didn't take long to reach F1. When Aston Martin scrapped its F1 project for 1960, Clark bounced back to sign for Lotus to race in F2. His pace was such that he was granted his F1 debut in the season's third round, the Dutch GP. The Scot qualified 11th out of 21, but his Lotus 18 retired from fifth when the transmission failed. He scored his first points next time out, at Spa-Francorchamps.

STARTING FROM THE FRONT

The predominance of Jim Clark and the Lotus 25 in 1963 led to his best seasonal tally of pole positions when he claimed the top spot in qualifying seven times in 10 rounds. He took pole position at Monaco, Zandvoort, Reims, Silverstone, the Nürburgring, Mexico City and East London. They didn't all result in wins, but he still managed seven of those that year.

Right **Overtaking no problem:** Jim powers through the field to regain the lead at the 1967 Italian GP at Monza.
Below **The beginning of the end:** Winning at the 1968 South African GP.

ARISE PRINCE JIM THE FIRST

Jim Clark was always going to be World Champion and an improvement in Lotus's reliability in 1963 allowed him the tools to do the job. Such was his form, winning four of the first six races, that the Scot was able to clinch his first title at the Italian GP with three rounds still to run. To become champion, he raced to his fifth win by 35 secs over Richie Ginther's BRM.

THE BEGINNING OF THE END

Going into 1968 the second campaign in which Lotus was powered by Ford's pace-setting Cosworth DFV engine, Jim Clark laid down his marker by dominating the season-opening South African GP at Kyalami. Such was Clark's advantage that he started from pole, demoted Jackie Stewart's fast-starting Matra on the second lap and led every remaining lap to beat teammate Graham Hill by 25.3 secs. Tragically, he died in an F2 race before the second round.

OVERTAKING NO PROBLEM

One of Jim Clark's most remarkable drives came at the 1967 Italian GP at Monza. He started from pole position and was leading before his Lotus had to pit to have a flat tyre replaced on the 13th of 70 laps, dropping him to 15th of the 16 remaining runners. Clark then tore through the field, making up an entire lap to retake the lead with seven laps to go, only to suffer fuel pump problems on the final lap and fall to third.

AN AIR OF INVINCIBILITY

||||||||||||||||||||||||||||||||

When Jim Clark was in his pomp, his rivals might have felt that second place behind his Lotus was the best that they could hope for. This would certainly have been the case in 1965 when Jim achieved his best winning sequence, following victory in the opening round in South Africa with five more wins in the next five races in Belgium, France, Britain, Holland and Germany.

CAREER STATS

Year	Team	Races	Wins	Points	Ranking
1960	Lotus	6	0	8	8th
1961	Lotus	8	0	11	7th
1962	Lotus	9	3	30	2nd
1963	Lotus	10	7	73	1st
1964	Lotus	10	3	32	3rd
1965	Lotus	9	6	54	1st
1966	Lotus	9	0	16	6th
1967	Lotus	11	4	41	3rd
1968	Lotus	1	1	9	11th

≫ IT COULD HAVE BEEN FOUR STRAIGHT

Jim Clark's death in 1968 scuppered any hopes of a third F1 title but, had his luck been better, he could have had four titles to his name by the end of 1965. All set to land the title in 1962, Jim's Lotus was sidelined by oil line failure in the final round. Although champion in 1963 and 1965, Clark came within an ace of taking the 1964 crown too, but suffered another oil line failure in Mexico City.

≫ TRACTOR BOY

Jim's earliest driving experiences weren't in anything as helpful as a racing kart. Instead, with his family being farmers in the Scottish borders, it was on tractors. Still, that can't have hurt…

Below **An air of invincibility:** Jim shows his smooth style as he guides his Lotus 25 to victory at Silverstone in 1965, the fourth of six wins in a row.

TOYOTA GRAND PRIX
OF LONG BEACH TOYO
TOYOTA G AND

GOOD YEAR

TOYO

Marlbo

EBEL
WATCHES

EBE
WATCH

parma

ICI
CHEMICALS
PLASTICS

GOOD YEAR

NIKI LAUDA

Niki Lauda was thought of as a "rent-a-driver", but he proved he was much more than that and became World Champion in 1975. A fiery accident almost claimed his life the next year, but he bounced back to be champion again in 1977 and then in 1984 after taking time out to start his own airline.

Below **Back in the saddle:** *After two years in retirement, Niki showed that he had lost none of his skill by winning at Long Beach in 1982 on his third race back.*

FACT FILE

Name: Niki Lauda

Nationality: Austrian

Date of birth: 22/2/49

F1 career span: 1971-1979, 1982-1985

Teams: March 1971-1972, BRM 1973, Ferrari 1974-1977, Brabham 1978-1979, McLaren 1982-1985

Races contested: 171

Wins: 25

Poles: 24

Fastest laps: 24

Points: 420.5

Championships: 1975, 1977 & 1984

CAREER STATS

Year	Team	Races	Wins	Points	Ranking
1971	March	1	0	0	-
1972	March	12	0	0	-
1973	BRM	15	0	2	17th
1974	Ferrari	15	2	38	4th
1975	Ferrari	14	5	64.5	1st
1976	Ferrari	14	4	68	2nd
1977	Ferrari	15	3	72	1st
1978	Brabham	16	2	44	4th
1979	Brabham	14	0	4	14th
1982	McLaren	15	2	30	5th
1983	McLaren	15	0	12	10th
1984	McLaren	16	5	72	1st
1985	McLaren	15	1	14	10th

MADE OF STERN STUFF

Niki Lauda was administered the last rites when hospitalized by the burns he suffered in the 1976 German GP. However, not only did he survive, but such was his recovery that he missed only two races before making his return at the Italian GP. Despite continuing to suffer great pain, Niki qualified fifth and drove an heroic race to fourth to keep his title hopes alive.

HIDING HIS LIGHT

Although he'd end his career with three world titles, Niki Lauda didn't arrive in F1 with a great reputation. Indeed, he used a bank loan to buy a drive in a semi-works March at his home grand prix at the Osterreichring in 1971. Unfortunately, he qualified only 21st out of 22 starters and rose no higher than penultimate place before retiring. It wasn't an auspicious start, but things got far better.

FANNING THE FLAMES

Niki achieved a unique feat when he won the 1978 Swedish GP, becoming the only person to win a grand prix with a car sucked to the ground by a giant fan. Starting third on the grid behind Lotus' pole-sitter Mario Andretti and his own teammate John Watson, he made it into the lead in his Brabham at mid-distance and waltzed clear when the Lotus slowed with engine problems. No fan car was allowed to compete in F1 again.

Above **Made of stern stuff:** Niki always wore a cap when out of the car after suffering facial burns in his accident in the 1976 German GP.
Below **Scraping home:** Second place behind McLaren teammate Alain Prost at Estoril in 1984 was just enough to give Niki his third world title.

FLIGHT OF FANCY

Top-level racing drivers, like any top-level athletes, are driven people. After winning his first two F1 titles Niki still had other ambitions, and so he set up his own airline.

SCRAPING HOME

Niki won the 1984 World Championship by the smallest margin in F1 history. His rival in that final round shoot-out at Estoril was none other than his McLaren teammate, Alain Prost. They arrived at the event with Lauda enjoying a 3½-point lead over his younger French rival. Prost dominated the race and won, but Lauda advanced from 11th to finish second, enough to take the title by half a point.

IN THE RAIN IN SPAIN

Niki's talent was masked by a poor-handling March in 1972, but he showed better form in a BRM in 1973. The turning point came when he landed a seat at Ferrari in 1974 and Niki stepped up from his first podium finish at the Argentinian GP to record his first win at the Spanish GP at Jarama. Although Niki started from pole, Ronnie Peterson moved his Lotus ahead in the rain but Niki profited when the Swede's engine failed.

BLOWING THE RUST AWAY

|||||||||||||||||||||||||||||||||||||||||||

Tempted back into racing after two years out of the sport while he set up his airline, Niki had quite a shock when he rolled out for McLaren at Kyalami for the 1982 season opener and qualified only 13th. But Niki demonstrated that the race craft that had helped him to world titles in 1975 and 1977 hadn't deserted him as he clawed his way forward to finish fourth. Two races later, he was a winner again.

Above **In the rain in Spain:** Niki guides his Ferrari 312B3 around Jarama's twists to score his first grand prix win in 1974. *Below* **For the fans:** Niki celebrates on the podium at Monza in 1975 after third place gave him his first world title. *Bottom* **Blowing the rust away:** Race craft rather than speed was key to Niki scoring points on his return at Kyalami in 1982.

ONE FOR THE FANS

Having turned Ferrari back into a winning team on his first year with them in 1974, Niki became the first Ferrari driver to be World Champion since John Surtees in 1964. Niki secured the title in front of the team's home crowd at the 1975 Italian GP, racing to third place behind teammate Clay Regazzoni and McLaren's Emerson Fittipaldi which was enough to keep him clear of Fittipaldi in the title battle with one round to run.

JUAN MANUEL FANGIO

Although approaching 39 when the World Championship kicked-off in 1950, Juan Manuel Fangio showed that skill counted more than age as he rattled off five F1 titles between 1951 and 1957 (and he didn't even compete in 1952 after a life-threatening accident before the opening round).

Below **His greatest drive:** *Juan Manuel looks drawn on the podium after a remarkable drive to victory in his Maserati in the 1957 German GP.*

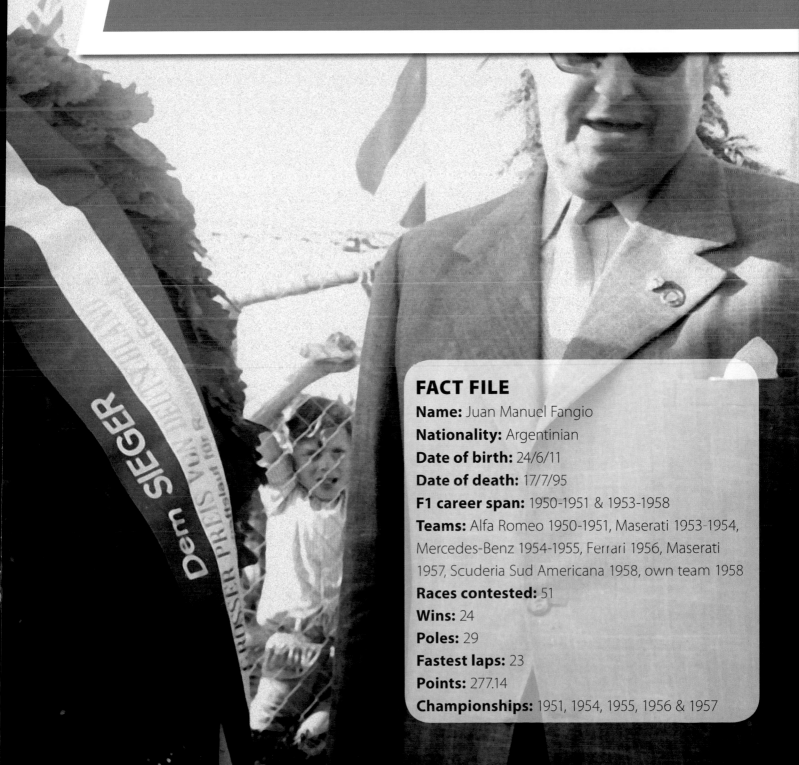

FACT FILE

Name: Juan Manuel Fangio

Nationality: Argentinian

Date of birth: 24/6/11

Date of death: 17/7/95

F1 career span: 1950-1951 & 1953-1958

Teams: Alfa Romeo 1950-1951, Maserati 1953-1954, Mercedes-Benz 1954-1955, Ferrari 1956, Maserati 1957, Scuderia Sud Americana 1958, own team 1958

Races contested: 51

Wins: 24

Poles: 29

Fastest laps: 23

Points: 277.14

Championships: 1951, 1954, 1955, 1956 & 1957

THE GREATEST CHASE

Juan Manuel Fangio's final win was his most dramatic. It came in 1957 at the German GP around the 14-mile Nürburgring Nordschleife. Despite qualifying his Maserati on pole, he completed the opening tour in third behind the Ferraris of Mike Hawthorn and Peter Collins. Two laps later, he was leading, but his gamble to stop for fresh tyres did not pay off when a slow pitstop dropped him to third. He then had to claw back 48 secs before passing both Ferraris on the penultimate lap to win and claim his fifth world title.

CAREER STATS

Year	Team	Races	Wins	Points	Ranking
1950	Alfa Romeo	6	3	27	2nd
1951	Alfa Romeo	7	3	37	1st
1953	Maserati	8	1	29	2nd
1954	Maserati & Mercedes	8	6	57.14	1st
1955	Mercedes	6	4	41	1st
1956	Ferrari	7	2	33	1st
1957	Maserati	7	4	46	1st
1958	Scuderia Sud Americana & Fangio	2	0	7	14th

》》FALLING AT THE FIRST

Juan Manuel Fangio had already tried his hand racing in Europe in 1948 and was back from his native Argentina to contest the inaugural World Championship in 1950. Racing for Alfa Romeo, he was part of an all-Alfa Romeo front row for the British GP at Silverstone. After running third in the opening stages behind Giuseppe Farina and Luigi Fagioli, he was up to second with seven laps to go when an oil pipe burst.

》》A LUCKY ESCAPE

As he was winding down his racing career in 1958, Juan Manuel elected to have a shot at the 1958 Indianapolis 500. He ran the qualifying tests and was accepted to practice for real. However, when his business required attention in Argentina, he decided not to continue with the race as he thought the car not competitive. This proved fortuitous when, right at the start, there was a 15-car pile-up in which Pat O'Connor died.

》》SHOPPING AROUND

Juan Manuel didn't sit still in his quest for F1 titles. Indeed, his five crowns were won with four different teams. His first, in 1951, was with Alfa Romeo who then quit the sport. Back from injury for 1953, he started the year with Maserati but transferred to Mercedes-Benz when the German team's cars were ready. He won with Mercedes again in 1955 before winning for Ferrari in 1956 then rounding it off with Maserati in 1957.

Below **The greatest chase:** The German crowd hails Juan Manuel after he'd hunted down and passed the Ferraris in 1957.

Above **The face of experience:** Juan Manuel won in France in 1954 after his 43rd birthday. *Left* **Shopping around:** After starting with Alfa Romeo, Juan Manuel kept changing teams. *Below* **Bouncing right back:** Juan Manuel's wins flowed from Monaco in 1950.

FAST TO THE VERY END

With Maserati closing its operation after his 1957 title, Juan Manuel raced on with independently-entered Maseratis. He raced in only two World Championship events in 1958 and in the second of these, the French GP at Reims he finished fourth after completing the entire race without the benefit of a clutch. Showing great respect, winner Mike Hawthorn backed off on the final lap rather than lap the great ace.

MUSEUM PIECE

There are racing museums dotted all around the world, but very few drivers have their own dedicated one. Juan Manuel does, though, in his hometown of Balcarce.

BOUNCING RIGHT BACK

After the disappointment of Silverstone, Juan Manuel Fangio bounced back to win at the second attempt in 1950. This was at Monaco, where he placed his Alfa Romeo 158 on pole position, set the race's fastest lap and led all the way for his first win. Fortune had smiled on him as there had been a nine-car pile-up behind him on the opening lap but he managed to thread his way through the wreckage on lap 2.

THE FACE OF EXPERIENCE

Racing drivers tended to be older in the early days and Juan Manuel was no exception, being 38 when the World Championship started in 1950. Armed with the experience of making cars last in the rough, long-distance races held on open roads in Argentina, he allied speed with mechanical sympathy and landed his first world title at the age of 40 in 1951. His final title, in 1957, came when he was 46.

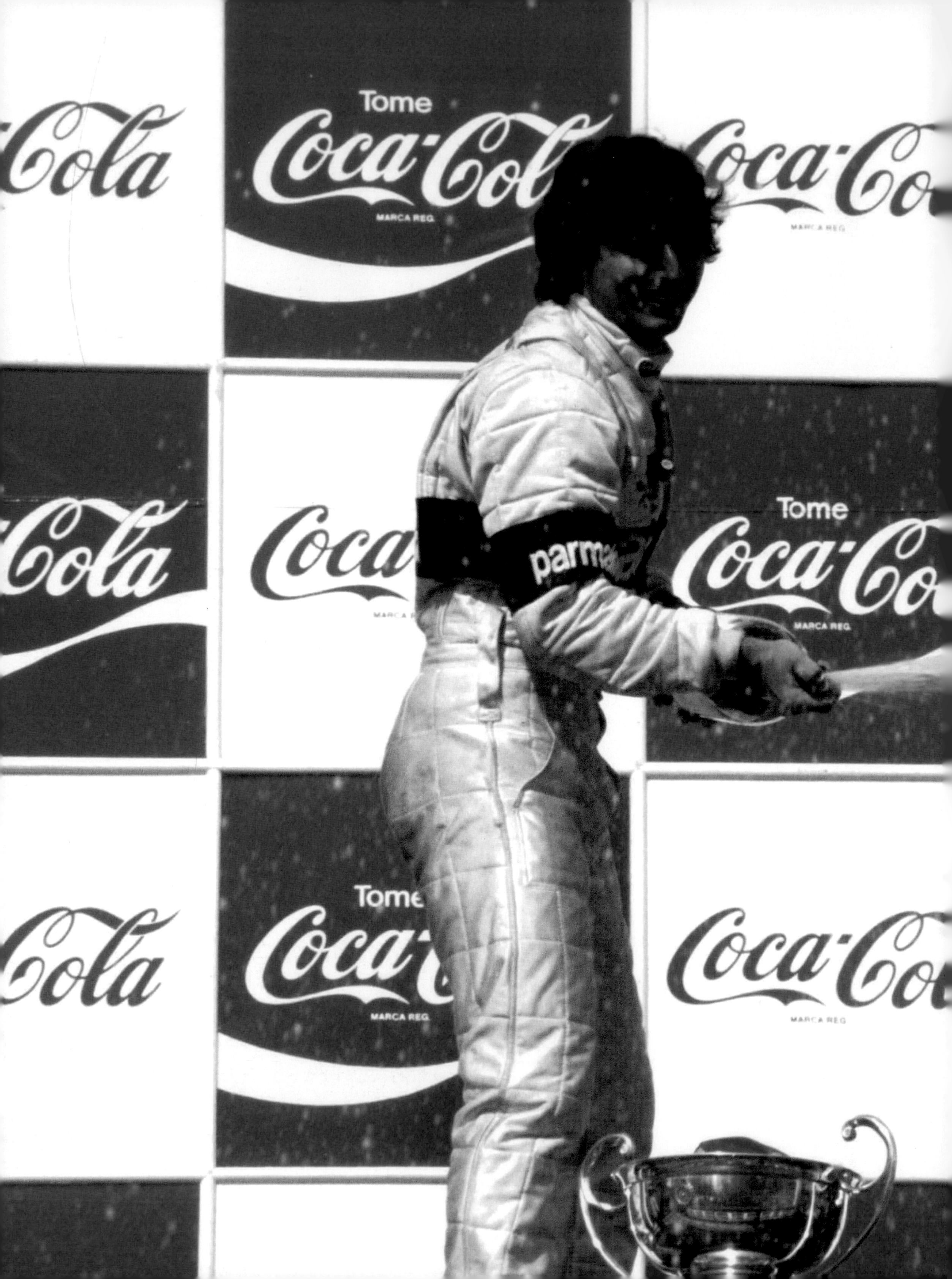
Tome
Coca-Cola
MARCA REG.
parma

NELSON PIQUET

Nelson Piquet was renowned for his speed and his irreverent humour. It was the speed that won out, though, for this pacy Brazilian won world titles with Brabham in 1981 and 1983, then outscored his Williams teammate Nigel Mansell to be crowned World Champion for a third time in 1987.

Below **Winning with a smile:** *Nelson gave the impression of seldom being serious out of the car, but his career tally of 23 wins proved that he was deadly serious when behind the wheel.*

FACT FILE
Name: Nelson Piquet
Nationality: Brazilian
Date of birth: 17/8/52
F1 career span: 1978-1991
Teams: Ensign 1978, BS Fabrications 1978, Brabham 1978-1985, Williams 1986-1987, Lotus 1988-1989, Benetton 1990-1991
Races contested: 203
Wins: 23
Poles: 24
Fastest laps: 23
Points: 485.5
Championships: 1981, 1983 & 1987

CLIMBING THE LADDER

Nelson Piquet was blessed with competitive machinery pretty much throughout his illustrious F1 career, but he made his World Championship debut in an Ensign at the 1978 German GP and qualified 21st out of 30. He moved on to drive a BS Fabrications-entered McLaren and struggled. His breakthrough came in the final race of the year, in Canada, when team owner Bernie Ecclestone entered him in a third Brabham.

OLD FRIENDS' REUNION

It really was a case of it being a small world on the podium at the 1990 Japanese GP. Nelson Piquet shared the stage with childhood friend and karting buddy Roberto Moreno who had just joined his compatriot in the Benetton team after Alessandro Nannini had been severely injured in a helicopter crash. Amazingly, Moreno duly finished second behind Piquet and so their mutual congratulation truly was heartfelt.

THE DAY IT ALL CAME GOOD

After increasingly impressive performances through 1979, his first full season of F1, Nelson stamped his mark at Long Beach in 1980. He not only qualified his Brabham on pole (his first), but held off a challenge by Renault's Rene Arnoux into the first corner before setting the fastest lap (his first) around the Californian street circuit on the way to his first grand prix win.

MAINLY A BRABHAM MAN

When people think of Nelson's F1 career, they usually think of Brabham, and that's not surprising as he drove for the team for seven of his 13 and a bit years in F1, from the end of 1978 until 1985. However, he also managed two-year stints with Williams, Lotus and then Benetton between leaving Bernie Ecclestone's team and his final race in 1991.

NEVER A HAT-TRICK

For a driver who claimed three F1 titles, Nelson achieved very few dominant runs. Indeed, he never scored more than two wins in a row across his 203 grands prix. These were at: the 1980 Dutch and Italian GPs; the 1981 Argentinian and San Marino GPs; the 1983 Italian and European GPs; the 1984 Canadian and US (Detroit) GPs; the 1986 German and Hungarian GPs; and the 1987 German and Hungarian GPs.

Above **The day it all came good:** Nelson (*middle*) rounded up a collection of firsts at the 1980 US GP West. *Below* **Never a hat-trick:** When Nelson won at Hockenheim in 1987, he might have hoped for a run of wins, but he never managed three in a row.

Right **Title rival can't compete:** Nelson was able to relax at Suzuka in 1987 and free to land the title, after Nigel Mansell's accident in qualifying left him unable to race.

TITLE RIVAL CAN'T COMPETE

The third and final time that Nelson won the F1 title came in 1987 when his greatest rival was his Williams teammate, Nigel Mansell. Heading to the penultimate race, at Suzuka, the Brazilian held a 12-point advantage (with nine points for a win), but his job was made a whole lot easier when Mansell crashed in qualifying and suffered heavy bruising which kept him from racing, making Nelson champion.

 ## SMEARING THE FAMILY NAME

Numerous F1 drivers are followed into racing by their offspring. Unfortunately, Nelson Jr's F1 career with Renault ended in disgrace after he agreed to crash in the 2008 Singapore GP to help team-mate Fernando Alonso.

BEATING THE FAVOURITE

Nelson didn't head to Caesar's Palace for the final round of 1981 as championship favourite. That fell to Williams racer Carlos Reutemann, who arrived in Las Vegas with a one-point advantage. However, Reutemann faded, perhaps overcome by nerves, while an exhausted Nelson did just enough on the last lap to hold off challengers to take the fifth place required to claim the first of his three titles.

Above **Beating the favourite:** Nelson was one of the few to enjoy F1's first visit to Las Vegas, as he won his first world title there. *Right* **Career stats:** Seven years with Brabham gave Nelson 13 wins, but he also won for Williams and Benetton.

CAREER STATS

Year	Team	Races	Wins	Points	Ranking
1978	Ensign & BS Fabrications	5	0	0	-
1979	Brabham	15	0	3	15th
1980	Brabham	14	3	54	2nd
1981	Brabham	15	3	50	1st
1982	Brabham	15	1	20	11th
1983	Brabham	15	3	59	1st
1984	Brabham	16	2	29	5th
1985	Brabham	16	1	21	8th
1986	Williams	16	4	69	3rd
1987	Williams	16	3	76	1st
1988	Lotus	16	0	22	6th
1989	Lotus	15	0	12	8th
1990	Benetton	16	2	44	3rd
1991	Benetton	16	1	26.5	6th

DAMON HILL

When Damon Hill took the world title in 1996, he became the first driver to follow in his father's wheeltracks to become World Champion. Graham's son also was the last champion to reach the top in F1 without having spent his childhood racing karts, instead starting in cars when already out of his teens.

Below **Happy to come second:** No one expected a top result from Arrows in Hungary in 1997, so Damon was delighted, even though he was passed for the lead on the final lap and ended up second.

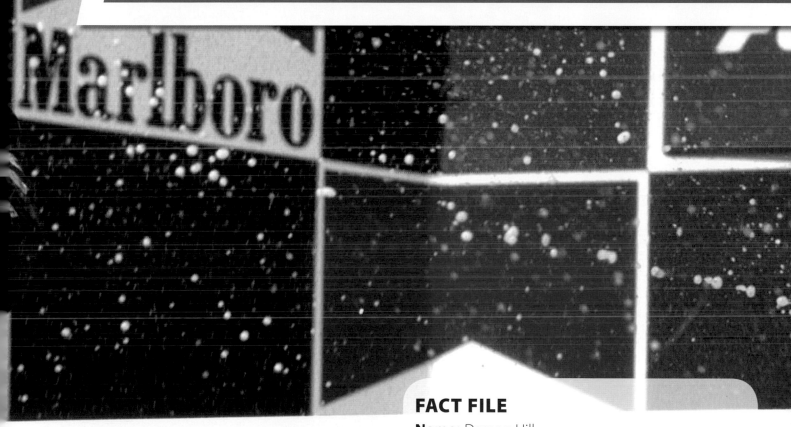

FACT FILE

Name: Damon Hill

Nationality: British

Date of birth: 17/9/60

F1 career span: 1992-1999

Teams: Brabham 1992, Williams 1993-1996, Arrows 1997, Jordan 1998-1999

Races contested: 116

Wins: 22

Poles: 20

Fastest laps: 19

Points: 360

Championships: 1996

TWO WHELS TO FOUR

Damon didn't race karts as a child, and his route into competition was unusual as he raced motorbikes before turning to four-wheeled competition taking the traditional route via Formula Ford.

CHAMPAGNE FOR DAMON

Damon did get one final taste of victory, in 1998 at the Belgian GP. This came after he'd been signed by Jordan and had enjoyed a couple of fourth-place finishes. The wet race at Spa began with a massive pile-up. Damon led the restarted race but was passed by a faster Michael Schumacher. Damon regained and retained the lead when the Ferrari driver hit David Coulthard.

SIXTH TIME LUCKY

Landing a drive in F1 has never been easy. Yet, Damon Hill discovered that it's best to attempt your graduation with a competitive team if you want to make it to the grid. Driving for Brabham, a team in decline by the time he joined in 1992, it took him six attempts from his debut at the Spanish GP before he qualified. Fittingly, Damon made his breakthrough on home ground at Silverstone.

A FLASH IN THE PAN

When Damon was dropped by Williams, it was felt that his days of winning were over. This was reinforced when he landed a 1997 drive for Arrows, a team that had never won a grand prix. However, Damon had an amazing Hungarian GP, qualifying third behind Michael Schumacher and Jacques Villeneuve. He led from lap 11 until he was slowed by hydraulic problems with less than a lap to go and had to let Jacques Villeneuve by to win.

THE ALL-IMPORTANT FIRST

Having collected five second-place finishes and come close to scoring his first grand prix win through the early races of 1993 (denied by engine failure at Silverstone and a tyre blow-out at Hockenheim), it all came right for Damon at the Hungarian GP. He was helped by pole-sitting team-mate Alain Prost having to start from the back of the grid, then he held off Ayrton Senna's McLaren into Turn 1 and led all the way.

Above **A flash in the pan:** The crowds could scarcely believe it when Damon led in an Arrows in Hungary in 1997. *Below* **The all-important first:** Hungary was where it first all came together for Damon, as he scored his maiden win there in 1993. *Bottom Left* **Champagne for Damon:** There was great satisfaction when victory came Damon's way at Spa in 1998 to give Jordan its first win.

CAREER STATS

Year	Team	Races	Wins	Points	Ranking
1992	Brabham	2	0	0	-
1993	Williams	16	3	69	3rd
1994	Williams	16	6	91	2nd
1995	Williams	17	4	69	2nd
1996	Williams	16	8	97	1st
1997	Arrows	17	0	7	12th
1998	Jordan	16	1	20	6th
1999	Jordan	16	0	7	11th

A GIANT STEP

The difference between the Williams that Damon raced in 1993 and the Brabham he piloted in 1992 couldn't have been more stark. For, although he failed to score in the opening round in South Africa, Damon enjoyed success next time out, at the Brazilian GP at Interlagos. Damon not only scored his first points but also raced to his first podium finish after surviving a mid-race deluge to trail Ayrton Senna home in second.

WINS AND A CROWN

When Damon claimed his world title in 1996, he did so in style. Having ended 1995 with victory in the final round in Adelaide, he extended this into his best winning sequence by adding victory in the first three races of 1996: the Australian: Brazilian; and Argentinian GPs. After winning five more, at: Imola; Montreal; Magny-Cours; Hockenheim; and Suzuka, 1996 became his most successful season in terms of wins.

BEATING HIS DAD

Damon had quite an act to follow when he followed his father into motor racing, as Graham Hill was a double World Champion. By the time Damon hung up his helmet with one F1 title to his name after eight seasons, though, he'd scored more wins (22 to 14); more pole positions (20 to 13); more fastest laps (19 to 10); and more points (360 to 289) than his father did in 18 seasons.

TAKING THE TITLE

||||||||||||||||||||||||||||||

Despite winning eight races in 1996, it was only at the finale that Damon could relax. The clincher at Suzuka pitted him against Williams teammate, Jacques Villeneuve and, with a nine-point advantage and 10 points for a win, Damon just had to be cautious. The title was pushed firmly his way when Villeneuve was slow away from pole and fell to sixth. Damon was left to lead and the title was his at two thirds distance when Villeneuve's car shed a wheel.

Below **Taking the title:** Damon raced into the history books at the 1996 Japanese GP when he raced clear at the start and went on to win and become the first and so far only second generation world champion.

PART 3

FAMOUS TEAMS

It takes more than a big budget to win in Formula 1, although it certainly helps. The teams that have succeeded and endured are those that are led from the top, with strong leadership helping Ferrari, McLaren and Williams cement their place at the top of almost all team records listings. Other teams have had their time at the top of the pile, but have since been consigned to the history books, their names remembered by only the most fanatical of today's fans.

Below **Cream rises to the top:** Five of F1's greatest teams – Williams, Lotus, Ferrari, McLaren and Brabham – show how competitive the racing was in 1985 as they line up in the first five grid positions for the French GP.

FERRARI

The most famous marque in motor racing, Ferrari has tasted success in each decade from the 1950s on, and the allure of its road-going sportscars adds to its appeal. In the early 2000s, the Italian team enjoyed its best spell, being all but invincible as Michael Schumacher starred, setting record after record.

Below **Red and rapid:** *Fernando Alonso showed his commitment to the Tifosi's cause when he dominated proceedings at Singapore for Ferrari in 2010, winning from pole position to boost his and the team's title hopes.*

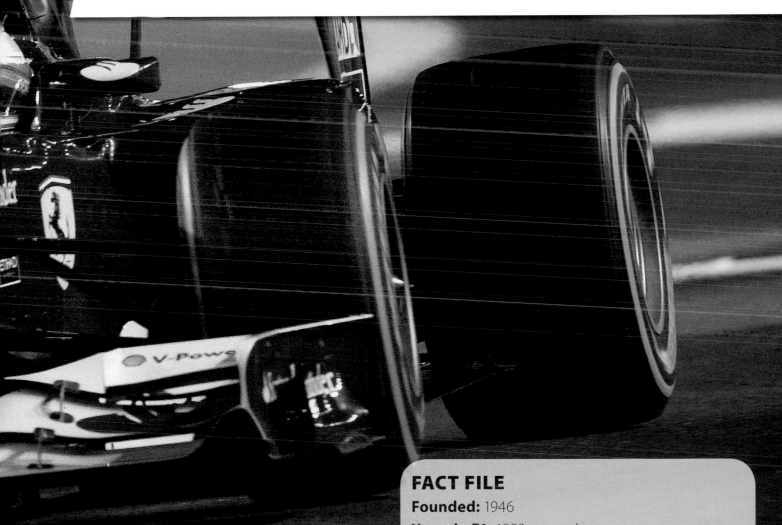

FACT FILE

Founded: 1946

Years in F1: 1950 onwards

Country: Italy

HQ: Maranello, Italy

Team principal: Stefano Domenicali

Constructors' titles: 1961, 1964, 1975, 1976, 1977, 1979, 1982, 1983, 1999, 2000, 2001, 2002, 2003, 2004, 2007, 2008

15 OUT OF 18

Ferrari made it six constructors' titles in succession in 2004, and did it in truly dominant style as it won 15 of the 18 rounds, almost exclusively through the efforts of World Champion Michael Schumacher who won 13. Teammate Rubens Barrichello won twice to be runner-up and this helped Ferrari finish with more than double the score of its closest rival, BAR. It's amazing therefore that it wasn't able to win again in 2005.

 ## TWO IN ONE GO

It took until the fourth round of the second World Championship for Ferrari to start a grand prix from pole position for the first time. This was thanks to the efforts of chunky Argentinian Jose Froilan Gonzalez for the 1951 British GP, and that wasn't the end of his glory at Silverstone as he then raced to Ferrari's first victory after swapping the lead with compatriot Juan Manuel Fangio before winning by 51 secs.

 ## TITLE NUMBER ONE

Alberto Ascari clinched the first of his two world titles in 1952 and this was the first of the 15 drivers' championship titles earned by nine Ferrari drivers through to Kimi Raikkonen's title in 2007. He wrapped up the championship after just five of the seven rounds, at the German GP at the Nürburgring, when he scored his fourth win in a row and then backed that up by winning the final two rounds.

 ## STARTING WITH A BANG

Ferrari didn't contest the first round of the inaugural World Championship in 1950, but it was at Monaco for the second one. Not only that, the Italian team came away with its first podium finish and first points as Alberto Ascari worked his way forward from seventh on the grid to finish second behind Juan Manuel Fangio's Alfa Romeo. The fact that he was a lap behind showed that Ferrari wasn't ready for that first win.

Left **Career Stats:** Fernando Alonso at the wheel of the F10 at the 2010 Singapore GP.

CAREER STATS

Year	Races	Wins	Points	Ranking	Year	Races	Wins	Points	Ranking
1950	5	0	N/A*	N/A*	1981	15	2	34	5th
1951	7	3	N/A*	N/A*	1982	16	3	74	1st
1952	7	7	N/A*	N/A*	1983	15	4	89	1st
1953	8	7	N/A*	N/A*	1984	16	1	57.5	2nd
1954	8	2	N/A*	N/A*	1985	16	2	82	2nd
1955	6	1	N/A*	N/A*	1986	16	0	37	4th
1956	7	5	N/A*	N/A*	1987	16	2	53	4th
1957	7	0	N/A*	N/A*	1988	16	1	65	2nd
1958	10	2	40	2nd	1989	16	3	59	3rd
1959	7	2	32	2nd	1990	16	6	110	2nd
1960	8	1	26	3rd	1991	16	0	55.5	3rd
1961	7	5	40	1st	1992	16	0	21	4th
1962	5	0	18	5th	1993	16	0	28	4th
1963	10	1	26	4th	1994	16	1	71	3rd
1964	10	3	45	1st	1995	17	1	73	3rd
1965	10	0	26	4th	1996	16	3	70	2nd
1966	7	2	31	2nd	1997	17	5	102	2nd
1967	10	0	20	4th	1998	16	6	133	2nd
1968	11	1	32	4th	1999	16	6	128	1st
1969	10	0	7	5th	2000	17	10	170	1st
1970	13	4	52	2nd	2001	17	9	179	1st
1971	11	2	33	4th	2002	17	15	221	1st
1972	12	1	33	4th	2003	16	8	158	1st
1973	13	0	12	6th	2004	18	15	262	1st
1974	15	3	65	2nd	2005	19	1	100	3rd
1975	14	6	72.5	1st	2006	18	9	201	2nd
1976	15	6	83	1st	2007	17	9	204	1st
1977	17	4	95	1st	2008	18	8	172	1st
1978	16	5	58	2nd	2009	17	1	70	4th
1979	15	6	113	1st	2010	19	5	396	3rd
1980	14	0	8	10th					

* There was no Constructors' Championship until 1958

SUCCESS ON A SAD DAY

The 1961 Italian GP at Monza will always be remembered as the race that claimed the life of popular German Ferrari driver Wolfgang von Trips. However, Ferrari also remembers it for another reason, as this was the race at which it landed its first constructors' title. This came through Phil Hill giving the team a home win. As his only rival for the title at the final round at Watkins Glen was von Trips, he too was crowned.

Above **Success on a sad day:** Phil Hill runs his Sharknose Ferrari high around the Monza banking in 1961, to win the race and the title, but team-mate Wolfgang von Trips had died earlier in the race. *Below* **Ferrari's greatest run:** Alberto Ascari was the main man in Ferrari's 14-race winning run across 1952 and 1953, winning 11 times, including here at Bremgarten in 1953.

›› TEAM WINS, DRIVER LOSES

Although Kimi Raikkonen won the drivers' crown In 2007, Ferrari's most recent constructors' title came in 2008 when the combined talents of Felipe Massa and Kimi Raikkonen were enough to help Ferrari outscore the team that fielded champion Lewis Hamilton, McLaren, as Heikki Kovalainen didn't score much in the second McLaren car. Ferrari clinched the crown at the dramatic final race at Interlagos. Although Massa won the race, it was Hamilton who grabbed the drivers' prize.

›› GOOD LUCK CHARM

Ferrari's prancing horse logo was created after Enzo Ferrari won a race in 1923 and was asked by the mother of First World War fighter ace Count Francesco Baracca to paint one on his car to bring him good luck.

FERRARI'S GREATEST RUN

Although Michael Schumacher gave Ferrari a huge number of wins in the 2000s, scoring eight in a row from 2003 into 2004, it was more than half a century before that Ferrari scored its best winning sequence. This was 14 races in a row, from Piero Taruffi's victory in the 1952 season-opener at Bremgarten to Alberto Ascari at the same Swiss circuit in 1953, with Ascari winning 11 of these and bagging two drivers' titles.

McLAREN

Founded by racer/engineer Bruce McLaren, this team was winning races in the late 1960s, taking titles in the 1970s, being reinvented by Ron Dennis in the 1980s and going on to dominate before the decade was out. Now the most professional team of all, it continues to chase Ferrari's records.

Below **American attack:** *James Hunt drove hard all through the 1976 season, heading to this win at Watkins Glen to become the second McLaren driver to become world champion.*

FACT FILE
Founded: 1963
Years in F1: 1966 onwards
Country: England
HQ: Woking, England
Team principal:
Constructors' titles: 1974, 1984, 1985, 1988, 1989, 1990, 1991, 1998

CAREER STATS

Year	Races	Wins	Points	Ranking	Year	Races	Wins	Points	Ranking
1966	6	0	3	9th	1989	16	10	141	1st
1967	6	0	3	10th	1990	16	6	121	1st
1968	12	3	59	2nd	1991	16	8	139	1st
1969	11	1	49	4th	1992	16	5	99	2nd
1970	12	0	36	4th	1993	16	5	84	2nd
1971	11	0	13	6th	1994	16	0	42	4th
1972	12	1	66	3rd	1995	17	0	30	4th
1973	15	3	68	3rd	1996	16	0	49	4th
1974	15	4	87	1st	1997	17	3	63	4th
1975	14	3	65	3rd	1998	16	9	156	1st
1976	16	6	88	2nd	1999	16	7	124	2nd
1977	17	3	65	3rd	2000	17	7	152	2nd
1978	16	0	16	8th	2001	17	4	102	2nd
1979	15	0	15	7th	2002	17	1	65	3rd
1980	14	0	11	7th	2003	16	2	142	3rd
1981	15	1	28	6th	2004	18	1	69	5th
1982	16	4	69	2nd	2005	19	10	182	2nd
1983	15	1	34	5th	2006	18	0	110	3rd
1984	16	12	143.5	1st	2007	17	8	0*	-
1985	16	6	90	1st	2008	18	6	151	2nd
1986	16	4	96	2nd	2009	17	2	71	3rd
1987	16	3	76	2nd	2010	19	5	454	2nd
1988	16	15	199	1st					

* All points annulled for alleged spying infringement

TAKING TO THE STREETS

Bruce McLaren gave his team its first grand prix outing at the 1966 Monaco GP and did well to qualify the new car 10th out of 16 starters. However, its Indianapolis-sourced Ford V8 was not only down on power but it was the cause of his early retirement in the race after an oil pipe came loose. A different engine was sought for the next race and this was the start of a team that would be a winning outfit within two years.

Above **Career Stats:** Mika Hakkinen in his 1998 championship-winning MP4/13. *Below* **McLaren's First Eleven:** Another masterclass from Ayrton Senna during his triumphant 1988 grand prix season.

MCLAREN'S FIRST ELEVEN

Beating your rivals is always gratifying, but asserting dominance throughout a season is extra satisfying. McLaren had a remarkable campaign in 1988 as its MP4/4 was the pick of the crop, and with Ayrton Senna and Alain Prost the team had the best drivers. So, perhaps it shouldn't come as a shock that the team won 11 on the trot, from the season-opening Brazilian GP at the start of April all the way through to the Belgian GP at the end of August.

THE BOSS TAKES FIRST WIN

Two years after McLaren's World Championship debut, having had Denny Hulme finish second at the 1968 Spanish GP, the team landed its first win at the next race, the Belgian GP at Spa-Francorchamps. Fittingly, this came at the hands of Bruce McLaren, who started that race from sixth on the grid, fell to 11th on the opening lap but then guided his M7A to victory when Jackie Stewart's Matra ran out of fuel on the final lap.

WINS FIRST, POLES SECOND

Despite taking its first win at the start of its third year in F1, McLaren didn't claim its first pole until the end of its seventh year. This breakthrough came at the 1972 Canadian GP at Mosport Park when Peter Revson scored the fastest lap and team-mate Denny Hulme helped the team take its first one-two on a grid. Sadly, Jackie Stewart soon propelled his Tyrrell to the front and the McLaren's had to settle for second and third.

THEY WEREN'T ALWAYS GREY

Younger fans will be surprised that McLarens have ever raced in any livery other than a predominantly silver-grey one. However, red and white were McLaren's colours for an incredible 23 years, thanks to backing from cigarette manufacturer Philip Morris's Marlboro brand. Red and white first adorned the flanks of a McLaren in 1974 and continued until 1996 when the West tobacco brand took over for 1997.

FIXTURES AND FITTINGS

David Coulthard and Mika Hakkinen raced at McLaren for so long that they became part of the furniture.

Hakkinen arrived in 1993 and was joined by Coulthard in 1996. By 2000, they'd become F1's longest serving driver pairing, racing as team-mates 99 times until the end of a sixth season in 2001, when Hakkinen took what he thought would be a sabbatical but turned into retirement from F1.

TRAGEDY AT GOODWOOD

McLaren was dealt a mighty blow in June 1970 when its founder Bruce McLaren was killed when testing at Goodwood. He was driving one of the Can-Am sportscars that helped finance the team's F1 programme.

Left **Wins first, poles second:** Pete Revson (left) claimed McLaren's first pole.
Above **Fixtures and fittings:** David Coulthard, Alex Wurz and Mika Hakkinen had long spells with the team.

TWO TITLES IN ONE YEAR

Grand Prix wins were flowing for McLaren in the 1970s and Emerson Fittipaldi helped the team advance to a new level in 1974 after arriving from Lotus. Not only did he win three times that year to become the team's first World Champion, but his team-mate Denny Hulme's tally of points was enough to help the team outscore Ferrari to claim the first of its eight constructors' championship titles to date.

Below **Two titles in one year:** Emerson Fittipaldi guided McLaren to the 1974 Drivers' and Constructors' titles.

WILLIAMS

When Frank Williams first ran a team in F1, money was short and it looked as though he'd never field a grand prix winner. Teaming up with Patrick Head changed all that and the team hit the front in the 1980s before enjoying another spell of domination in the 1990s that it's still hoping to replicate.

Below **Mansell on the move:** *Williams hit uncharted heights when Nigel Mansell dominated the 1992 World Championship in its Renault-powered FW14B, including a victory at Silverstone, one of his nine that year.*

FACT FILE

Founded: 1968

Years in F1: 1972 onwards

Country: England

HQ: Grove, England

Team principal: Sir Frank Williams

Constructors' titles: 1980, 1981, 1986, 1987, 1992, 1993, 1994, 1996, 1997

FRANK'S BAD BREAK

Frank Williams' life took an unwanted turn in 1986 when he was involved in a car crash on the way back from testing at Paul Ricard that broke his neck, leaving him wheelchair-bound.

HANGING ON TO HIS DRIVE

Williams is a team that likes to keep its drivers on their toes – it famously let both Nigel Mansell and Damon Hill know during their title-winning campaigns (1992 and 1996) that they would not be needed for the following year. So Riccardo Patrese, Williams' longest-serving driver, did well to stay for five full seasons. The Italian clocked-up 80 grand prix starts between 1988 and 1992 before being replaced by Hill.

A RUN THE TEAM WANTS TO END

When Juan Pablo Montoya won the Brazilian GP in 2004, it was Williams' first win for more than a year, and it had been taken in front-running style, without the retirements of others. However, unlikely as it might have seemed in the post-race euphoria at Interlagos, the team would claim no more wins up to the end of the 2010 World Championship as it slipped down the rankings, even losing a works engine deal before 2010..

Above **A run the team wants to end:** Juan Pablo Montoya was Williams' most recent winner, at Interlagos in 2004. *Below* **Hanging on to his drive:** Riccardo Patrese (trailing Williams teammate Nigel Mansell) enjoyed two victories in 1991.

A TROUBLED BEGINNING

Defining when Williams started in F1 is slightly hazy, as Frank Williams fielded cars as long ago as 1969. However, the first time he entered a car that was unique to his team came in 1972, at the British GP at Brands Hatch, when Henri Pescarolo was slowest of the qualifiers in his Politoys FX3. Unfortunately, it was written-off on the third lap and it would be another seven years until Williams scored its breakthrough win.

MADE IN BRITAIN

Alan Jones was Williams' lead driver in 1979, but it was teammate Clay Regazzoni who claimed the team's first grand prix victory. This came at the British GP at Silverstone. Up until lap 38 of 68 it looked as though the pole-starting Australian would be winner, but then his water pump failed and Regazzoni was free to canter home. As the team had a Saudi sponsor, Regazzoni had to decline the champagne celebration.

THE FIRST AND MOST-LOVED

Alan Jones is a driver long-departed from Williams, but his memory lives on with founders Frank Williams and Patrick Head. Not only was he the team's first title-clincher but he also provided the template of a perfect Williams driver – an uncompromising, unflinching racer who wouldn't moan. Jones wrapped up the 1980 title when he raced to victory at the penultimate race, the Canadian GP at Montreal.

Above **The first and most-loved:** Alan Jones's fourth win of 1980, in Canada, made him Williams' first world champion.
Below **Career stats:** Nigel Mansell has scored most victories for Williams, with 28 spread across three spells with the team.

 ### PROVING IT WAS NO FLUKE

The best way for Alan Jones to expunge any disappointment at not having been the driver to give Williams its first win was to win the next race, the 1979 German GP at Hockenheim. Having got the jump on Jean-Pierre Jabouille's pole-sitting Renault, Jones then led every lap to take victory. Clay Regazzoni completed Williams' first one-two finish, advancing when Jabouille spun and then passing Jacques Laffite's Ligier.

 ### IT CAME TO A SUDDEN STOP

When Williams secured the 1997 constructors' championship title at the European GP at Jerez, it was the team's fifth title in six years, so more were sure to follow. Amazingly, as McLaren came back to form, Williams' form faded and the 1997 success, shaped by champion Jacques Villeneuve and team-mate Heinz-Harald Frentzen, remains the most recent time that Williams reached the top of the pile.

CAREER STATS

Year	Races	Wins	Points	Ranking	Year	Races	Wins	Points	Ranking
1972	1	0	0	–	1992	16	10	164	1st
1973	15	0	2	10th	1993	16	10	168	1st
1974	15	0	4	10th	1994	16	7	118	1st
1975	12	0	6	9th	1995	17	5	118	2nd
1976	13	0	0	–	1996	16	12	175	1st
1978	16	0	11	9th	1997	17	8	123	1st
1979	15	5	75	2nd	1998	16	0	38	3rd
1980	14	6	120	1st	1999	16	0	35	5th
1981	15	4	95	1st	2000	17	0	36	3rd
1982	15	1	58	4th	2001	17	4	80	3rd
1983	15	1	38	4th	2002	17	1	92	2nd
1984	16	1	25.5	6th	2003	16	3	144	2nd
1985	16	4	71	3rd	2004	18	1	88	4th
1986	16	9	141	1st	2005	19	0	66	5th
1987	16	9	137	1st	2006	18	0	11	8th
1988	16	0	20	7th	2007	17	0	33	4th
1989	16	2	77	2nd	2008	18	0	26	8th
1990	16	2	57	4th	2009	17	0	34.5	7th
1991	16	7	125	2nd	2010	19	0	69	6th

LOTUS

This British team was the one to watch through the 1960s and 1970s. Team founder Colin Chapman's ideas revolutionized F1, leading to periods of domination with Jim Clark and then, in the late 1970s, with Mario Andretti. However, Chapman died and the team fell away after a late flurry with Ayrton Senna.

Below **Black beauties:** *The Lotus 79 was the class of the field in 1978 as it took its ground-effect capabilities ever further ahead of the rival teams, allowing Mario Andretti and Ronnie Peterson to pull away, as shown here at the Spanish GP at Jarama, a race they dominated.*

FACT FILE

Founded: 1952

Years in F1: 1958-1994 then 2010 onwards

Country: England

HQ: Hingham, England

Team principal: Tony Fernandes

Constructors' titles: 1963, 1965, 1968, 1970, 1972, 1973, 1978

STARTING WITH A WHIMPER

When Cliff Allison and Graham Hill turned up at Monaco for the second grand prix of 1958, qualifying their Lotus 12s 13th and 15th, they were both roughly 5 secs off the pace. Allison ultimately finished 13 laps down on Maurice Trintignant's winning Cooper and Hill not at all, revealing few signs that this new marque was going to be the lead team of the following decade, but history relates that this is what Lotus would become.

NOT A ONE-HORSE TEAM

For many of its early years, Lotus had one driver who was its clear lead. Or maybe that was simply what happened because it was running Jim Clark… Despite having winning form from 1961, it took until 1967 for the team to take its first one-two in qualifying. This came at the British GP when Clark took pole ahead of Graham Hill as they were the only two who were using the new dominant engine, the Ford Cosworth DFV.

THE END OF THE LINE

When a team is at the top of its game, it's hard to imagine its winning ability coming to an end. Jim Clark's death in 1968 knocked Lotus back, but Ayrton Senna's departure to McLaren for 1988 sealed the teams' fate, with the final Lotus win coming at the 1987 Detroit GP when Senna made his tyres last to outwit Williams' Nigel Mansell. His best results in the remaining 11 rounds were a pair of second places.

BLAZING A TRAIL

It was always a question of when, not if, Lotus was going to land a constructors' title. Having finished second three years in a row, it all came right in 1963. And how! Almost entirely through the efforts of Jim Clark, who won seven of the 10 rounds, and with the advances wrought by Lotus introducing F1's first monocoque, both team and driver wrapped up their titles with victory at Monza with three rounds still to run.

Top **The end of the line:** Ayrton Senna heads for Lotus's final win, at Detroit in 1987. *Above* **Blazing a trail:** Both Jim Clark and team boss Colin Chapman (on car) had reason to celebrate at Monza in 1963. *Below* **Beating the works team:** Stirling Moss scores the first Lotus win in a privately entered Lotus at Monaco in 1960.

BEATING THE WORKS TEAM

Statisticians can be confused by Lotus's very early days in F1 as the most successful Lotus entry wasn't fielded by the works team, but by privateer Rob Walker instead. He had Stirling Moss as his driver and Moss scored not only the first pole position (Monaco 1960) and first win at the same race, but the marque's first fastest lap as well at the following race at Zandvoort. Then the works Lotus team got up to speed.

ELIO HANGS AROUND

In terms of years, Jim Clark was the longest-serving Lotus driver, racing with the team from 1960 to the start of 1968. That encompassed 72 grands prix up to his death. Mario Andretti was at Lotus for five years in the 1970s and managed three more, 75. Then along came Elio de Angelis in 1980 and he raced for Lotus on a record 90 occasions before moving on to Brabham in 1986.

CAREER STATS

Year	Races	Wins	Points	Ranking	Year	Races	Wins	Points	Ranking
1958	9	0	3	6th	1977	17	5	62	2nd
1959	8	0	5	4th	1978	16	8	86	1st
1960	8	0	34	2nd	1979	15	0	39	4th
1961	8	3	32	2nd	1980	14	0	14	5th
1962	9	3	37	2nd	1981	15	0	22	7th
1963	10	7	58	1st	1982	16	1	30	5th
1964	10	3	40	3rd	1983	15	0	11	7th
1965	10	6	56	1st	1984	16	0	47	3rd
1966	9	1	21	5th	1985	16	3	71	3rd
1967	11	4	50	2nd	1986	16	2	58	3rd
1968	12	5	62	1st	1987	16	2	64	3rd
1969	11	2	47	3rd	1988	16	0	23	4th
1970	12	6	59	1st	1989	16	0	15	6th
1971	11	0	21	5th	1990	16	0	3	7th
1972	12	5	61	1st	1991	16	0	3	9th
1973	15	7	92	1st	1992	16	0	13	5th
1974	15	3	42	4th	1993	16	0	12	6th
1975	14	0	9	7th	1994	16	0	0	-
1976	16	1	29	4th	2010	19	0	0	-

HATS OFF TO THE WINNER

Team founder Colin Chapman had a trademark celebration for any win in the 1970s – he would climb over the pitwall, onto the track and hurl his black corduroy cap into the air.

Right **Career Stat:** Emerson Fittipaldi took nine wins and the 1972 world title for Lotus. *Below* **Triumph and tragedy:** Ronnie Peterson raced to a dominant win in Austria in 1978, but he died two races later.

TRIUMPH AND TRAGEDY

Lotus's most recent title came off the back of one of Colin Chapman's many technical innovations. Having introduced ground effects in 1977, Mario Andretti and Ronnie Peterson took control in 1978. With win following win, the team landed the title by the 12th of the 16 rounds. Sadly, Peterson would die two races later.

BRABHAM

Jack Brabham was a double World Champion when he started making and racing his own cars. Success soon followed and he became the only man to win a world title in a car bearing his name. He then sold the team and it landed more titles in the 1980s through Nelson Piquet. Yet, a decade later, it had folded.

Below **Car and driver:** *Jack Brabham leads John Surtees and Jochen Rindt at Silverstone in 1966. It was the second of four races he would win that year to become the only driver to win a world title in a car bearing his own name.*

FACT FILE

Founded: 1961
Years in F1: 1962-1987 & 1989-1992
Country: England
HQ: Chessington, England
Team principal: N/A as team closed in 1992
Constructors' titles: 1966, 1967

OVER AND FINALLY OUT

The end of Brabham came during 1992. Once Eric van de Poele jumped ship, the team was left with just one entry for Damon Hill for the Hungarian GP and he came home 11th and last.

Then, with none of the five potential offers to buy the team coming to fruition and backer Landhurst Leasing going into liquidation, the team failed to turn up for the following race at Spa-Francorchamps and its 30-year history came to an end.

NO FINISH, BUT PROMISE

Jack Brabham ran a Lotus for the first five races of his 1962 World Championship campaign before the first of his eponymous chassis was ready. The car made its debut at the German GP, Jack qualified towards the tail end of the 30-car grid and pulled off at two-thirds distance with throttle linkage failure. There had been flashes of promise and a pair of second-place finishes in the next two races gave him succour.

SHORTER STAY, MORE RACES

Jack Brabham raced for his own team from its foundation in 1962 until he retired from racing in 1970. However, although his span was the longest, at nine years, the ever greater number of grands prix each year through the 1980s meant that Nelson Piquet clocked-up more grand prix appearances for Brabham. The Brazilian raced for the team on 95 occasions from 1979 to 1985.

Below **Right engine, two titles:** Jack Brabham drew a blank at the 1966 Italian GP, but still claimed the title and teammate Denny Hulme added another in 1967. *Bottom* **Career stats:** Jack Brabham (on car) and Denny Hulme starred in the 1960s.

CAREER STATS

Year	Races	Wins	Points	Ranking
1962	3	0	6	7th
1963	10	0	28	3rd
1964	10	2	30	4th
1965	10	0	32	3rd
1966	9	4	42	1st
1967	11	4	63	1st
1968	12	0	10	8th
1969	11	2	49	2nd
1970	13	1	35	4th
1971	11	0	5	9th
1972	12	0	7	9th
1973	15	0	22	4th
1974	15	3	35	5th
1975	14	2	54	2nd
1976	16	0	9	9th
1977	17	0	27	5th
1978	16	2	53	3rd
1979	15	0	7	8th
1980	14	3	55	3rd
1981	15	3	61	2nd
1982	15	2	19	9th
1983	15	4	72	3rd
1984	16	2	38	4th
1985	16	1	26	5th
1986	16	0	2	9th
1987	16	0	10	8th
1989	16	0	8	8th
1990	16	0	2	8th
1991	16	0	3	9th
1992	3	0	0	-

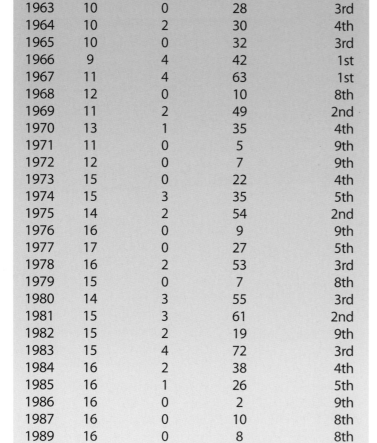

RIGHT ENGINE, TWO TITLES

The best time to make an impression is when there's a major change to F1's technical rules and this is what Brabham managed in 1966 when engine capacity was doubled to 3000cc. Brabham's decision to fit Repco engines proved the best he ever made, and they powered him to the team's first world title in 1966 before teammate Denny Hulme made it two titles on the trot for the team in 1967.

THE EMPLOYEE NOT THE BOSS

When the Brabham team scored its first win in 1964, it wasn't Jack Brabham who was first past the chequered flag but Dan Gurney. The American driver gave the team its breakthrough result in the French GP at Rouen-les-Essarts in a race that had belonged to Lotus's Jim Clark until his engine blew. Gurney went on to win, with Jack finishing third on a day of mixed emotions for the ever-competitive Australian.

⟫ THE END OF THE LINE

So successful was the team as the 1970s fed into the 1980s, it seemed unlikely that Brabham's form would ever dip. But the ascent of McLaren, then Williams, left Brabham off the pace and its 35th and final win came in the 1985 French GP thanks to Nelson Piquet. Then, after two winless years, Brabham dropped out of the championship before coming back with a new owner to commence a slide into oblivion.

Above **The employee not the boss:** American Dan Gurney races towards the Brabham team's first win, at the 1964 French GP.
Below **Lucky thirteen:** Nelson Piquet heads for victory at Brands Hatch in 1983, the 10th of his 13 wins for Brabham during a seven-year spell that yielded two drivers' titles.

⟫ BERNIE'S THE BOSS

F1 ringmaster Bernie Ecclestone bought Brabham from Ron Tauranac at the end of 1971 and ran the team until 1988. After that, the team changed hands several times before folding in 1992.

LUCKY THIRTEEN

Nelson Piquet proved to be Brabham's most successful driver, winning 13 grands prix for the team and two world titles, in 1981 and 1983. This put him well clear of team founder Jack Brabham. Infuriatingly for Brabham, there was only one Australian GP during Piquet's spell and he retired from that, meaning that proud Aussie Jack never had a home win.

RENAULT

Renault won the first ever grand prix, the French GP of 1906, and made its first World Championship appearance in 1977 when it introduced turbocharged engines. Renault became a winning team in 1979 but bowed out after 1985. It returned in 2002 when it took over the Benetton team.

Below **Yellow car on a golden day:** *Winning at home was always important for Renault, so Rene Arnoux delighted the bosses when he led home Alain Prost in a Renault one-two at Paul Ricard in 1982.*

FACT FILE

Founded: 1977

Years in F1: 1977-1985 & 2002 onwards

Country: France

HQ: Enstone, England

Team principal: Gerard Lopez

Constructors' titles: 2005, 2006

A REALLY LONG WAIT

Although the French hosted the first grand prix, back in 1906 (won by a Renault incidentally), the nation really took its time to get going in Formula 1. Indeed, although Bugatti, Gordini and Talbot tried to win for the glory of France in the 1950s, it took until 1979 for that first race win and a further 26 years for the first title to be won by a French team. Mind you, by this point, it was a French team operating out of Britain.

FIRST POINTS, BUT ONLY JUST

The almost ceaseless mechanical failures that blighted Renault's debut season in 1977 were reduced for its second campaign and Jean-Pierre Jabouille claimed the team's first points at the 1978 US GP at Watkins Glen. He qualified ninth but advanced as others fell off and was fourth at flagfall. It could have been third but his engine spluttered with eight laps to go. He let Jody Scheckter's Wolf by, then just limped home.

CAREER STATS

Year	Races	Wins	Points	Ranking
1977	5	0	0	-
1978	14	0	3	12th
1979	15	1	26	6th
1980	14	3	38	4th
1981	15	3	54	3rd
1982	16	4	62	3rd
1983	15	4	79	2nd
1984	16	0	34	5th
1985	16	0	16	7th
2002	17	0	23	4th
2003	16	1	88	4th
2004	18	1	105	3rd
2005	19	7	191	1st
2006	18	8	206	1st
2007	17	0	51	3rd
2008	18	2	80	4th
2009	17	0	26	8th
2010	19	0	163	5th

Above **Career stats:** Fernando Alonso took two drivers' titles for Renault, in 2005 and 2006, and 17 wins. *Below* **Now that's something new:** Jean-Pierre Jabouille laps Silverstone on Renault's debut in 1977, but he wasn't around at the finish.

AT HOME AND AWAY

Renault's two spells in F1 are distinct as the first, from 1977 to 1985, was based in France and the second, from 2002, was based in Britain, having taken over the Benetton team premises and personnel.

NOW THAT'S SOMETHING NEW

There was considerable interest when Renault made its F1 debut midway through 1977. This wasn't just because an all-new team arrived for the British GP at Silverstone with an all-new car, but also because the yellow racer was powered by the first turbocharged engine in F1. Jean-Pierre Jabouille qualified 21st and was making progress when the car pulled off with, you've guessed it, turbocharger failure…

TOPPING THE TON

|||||||||||||||||||||||||||||||||||||||

Even before he returned for his second spell with the team in 2008, Fernando Alonso had become Renault's longest-serving driver. Before he left for his troubled year with McLaren in 2007, the Spaniard had raced 71 times for the team, more than long-term Renault racers Rene Arnoux, Jean-Pierre Jabouille and Alain Prost. Alonso's two-year second stint in 2008 and 2009 then boosted that total to 106 grands prix.

Above **Topping the ton:** Fernando Alonso waves to the fans at Interlagos in 2006. He raced more than 100 times for Renault.
Below **Landmark flying laps:** Rene Arnoux lost out to Gilles Villeneuve in the 1979 Franch GP, but he did set the fastest lap.

 ### DOING IT IN STYLE

When Renault scored its breakthrough victory, it did so in style. This wasn't simply because it did so on home ground when Jean-Pierre Jabouille was first to the chequered flag in the 1979 French GP at Dijon Prenois, but because the battle over second place was all but explosive in the closing laps, with team-mate Rene Arnoux and Ferrari's Gilles Villeneuve changing places at almost every bend and entertaining royally.

 ### BEING DOUBLY HONOURED

Despite Renault's successes in the late 1970s and early 1980s in the days when the team was wholly French, it took until 2005 for the now British-run team representing the French marque to take its first constructors' championship. Then, like buses, a second title came along straight after it, with Fernando Alonso's second place behind Ferrari's Felipe Massa in the 2006 Brazilian GP at Interlagos sealing the deal.

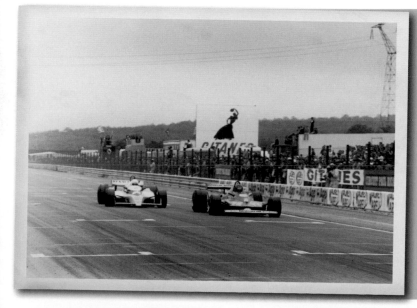

LANDMARK FLYING LAPS

Renault brought turbocharged engines into F1 in 1977 and their power soon made them almost untouchable around a lap. For races, the boost had to be turned down, not just to increase fuel consumption but to ensure they didn't blow. So, although Renault's first pole came at the 1979 South African GP, it took another five races before it took its first fastest lap, through Rene Arnoux in the French GP, a race won by team-mate Jean-Pierre Jabouille.

BENETTON

The team was born out of the Toleman team after it ran into financial difficulties in 1985 and was bailed out by the Benetton knitwear company. Racing as Benetton from 1986, it took Michael Schumacher to titles in 1994 and 1995 but disappeared when taken over by Renault for 2002.

*Below **Benetton's guiding light:** Michael Schumacher sends the crowds wild as he heads for his first win at home, at Hockenheim in 1995, putting him on course for his second title as well as Benetton's lone constructors' crown.*

FACT FILE

Founded: 1986

Years in F1: 1986-2001

Country: England

HQ: Enstone, England

Team principal: N/A, as team defunct

Constructors' titles: 1995

END OF YEAR, END OF NAME

The record books show that Benetton's last grand prix was at the final round of the 2001 World Championship, the Japanese GP, as Renault's buy-in meant that the Enstone-based team would be known as Renault from 2002 onwards. It hadn't been a good season for either Giancarlo Fisichella or Jenson Button, and although they qualified sixth and ninth at Suzuka, neither scored, with Button seventh and Fisichella on the sidelines.

Left **End of year, end of name:** Jenson Button was the last driver to finish a race in a Benetton car, finishing seventh at Suzuka in the 2001 season finale.

STRAIGHT INTO THE POINTS

Benetton wasn't a brand new team when it made its debut at the 1986 season-opener in Brazil, rather a re-badged version of the team that had finished 1985 as Toleman. However, the investment that poured in over the close-season resulted in a superior car and Gerhard Berger qualified 16th before racing through the field to score a point for sixth, four places up on team-mate, Teo Fabi. More points would follow.

LIGHT THE TOUCHPAPER

Very few teams show pace-setting speed in their first season, but Benetton did. Propelled by turbocharged BMW engines, the green cars with multi-coloured flashes on their engine covers certainly had ample power, most especially with the boost turned up for qualifying. This resulted in the team's first pole position at the 1986 Austrian GP when Teo Fabi and Gerhard Berger shared an all-Benetton front row.

FIRST YEAR WINNERS

It took until the penultimate grand prix of its first season racing as Benetton (after its development years racing as Toleman) for the team to secure its first win. This came at the Mexican GP in 1986 when Gerhard Berger qualified fourth, gained a place at Nigel Mansell's expense on the opening lap, then kept his cool to run non-stop to victory on his Pirelli tyres while his Goodyear-shod rivals had to pit for fresh rubber.

Above **First year winners:** Gerhard Berger used his tyres sensibly in the Mexican heat in 1986 to give Benetton its first victory one race before the end of its maiden campaign. *Right* **The first and the last:** Berger surprised everyone when he came back from missing three races in 1997 to win the German GP for what would be Benetton's final grand prix success.

THE FIRST AND THE LAST

Not only did Gerhard Berger score Benetton's first win in 1986, but he returned to the team after nine years away racing for Ferrari (twice) and McLaren to be the driver who gave Benetton its last. This came in 1997 at the German GP at Hockenheim. Early season form hadn't suggested such an outcome would be possible, and he missed three races with a sinus problem, before bouncing back with this popular win from pole.

CAREER STATS

Year	Races	Wins	Points	Ranking
1986	16	1	19	6th
1987	16	0	28	5th
1988	16	0	39	3rd
1989	16	1	39	4th
1990	16	2	71	3rd
1991	16	1	38.5	4th
1992	16	1	91	3rd
1993	16	1	72	3rd
1994	16	8	103	2nd
1995	17	11	137	1st
1996	16	0	68	3rd
1997	17	1	67	3rd
1998	16	0	33	5th
1999	16	0	16	6th
2000	17	0	20	4th
2001	17	0	10	7th

FIRST DRIVER THEN TEAM

||||||||||||||||||||||||||||||||||||

Michael Schumacher won the drivers' championship for Benetton in a controversial 1994 season, but the team had to wait until he secured the championship again in 1995 before it could celebrate its own crown. This constructors' championship was wrapped up at the Japanese GP when Schumacher qualified on pole and then led every lap (apart from when pitting). He had already claimed the drivers' title two races earlier.

Above **Career stats:** Michael Schumacher was Benetton's driving force, giving the team 19 wins between 1992 and 1995.

Below **First driver then team:** Michael Schumacher's victory in Germany in 1995 was an important ingredient in his second title and the team's first.

⟫ TOP OF ALL THE LISTS

Not only was Michael Schumacher Benetton's longest-serving driver, with 68 starts between his transfer from Jordan towards the end of the 1991 season

and the end of 1995, but he was the team's most successful driver by some margin. His tally, before he left to race for Ferrari in 1996, was two drivers' titles, 19 wins, 10 pole positions, 24 fastest laps and 313 points.

⟫ EARNING HIS COLOURS

Benetton is an Italian knitwear company that expanded across the world in the 1980s, with long-time F1 boss Flavio Briatore handed the reins as a reward for establishing the brand in the USA.

TYRRELL

Once a racer, then a team manager, Ken Tyrrell helped Matra to succeed in F1 before founding his own marque in 1970. Jackie Stewart grabbed two drivers' and one constructors' title to establish the team, but it was never as competitive again and was bought by British American Racing in 1998.

Below **Alpine star:** *Jackie Stewart was the driver on whom Tyrrell's successes were built and his strong form in 1973, such as this charge to the podium in Austria, helped him to his second drivers' title with the team.*

FACT FILE

Founded: 1960

Years in F1: 1970-1998

Country: England

HQ: Ockham, England

Team principal: N/A as team defunct

Constructors' titles: 1971

Below **Career stats:** Jackie Stewart helped Tyrrell to its only constructors' championship in 1971 by winning six of the 11 rounds, in Spain, Monaco, France, Britain, Germany and Canada.

VICTORY RUN THWARTED

Although Tyrrell started 1970 running a March chassis for Jackie Stewart, it wasn't until the Canadian GP, the 11th of 13 races, that the Scot was sent out to race in the team's first chassis, the Tyrrell 001. Stewart delighted the team by qualifying on pole, something he'd managed three times in the March with which they'd started the year. Then, heading to victory, his stub-axle failed just before half distance.

MAKING YOUR OWN LUCK

Jackie Stewart raced to five wins and a second in the first seven rounds of 1971. So great was his advantage that he secured the drivers' title and Tyrrell wrapped up the constructors' title at the eighth round of 11. Ironically, the team's first title was claimed at the Austrian GP, in which Stewart retired, albeit because he lost a wheel just a few laps after his closest rival, Ferrari's Jacky Ickx, had dropped out.

CAREER STATS

Year	Races	Wins	Points	Ranking
1970	3	0	0	-
1971	11	7	73	1st
1972	12	4	51	2nd
1973	14	5	82	2nd
1974	15	2	52	3rd
1975	14	1	25	5th
1976	16	1	71	3rd
1977	17	0	27	5th
1978	16	1	38	4th
1979	15	0	28	5th
1980	14	0	12	6th
1981	15	0	10	8th
1982	16	1	25	6th
1983	15	1	12	7th
1984	12	0	0*	-
1985	16	0	7	9th
1986	16	0	11	7th
1987	16	0	11	6th
1988	15	0	5	8th
1989	16	0	16	5th
1990	16	0	16	5th
1991	16	0	12	6th
1992	16	0	8	6th
1993	16	0	0	-
1994	16	0	13	6th
1995	17	0	5	8th
1996	16	0	5	8th
1997	17	0	2	10th
1998	16	0	0	-

* All results were stripped from the team in 1984 as illegal fuel was found in its cars at the Detroit GP

IMPRESSING THE BOSSES

If you're powered by Ford, winning the Detroit GP isn't a bad way to impress the right people on the streets of the world's automotive capital. This is what happened to Tyrrell in 1983 when Michele Alboreto worked his way forward from sixth to third, then gained a place when Rene Arnoux retired his Ferrari from the lead. When new leader Nelson Piquet's Brabham picked up a puncture, Alboreto secured the team's 23rd and final win.

Above **Impressing the bosses:** Michele Alboreto is pursued by Keke Rosberg's Williams in Detroit in 1983, but he stayed ahead to score what proved to be Tyrrell's final win.

ENDING WITH A WHIMPER

Tyrrell's time in F1 came to an end at the 1998 Japanese GP at Suzuka after 29 years. Sadly, this once proud team, whose World Championship entry was taken over by BAR, went out with a whimper when Ricardo Rosset failed to qualify and Toranosuke Takagi crashed out just after mid-distance in a collision with Minardi's Esteban Tuero. That they were scrapping over last place emphasised how far the team had fallen.

STAYING CLOSE TO HOME

F1 standards have changed out of all recognition, but even in its day it came as a shock to learn that Ken Tyrrell ran his successful team from sheds alongside his family's timber yard business.

LIFE WITH 'UNCLE KEN'

Ken Tyrrell was a benevolent if sometimes sparky team principal, but almost all of his drivers liked his avuncular manner. Patrick Depailler certainly did, as he became Tyrrell's longest-serving driver, staying with the Surrey-based team for five years from 1974, having first competed in a pair of races for Tyrrell in 1972. In all, he contested 80 grands prix during that time.

WITHDRAWAL HITS TITLE HOPE

Tyrrell was on course for its second constructors' title in 1973 after a year-long battle with Lotus. However, Francois Cevert's death in qualifying for the final round, the United States GP, led Ken Tyrrell to withdraw the team. This left the way clear for Ronnie Peterson to win for Lotus to gift them the crown, meaning that Tyrrell's final title was the drivers' one that Jackie Stewart claimed three races earlier at the Austrian GP.

Left **Life with "Uncle" Ken:** Ken Tyrrell poses with the team's 1974 challenger, the 007.

GETTING BACK ON TRACK

With Jackie Stewart's retirement at the end of 1973, and Francois Cevert's tragic death, it was left to Tyrrell's new guard of Patrick Depailler and Jody Scheckter to keep the team at the front. It all came together for the pair in the seventh round, the Swedish GP at Anderstorp, when they claimed the team's first one-two in qualifying before the South African got the jump on the Frenchman and led all the way.

Below **Getting back on track:** After giving Tyrrell its first win of 1974 in Sweden, Jody Scheckter was a winner again three races later in the British GP at Brands Hatch.

BRM

Considerable hope was placed on this well-funded British team as it took on the continental challenge through the 1950s, but it only hit the high notes in the early 1960s when Graham Hill took it to glory. Then, the team went into gradual decline until folding after a disastrous 1977 campaign.

Below **Heading to glory:** *Graham Hill races to victory in the 1962 Italian GP at Monza to put himself into an almost unassailable position in the drivers' championship and help BRM towards its only constructors' title.*

FACT FILE

Founded: 1947

Years in F1: 1951-1977

Country: England

HQ: Bourne, England

Team principal: N/A as team defunct

Constructors' titles: 1962

TAKING POINTS NOT PLAUDITS

There was a great deal of national interest at the 1951 British GP at Silverstone when BRM made its World Championship debut. The marque had invested a considerable amount in trying to take on the mighty Italian teams, Alfa Romeo and Ferrari, yet Reg Parnell and Peter Walker started on the back row after failing to set a time in qualifying. Impressively, they finished fifth and seventh, albeit four and five laps down.

BRM'S ONE AND ONLY

BRM's not inexpensive bid for World Championship glory was achieved in 1962, and it's a good thing too as the team had been threatened with a "win or bust" message from the people paying the bills. BRM's Graham Hill led the way, and the retirement of Lotus ace Jim Clark in the final round, the 1962 South African GP at Kyalami, was enough for both Hill and BRM to triumph.

Below **Two out of three:** Harry Schell races to BRM's first podium at Zandvoort in 1958, a year before Jo Bonnier scored BRM's first win there.

CAREER STATS

Year	Races	Wins	Points	Ranking
1951	1	0	N/A*	N/A*
1956	1	0	N/A*	N/A*
1957	3	0	N/A*	N/A*
1958	9	0	18	4th
1959	7	1	18	3rd
1960	8	0	8	4th
1961	8	0	7	5th
1962	9	4	42	1st
1963	10	2	36	2nd
1964	10	2	42	2nd
1965	10	3	45	2nd
1966	9	1	22	4th
1967	11	0	17	6th
1968	12	0	28	5th
1969	10	0	7	5th
1970	13	1	23	6th
1971	11	2	36	2nd
1972	12	1	14	7th
1973	15	0	12	6th
1974	15	0	10	7th
1975	10	0	0	-
1976	1	0	0	-
1977	2	0	0	-

* There was no constructors' championship until 1958

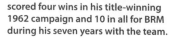

Above **Career stats:** Graham Hill scored four wins in his title-winning 1962 campaign and 10 in all for BRM during his seven years with the team.

WHAT A WASTE OF MONEY

BRM's attempts to get its over-complicated V16 to race were a source of constant embarrassment and the public grew tired of them, throwing money over the fences at the car at Silverstone after it failed on the grid.

HILL'S BRM MAJORITY

Graham Hill was not only BRM's sole World Champion and the driver who scored its most wins but also the longest-serving. The Londoner joined BRM from Lotus for 1960 and stayed on for seven seasons, winning the 1962 drivers' title. After 64 starts for BRM, Hill returned to Lotus for 1967. His nine grand prix victories, including three at Monaco, were more than half of BRM's tally.

TWO OUT OF THREE

BRM flirted with the World Championship in its early days in the 1950s, and 1958 was its first real bid for championship glory. Pleasingly, there was early reward when Harry Schell qualified seventh and then raced to BRM's first podium finish at the third round, the Dutch GP at Zandvoort. He finished almost 48s behind winner Stirling Moss's Vanwall, but with team-mate Jean Behra third, it was a good day.

COMING UP TRUMPS IN MONACO

One of BRM's most famous wins turned out to be the team's final one. It came at the Monaco GP in 1972 and the driver taking the plaudits was Jean-Pierre Beltoise. The Frenchman had qualified fourth, but on the run to the first corner in the pouring rain he blasted into the lead. At Monaco, where passing is hard in the dry and nigh on impossible in the wet, that was enough. Eighty laps later, he was victorious.

Above **Coming up trumps in Monaco:** Jean-Pierre Beltoise blasts his P160B through Monaco's tunnel in a feisty drive to victory in which he led every lap. It was to be his only F1 win and BRM's last. *Below* **BRM's weekend of weekends:** Jo Bonnier leads the field into Tarzan on the opening lap in 1959 and, although passed on lap 2, was back in front by the finish.

BRM'S WEEKEND OF WEEKENDS

|||||||||||||||||||||||||||||||||||||||||||

After years of not delivering, everything came together for BRM in one weekend at the Dutch GP early in the 1959 season. Not only did Jo Bonnier give BRM its first pole position, but he then went on to score its first win. Stirling Moss must have been kicking himself, as he'd spent the previous week testing and developing the BRM. However, it was a flash in the pan as the next win didn't come until 1962.

OVER AND VERY MUCH OUT

BRM didn't achieve what it ought, but its end was a fiasco, as this once-fancied team faded into oblivion at the start of 1977. Larry Perkins was the unfortunate soul who had to see it out of the door and endured the embarrassment of arriving for the opening race in Argentina without a car when it wouldn't fit into the plane's hold. The death knell came two races later, at the South African GP at Kyalami when he finished in 15th and last place, five laps down.

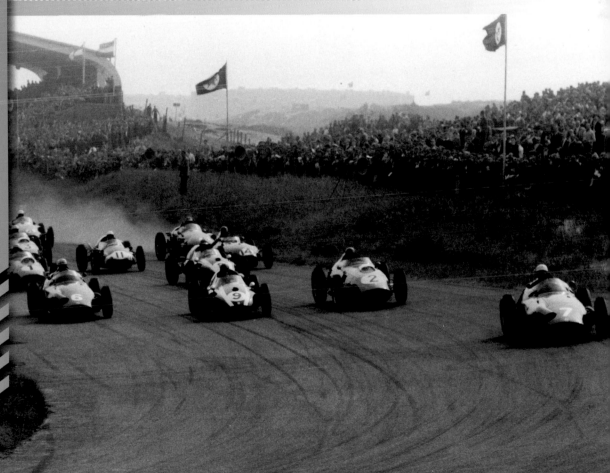

COOPER

This was the team that bucked traditional thinking when it entered cars with an engine behind the driver rather than in front and proved that big wasn't best. However, after title glory in 1959 and 1960, its form rather dropped away and instead made its money from selling chassis for others to drive.

Below **Black Jack:** *Jack Brabham had a great run to help himself to the drivers' title and Cooper to the constructors' crown in 1960, although a mechanical problem slowed his progress in the final round, the US GP at Riverside.*

FACT FILE

Founded: 1946

Years in F1: 1953-1968

Country: England

HQ: Surbiton, England

Team principal: N/A as team defunct

Constructors' titles: 1959, 1960

A FOOT IN THE DOOR

Harry Schell's family team entered a Cooper in the 1950 Monaco GP and assorted privateers ran Coopers in 1952. However, it was in 1953 that the Cooper Car Co finally entered a works team, starting by running a car for Adolfo Schwelm-Cruz in the season-opening race in Buenos Aires. He was the first to retire, when his car shed a wheel, and teammates John Barber and Alan Brown finished a distant eighth and ninth.

COOPER'S HIGH FIVE

Cooper's best winning sequence came in the second year in which it won the constructors' championship, 1960. Much of the momentum required to vanquish Lotus came from this five-race winning streak that started when Jack Brabham won the Dutch GP, then added the next four in Belgium, France, Britain and Portugal.

BEATEN BY A CUSTOMER

Imagine the mixed feelings you'd experience if your marque defeated the big guns to score its maiden victory, yet the car wasn't run by your works team but a private entry. This was what happened to Cooper in 1958 when Rob Walker Racing's Stirling Moss went to the season-opener in Argentina in a Cooper and came away victorious. It would take just over a year for Jack Brabham to win for Cooper Car Co, at Monaco.

OVER AND ALMOST OUT

The last grand prix entered by Cooper Car Co was the 1968 Mexican GP. Vic Elford and Lucien Bianchi qualified 17th and 21st, but only Elford was able to finish, in eighth place. With money tight, that was the end of the works team. A Cooper made one last visit to a World Championship round in the Monaco GP the following year when Elford finished seventh for Colin Crabbe's Antique Automobiles Ltd team.

SUPER COOPER

John Cooper created a special Mini in 1961. Known as the Mini Cooper, it offered a more powerful engine, better brakes and was the car every young man about town wished to drive.

Above **Beaten by a customer:** Stirling Moss gave Cooper its first win, for Rob Walker Racing in Argentina in 1958. *Below left* **Career stats:** Jack Brabham won two races on his way to the 1959 title with Cooper. *Below* **One, two, nothing:** Brabham had good reason to smile in both 1959 and 1960.

CAREER STATS

Year	Races	Wins	Points	Ranking
1953	3	0	N/A*	N/A*
1955	1	0	N/A*	N/A*
1957	5	0	N/A*	N/A*
1958	9	2	31	3rd**
1959	8	5	40	1st**
1960	8	6	48	1st
1961	8	0	14	4th
1962	9	1	29	3rd
1963	10	0	25	5th
1964	10	0	16	5th
1965	10	0	14	5th
1966	9	1	30	3rd
1967	11	1	28	3rd
1968	12	0	14	6th

* There was no constructors' championship until 1958

** Including the results of privateer Cooper-fielding team Rob Walker Racing as the constructors' series points were awarded according to the make of car rather than the team running it

ONE, TWO, NOTHING

Cooper won two constructors' titles, in 1959 and 1960. Jack Brabham led the team's attack, winning the drivers' championship in both those years, ably supported by Bruce McLaren. However, the Australian left Cooper and Kiwi McLaren soldiered on. The rise of Lotus and resurgence of Ferrari left it fighting for the minor point-scoring places through until Cooper's demise at the end of 1968.

FOLLOWING THE LEADER

You might have thought that Jack Brabham would hold the record as Cooper's longest-serving driver. However, it is Bruce McLaren, his teammate when Jack won the drivers' titles in 1959 and 1960 who comes out far ahead, 64 to 39. The Kiwi joined Cooper at the tail end of 1958 and stayed on until the close of the 1965 season before he, like Brabham before him, headed off to found his own marque.

Above **Following the leader:** Bruce McLaren steers his Cooper T60 Climax to victory in the 1962 Monaco Grand Prix.
Below **A win/win situation:** A privately entered Cooper driven by John Love was heading for victory in the 1967 South African GP until it had to pit for fuel and Pedro Rodriguez came through to win for the works team.

A WIN/WIN SITUATION

The season-opening 1967 South African GP is a race remembered for a "what if" performance as it was the most famous upset in F1 history. John Love, a driver from neighbouring Rhodesia (now Zimbabwe) was heading for victory in a privately entered Cooper when he had to pit for fuel with seven laps to go. Love's hiccough left the way clear for one of the works cars, driven by Pedro Rodriguez, to come through to victory.

There are great drivers, great teams and undoubtedly great circuits where the race action has been staged over the decades. The newer circuits outside Europe may possess the latest facilities, but the likes of Monza, Monaco, Silverstone, Spa-Francorchamps and the Nürburgring are steeped in history, packed with the memories of legendary races they have hosted. Some of these are wide open and flat-out, producing mind-boggling average speeds, others narrow and waiting to bite at every tight corner.

Below **Threading the needle:** The insertion of chicanes has broken the high-speed flow at Monza, but it certainly adds to the action on the opening lap. Lewis Hamilton leads Kimi Raikkonen and Adrian Sutil out of the Variante Del Rettifilio in 2009.

MONZA

This historic parkland circuit has always been blessed with superlatives, from the fastest race average speed, fastest straightline speed, the closest group finish and even the greatest number of lead changes during a grand prix. And, being in Italy, every second of Ferrari action at Monza is cheered on by the fanatical *Tifosi*.

ALFA COMPLETES DOMINATION

The pattern was set when the World Championship came to Monza for the first time in 1950 to round out its inaugural season: Alfa Romeo would win as it had in the previous five races. Indeed, Giuseppe Farina controlled proceedings, but Ferrari challenged for the first time, with Alberto Ascari running second until his engine overheated. After taking over teammate Dorino Serafini's car, Ascari recovered to bag second place.

A ROYAL APPOINTMENT

Motor racing circuits tend to be built on greenfield sites, but Monza is a little different, as it was built in 1922 on the parkland surrounding Monza royal palace, which explains the mature trees that surround it, adding to its appeal.

WHO'S LEADING THIS LAP?

While the 1971 Italian GP had the most drivers taking a turn at leading the race with eight, the 1965 Italian GP had a greater number of changes of the lead. With a total of 39 lead changes – 14 more than in 1971 – it is no surprise that it stands out as Monza's most memorable race. Jim Clark led from the off in 1965, but Graham Hill, Jackie Stewart and John Surtees all took turns in the lead before Stewart won for BRM.

FANGIO'S HAT-TRICK

Juan Manuel Fangio is the only driver to have achieved three wins in a row at Monza, the great Argentinian achieving this hat-trick between 1953 and 1955. He took the first of these for Maserati, hitting the front out of the final corner when race-leader Giuseppe Farina crashed out. Fangio then added the next two while leading the Mercedes-Benz attack, albeit with a fortunate win in 1954 when others retired and a clear run in 1955.

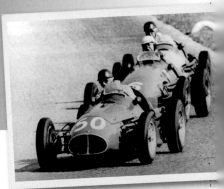

Right **Fangio's hat-trick:** Juan Manuel Fangio races his works Maserati towards victory at Monza in 1953.

Above **Track facts:** Monza is located in a royal park to the north-west of Milan and its lay-out can be made out, as well as that of the oval circuit cutting the through the trees.

TRACK FACTS

Opened: 1922

Country: Italy

Location: 10 miles north-west of Milan

Active years in F1: 1950-1979, 1981 onwards

Most wins/driver: Michael Schumacher, 5 (1996, 1998, 2000, 2003, 2006)

Most wins/team: Ferrari, 18 (1951, 1952, 1960, 1961, 1964, 1966, 1970, 1975, 1979, 1988, 1996,1998, 2000, 2002, 2003, 2004, 2006, 2010)

Lap length: 3.600 miles

Number of turns: 11

Lap record: 1m21.046s, 159.909mph, Rubens Barrichello (Ferrari), 2004

Right **Slowing down the cars:** The new chicane at Roggia caught Clay Regazzoni out in 1972. *Below* **Exit of Parabolica:** Jenson Button guides his McLaren through this final corner of Monza's lap in 2010 en route to second place.

EXIT OF PARABOLICA

The final corner of Monza's lap, the Parabolica, is a long, long corner. Approached at 210mph, this is a fourth gear bend, with drivers still travelling at 130mph as they turn through this right-hander. Exit speed is critical, and drivers should be changing up to fifth gear and hitting 150mph by the exit, as they need to carry as much speed as possible onto the start/finish, straight past the grandstand and on down to the first chicane.

THREE FOR TWO

Lotus and Ferrari share the bragging rights for the longest victory sequence, with the British team having won at Monza three years running from 1972 to 1974, all with its increasingly venerable Lotus 72. Emerson Fittipaldi claimed the first of these, then Ronnie Peterson added the next two. Ferrari's run came 30 years later, as Rubens Barrichello won in 2002 and 2004, with Michael Schumacher taking the flag in 2003.

DELIGHTING THE TIFOSI

Fangio, Moss, Peterson, Piquet and Prost have all won three grands prix at Monza. Rubens Barrichello has claimed four victories, but the driver who really put Ferrari back on the map from the late 1990s, Michael Schumacher, is top of the pile, with five wins. These came in 1996, 1998, 2000, 2003 and 2006. To the delight of the *Tifosi*, Ferrari is the team with the greatest winning record, having taken 19 wins.

SLOWING DOWN THE CARS

Packs of cars slipstreaming around the lap at Monza was a recipe for disaster and so the circuit lay-out was slowed with the insertion of three chicanes for 1972 – one on the run to Curva Grande (the original first corner), another at Roggia and a third at Vialone. As a result Emerson Fittipaldi's race-winning average in his Lotus in 1973 was fully 19.16mph slower than the previous year's mark.

GOING FASTEST AND FASTER

Monza has always been an ultra high-speed circuit. Ferrari's Phil Hill was the first to set an average speed of more than 130mph in 1960. John Surtees topped 140mph in his Honda in 1967.

Just four years later, in the closest group finish ever, Peter Gethin was first with a winning average of over 150mph. Three chicanes were inserted in 1972 and it wasn't until 2003 that Michael Schumacher's average speed topped 150mph with them in place …

MONACO

By rights, there should no longer be a grand prix at Monaco as its streets are too narrow for contemporary F1 cars, but to discard it would strip the World Championship of the race with the strongest identity. The yachts and beautiful people add glamour, and F1 would be the poorer without it.

IN A CLASS OF HIS OWN

Juan Manuel Fangio was very much the star of the show at Monaco's first World Championship race in 1950. Not only did he put his Alfa Romeo 158 on pole position by 2.6 secs from teammate Giuseppe Farina but he also shot off to win the race by a lap, setting the fastest lap as he went. His advantage over the slowest qualifier, Johnny Claes in a Ecurie Belge Talbot, was 20.8 secs.

EVERY WHICH WAY BUT...

There has been some enthralling racing at Monaco, but Nigel Mansell's pursuit of Ayrton Senna in 1992 was debatably even more exciting than Jochen Rindt's successful chase of Jack Brabham in 1970. Mansell had led from the start, but what made it Monaco's most memorable race was when a wheel weight came loose and Mansell had to pit for new tyres. On rejoining, with six laps to go, he was 5 secs down on Senna, then closed in and was all over him but just couldn't find a way past.

MONACO'S DARKEST DAY

The 1967 Monaco GP was shaping up into a hugely exciting battle between Denny Hulme's Brabham and Lorenzo Bandini's Ferrari when the Italian began to close in. After Hulme's teammate Jack Brabham retired with engine failure, the Kiwi driver must have been dreading the same. Then, on lap 83, Bandini crashed at the chicane, flipped and was trapped underneath as his car caught fire. He died three days later.

SIX IN SUCCESSION

McLaren enjoyed an amazing run at Monaco when its drivers won in the principality six years running from 1988 to 1993. Alain Prost inherited victory in the first of these when team-mate Ayrton Senna crashed inexplicably out of a clear lead. Senna then made amends and won the next five races here. Incredibly, Senna's victory at Monaco in 1987 for Lotus was the only non-McLaren win in the 10 years from 1984.

McLAREN'S MONTE MAGIC

One might have thought, given its lengthy history in F1, that Ferrari would be the team with the most wins at Monaco, but the Italian team has underachieved there by its own standards. For, while it has 18 wins on home ground at Monza, it has won only eight times at Monaco since 1950. McLaren is way clear at the top of the pile at Monaco, having recorded 15 wins up to and including the 2010 season.

THE PRINCE'S PLEASURE

Like Monza, Monaco has a royal connection. Not only was cigarette manufacturer Antony Noghes given permission to stage racing on a street circuit by Prince Louis II, but the Grimaldis' castle overlooks the circuit from on high.

GETTING CLOSE TO THE TON

The fastest ever Monaco GP took place in 2007 when Fernando Alonso won for McLaren at an average speed of 96.655mph, helped in no small part by the race taking place without interruption from the safety car. Lewis Hamilton was confident that he could have gone faster, if only he'd been allowed to attack. By way of comparison, the slowest Monaco GP, in 1950, was won by Juan Manuel Fangio at 61.331mph.

Above **Six in succession:** When Alain Prost won at Monaco, McLaren had no way of knowing that it would triumph in the next five races there as well.
Left **Getting close to the ton:** The McLarens of Fernando Alonso and Lewis Hamilton dominated in Monaco's fastest ever grand prix in 2007.

Below **Track facts:** The way in which the circuit has to thread its way between Monaco's buildings, twisting around tight corners, is clear from this view of the stretch from Mirabeau to Portier.

TRACK FACTS

Opened: 1922

Country: Monaco

Location: Monte Carlo

Active years in F1: 1950, 1955 onwards

Most wins/driver: Ayton Senna, 6 (1987, 1989, 1990, 1991, 1992, 1993)

Most wins/team: McLaren, 15 (1984-1986, 1988-1993, 1998, 2000, 2002, 2005, 2007-2008)

Lap length: 2.075 miles

Number of turns: 19

Lap record: 1m14.439s, 100.373mph, Michael Schumacher (Ferrari), 2004

CASINO SQUARE

||||||||||||||||||||||||||||||||||||||||

One of the most glamorous of Monaco's glamorous spots, Casino Square, passes in a flash for the drivers when the grand prix circus comes to town. The cars arrive over a brow into the preceding corner, Massenet, then feel funnelled by crash barriers and a patch of shade before bursting back into the sunlight as they enter the square.

WHEN CARS USED TO BREAK

People often view "the olden days" through rose-tinted spectacles, as it tends to be forgotten that the cars were nowhere near as reliable as today. Take the 1966 Monaco GP when there were just four classified finishers from the 16 starters. Certainly, this was the first race of the new 3-litre engine regulations but this was a pathetic result. Actually, two other cars were still circulating, but they were 25 and 27 laps adrift…

Below **Casino Square:** Ukyo Katayama flashes through this famous square in his Tyrrell in 1995, but he never managed to get the roll of the dice at Monaco.

SILVERSTONE

The site of the first ever World Championship round in 1950, Silverstone is more than the home of the British GP. It's one of the true homes of motor racing not just because of its long history but also because the majority of the teams are based in England, making this their home race.

 ## AND THEY'RE OFF...

Silverstone had the honour of hosting the first round of the first World Championship in 1950. Watched by the royal family from a private grandstand, the race was an Alfa Romeo benefit as not only did its cars fill the first four places on the grid but Giuseppe Farina led home an Alfa one-two-three ahead of Luigi Fagioli and Reg Parnell, with teammate Juan Manuel Fangio dropping out with a connecting rod failure.

 ## WINNING BY MILES

The greatest winning margin for a British GP at Silverstone was an entire lap, and this has happened three times. This first occurred in 1969 when Matra racer Jackie Stewart trounced the field, with Jacky Ickx the best of the rest for Brabham. The previous biggest winning margin had been in 1956 when Juan Manuel Fangio had beaten his Ferrari teammates Peter Collins and Alfonso de Portago by 1 min 32 secs.

 ## SKITTLES AT SILVERSTONE

When Jody Scheckter hit F1, he was desperate to make an impression and his over exuberance at the start of the 1973 British GP led to an accident that certainly won't be forgotten. Having started sixth in his McLaren, the young South African ran wide coming out of Woodcote at the end of lap 1 scattering those behind, leaving seven cars unable to take the restart and Andrea de Adamich with leg injuries.

 ## FEW REACH THE FINISH

The fewest finishers in a British GP at Silverstone came in 1958 when only nine cars were still circulating at the chequered flag as Peter Collins led a Ferrari one-two. There were even fewer cars still running in 1975, seven, when the race was stopped after a downpour had cars sliding off all around the circuit. However, as the race was red-flagged, the result was declared from a lap before, when 18 cars were still circulating.

Below **Track facts:** Silverstone's origins as an airfield are clear to see from an aerial shot, with the main runway running from Copse (*bottom left*) to Stowe (*top right*).

TRACK FACTS

Opened: 1948

Country: England

Location: 16 miles south-west of Northampton

Active years in F1: 1950-1954, 1956, 1958, 1960, 1963, 1965, 1967, 1969, 1971, 1973, 1975, 1977, 1979, 1981, 1983, 1985, 1987 onwards

Most wins/driver: Alain Prost, 5 (1983, 1985, 1989, 1990, 1993)

Most wins/team: McLaren, 12 (1973, 1975, 1977, 1981, 1985, 1988-1989, 1999-2001, 2005, 2008)

Lap length: 3.666 miles

Number of turns: 18

Lap record: 1m30.874s, 145.018mph, Fernando Alonso (Ferrari), 2010

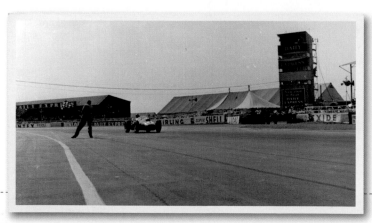

Left **Few reach the finish:** Peter Collins takes the chequered flag to win the 1958 British GP for Ferrari, but only nine of the 20 starters made it to the finish.

APPROACH TO STOWE

Silverstone is an open, airy place. However, at no point does the circuit feel as broad as it does on the Hangar Straight where the drivers race down towards the grandstands and the fast right-hander at Stowe. Arriving at 190mph, the drivers have to drop down two gears to fifth and try to stop themselves from running wide as the track kinks back slightly on itself and drops into the dip known as the Vale.

WINNING FOR BRITAIN

There have been many great races at Silverstone and each generation has a favourite. What can't be denied is that the 1987 British GP was one of the most memorable. This was in a period of Williams' superiority and the battle within the team between Nigel Mansell and Nelson Piquet was as fierce as it was with rivals. With the packed crowd urging him on, Mansell's jinking move to take the lead with two laps to go was brilliant.

FLYING ROUND THE TRACK

Silverstone set something of a trend when its circuit was marked out around the perimeter roads of an airfield in 1948. The airfield had become disused in the wake of the Second World War and the race circuit gave it a new lease of life.

TWO TEAMS LAND TWELVE

Silverstone is a circuit that has yielded most to champions. Alain Prost holds the record for the most wins by a driver, five, between his first there for Renault in 1983 (*below*) and his last for Williams 10 years later. Ferrari and McLaren are the teams that have won at Silverstone most often, taking 12 wins apiece, albeit with Ferrari scoring its first win there in 1951. McLaren's Silverstone breakthrough came in 1973.

SEVEN SETS OF PAIRS

The best victory sequence of any driver at Silverstone is, amazingly, just two, and seven drivers have achieved this since Alberto Ascari's double in 1952 and 1953. Ferrari scored six wins in a row at Silverstone in the 1950s bookended by Gonzalez in 1951 and Peter Collins in 1958. However, the wins were not consecutive as the British GP was held at Aintree in 1955 and 1957, when Mercedes and then Vanwall won.

Below **Two teams land twelve:** Alain Prost races to the first of his five British GP wins, for Renault in 1983.
Bottom **Approach to Stowe:** Nineteen cars trail Jacques Villeneuve into Stowe.

SPA-FRANCORCHAMPS

A win at this Belgian circuit is a feather in any driver's cap. It's a real drivers' circuit, challenging them like few others as it follows the route of much of the circuit that opened in 1924. It has gradient changes, fast corners and often changeable weather to add plenty of extra twists and drama.

 ### FANGIO DRAWS FIRST BLOOD

The fourth round of the inaugural World Championship in 1950 brought the teams to Spa-Francorchamps, and Giuseppe Farina and Juan Manuel Fangio shared a lap time to be equal fastest in qualifying. It was the Argentinian who led away and records show that Raymond Sommer led in his Talbot-Lago, but this was only when Alfa Romeo's star duo pitted for fuel. Thereafter, Fangio came back to score his second win.

 ### VICTORY WITH TIME TO SPARE

Despite the fastest lap of the 1963 Belgian GP being covered in just under 4 mins, Jim Clark's winning margin over Cooper driver Bruce McLaren was 4 mins 54 secs. This was the largest winning margin in the history of the race and was achieved after rain hit late in the race once the Lotus driver had made his break and McLaren was just a fraction under a lap behind as they completed the circuit at a reduced pace.

 ### ALL TOGETHER NOW...

Some accidents involve a driver throwing his car off the circuit, others one car hitting another. Then there are pile-ups, and the 1998 Belgian GP produced one of these. It happened, as most do, on the first lap and was triggered by David Coulthard after his McLaren had been tagged by a Ferrari. In all, 12 cars were involved and four were too damaged to take the restart, which also resulted in a first corner accident...

 ### YIELDING ONLY TO THE GREATS

Proving that Spa-Francorchamps is a circuit that is one of the ultimate tests of driving ability. The only drivers to have managed four wins apiece are two of the all-time greats, Jim Clark and Ayrton Senna. The Brazilian's run of four consecutive victories followed Alain Prost's win in 1987, making McLaren the team with the longest winning run here, with five victories through until 1991.

 ### SOMETIMES EASY, SOMETIMES HARD

As Spa-Francorchamps has a long lap, you'd expect it to have a high record number of finishers on the winning lap. It does, with 14 drivers managing this in 2009 when Kimi Räikkönen led home Giancarlo Fisichella by less than a second after the safety car had been deployed for a first lap accident. The fewest was just two, and it was no freak result, as it also happened in 1953, 1954, 1960, 1963, 1965, 1966 and 1987.

 ### SPA'S UPS AND DOWNS

Not a lot of circuits offer much in the way of gradient changes, but Spa-Francorchamps does. What made the original circuit so unusual, though, was that its 9.2-mile long lap spanned not one but two valleys, cresting the hill in between.

TRACK FACTS

Opened: 1924

Country: Belgium

Location: 20 miles south-east of Liege

Active years in F1: 1950-1956, 1958, 1960-1968, 1970, 1983, 1985-2002, 2004-2005, 2007 onwards

Most wins/driver: Michael Schumacher, 6 (1992, 1995-1997, 2001-2002)

Most wins/team: Ferrari, 12 (1952-1953, 1956, 1961, 1966, 1996-1997, 2001-2002, 2007-2009)

Lap length: 4.352 miles

Number of turns: 19

Lap record: 1m47.263s, 146.065mph, Sebastian Vettel (Red Bull), 2009

Below **Track facts:** The fearsome stretch of the original layout, between the Masta Kink and Stavelot, shows the blast back up the hill to the current circuit exiting at the top right.

EAU ROUGE

This is a corner for which television does no justice. You really have to watch trackside at Spa-Francorchamps to appreciate how steep the drop down from La Source is then how much steeper the climb is from the start of the left-right flick as the drivers point their cars at the horizon and attempt to hit the right line over the crest to carry as much speed onto the long ascent to Les Combes.

THE BLINK OF AN EYE

The closest ever finish to a Belgian GP came in 1961 when Phil Hill pipped team-mate Wolfgang von Trips by just 0.70s as Ferrari drivers filled the top four places. The Ferraris were dominant and swapped the lead before first Olivier Gendebien then Richie Ginther dropped back, leaving von Trips and Hill to jostle for position until the American took the lead with five laps to go and stayed there, just, to the finish.

SCHUMACHER LOVES SPA

The closest grand prix circuit to Michael Schumacher's childhood home in Kerpen is actually this one in Belgium. And he loved it, not only making his F1 debut here, but scoring his first F1 win in 1992, then adding five more. Thanks to winning at Spa-Francorchamps as early as 1952, through Alberto Ascari, Ferrari is the most successful team, its 12 wins putting it one ahead of McLaren up to and including 2010.

Below **Schumacher loves Spa:** Twelve months after his F1 debut at Spa for Jordan, Michael Schumacher was able to celebrate his first win with Benetton.

Below **Eau Rouge:** Graham Hill powers through the uphill sweeper in his BRM in 1965 leading the obscured Jim Clark, who soon passed him. *Inset* **The blink of an eye:** Ferrari Dino 156s filled the first four places in 1961, with Phil Hill (4) taking the win.

NÜRBURGRING

There are two Nürburgrings. The first is a 14-mile long monster which trails through forests and was deemed too dangerous for F1 in 1976. The second, the thoroughly modern circuit used today, was built over a small area of the original and has been much modified but now at least the "new" Nürburgring provides a challenge.

Above **Track facts:** The opening corner underwent considerable modification for 2002, with the previous right/left Castrol S replaced by a hairpin leading into a long left, a gently sloping hairpin and then a tight right, all overlooked by the attractive grandstand (*right*).

TRACK FACTS

Opened: 1926

Country: Germany

Location: 35 miles north-west of Koblenz

Active years in F1: 1951-1954, 1956-1958, 1961-1969, 1971-1976, 1985, 1995-2007, 2009

Most wins/driver: Michael Schumacher, 5 (1995, 2000-2001, 2004, 2006)

Most wins/team: Ferrari, 14 (1951-1953, 1956, 1963-1964, 1972, 1974, 1985, 2000-2002, 2004, 2006)

Lap length: 3.199 miles

Number of turns: 15

Lap record: 1m29.468s, 128.721mph, Michael Schumacher (Ferrari), 2004

ECONOMY BEATS THIRST

Germany didn't host a World Championship round in 1950, but got its first GP a year later when the Nürburgring hosted the fifth round of seven. Alberto Ascari had won an F2 race there for Ferrari 12 months earlier and used that experience to good effect to win in 1951. Juan Manuel Fangio led the early laps in his Alfa Romeo before Ascari took the lead. As his Ferrari needed only one pitstop and the Alfas needed two, Ascari won.

STEWART'S MASTERCLASS

Jackie Stewart achieved the Nürburgring's largest winning margin in 1968 when he excelled in appalling conditions. Despite qualifying sixth, the Scot took the lead in his Matra on the first lap and then extended his advantage with each of the following 13 laps of the giant Nordschleife circuit. By flagfall, he was 4 mins 3.2 secs ahead of Graham Hill who'd spun his Lotus, got out, turned it around the right way then carried on...

THE FASTEST OF THE BRAVE

The Nürburgring Nordschleife was very fast in places, with the trees lining the route making it feel all the faster. In the 22 occasions that the full circuit was used (up until it was adjudged too dangerous after the 1976 German GP), the fastest race-winning average speed was achieved in 1975 by Carlos Reutemann when he won for Brabham by more than a minute and a half from Jacques Laffite's Williams.

PROVING ITS DANGERS

There were already considerable concerns before the 1976 German GP that the Nürburging Nordschleife circuit was too dangerous for F1. Ironically, one of the main voices requesting change was Niki Lauda, who crashed on lap 2 at Bergwerk and had to be hauled from his burning Ferrari by fellow drivers, suffering major burns. The German GP only returned to the circuit once it had been shortened and made safer.

A TEST FOR CARS AND DRIVERS

The Nürburgring Nordschleife put a strain not only on the cars but the drivers too, with its undulating course containing blind brows among its 176 corners and hazards. The fewest finishers of any of the German GPs held around its 14-mile layout between 1951 and 1976 was just five and one non-classified runner in 1956. Surprisingly, the race, won by Juan Manuel Fangio for Ferrari, lost only two of the retirees to accidents.

FERRARI BEST ON THE NEW

Grands prix held on the shorter Nürburgring used since 1984 have Michael Schumacher as the most frequent winner with six – from his 1994 victory for Benetton to the one in 2006, the last of four in a Ferrari. Adding two more from the 16 races held on the 3.199-mile circuit, by Michele Alboreto in 1985 and Rubens Barrichello in 2002, makes Ferrari the most successful team on this track too.

Above **Ferrari best on the new:** Ferrari, and Michael Schumacher in particular, have enjoyed many a celebration at the Nürburgring. *Below* **NGK Schikane:** Low kerbs and an uphill entry encourage drivers to attack.

FERRARI BEST ON THE OLD

Taking only the Nürburgring Nordschleife, the best winning sequence was achieved by Juan Manuel Fangio when he won in a Mercedes in 1954, in a Ferrari in 1956 and in a Maserati in 1957 (there was no 1955 German GP). Ferrari won three in a row in its own right at the start of the decade, winning the first three German GPs from 1951 to 1953 through Alberto Ascari (twice) then Giuseppe Farina.

GOING ROUND THE BEND

The original 14.1-mile Nürburgring Norschleife circuit wasn't the longest circuit ever used in the World Championship, as Pescara was longer at 15.894 miles, but it had the most corners, at 176 per lap… If the 4.8-mile Sudschleife was added, it had more than 200.

NGK SCHIKANE

This chicane acts as a magnet to incident. It's approached up a kinked straight that drops from the Bit Kurve, reaches its lowest point at ITT Bogen, then climbs all the way to the turn-in point. If a driver carries too much speed, he will miss the racing line, clatter the kerbs and fail to get in position to accelerate through the right-hand part out of which there is just a short run to the final corner.

MONTREAL

The Circuit Gilles Villeneuve is one of the very best examples of a circuit close enough to a metropolis to attract a capacity crowd. Over the years this circuit, on an island in a river, has produced great racing, but it is better known for being a car-breaker and having a chicane that bites.

THE DREAM START

Imagine the excitement when Quebec welcomed its greatest star to its greatest city, as Montreal did for its first grand prix in 1978. Gilles Villeneuve qualified his Ferrari third behind Jean-Pierre Jarier's Lotus and Jody Scheckter's Wolf. Having slipped behind Alan Jones' Williams, he regained third when Jones had a puncture. Then he passed Scheckter. Jarier held a 30s lead but retired, leaving Villeneuve to score his first win.

Below **Final chicane:** The wall at the exit claimed two world champions in 1999, when Jacques Villeneuve copied the example set by Michael Schumacher five laps earlier.

RAIN, RAIN, GO AWAY

Safety car deployments are all too common in grands prix held at the Circuit Gilles Villeneuve and the slowest race came in 1981 when Jacques Laffite's winning average speed in his Ligier was just 85.310mph, more than 22mph down on the previous year. Ironically, this wasn't a race in which the safety car was needed instead it was so slow because torrential rain had the cars aquaplaning all over the circuit.

Below **Rain, rain, go away:** Jacques Laffite splashes his Ligier through the wet en route to victory at an average of just 85mph in 1981.

FINAL CHICANE (TURN 13)

All a driver can see straight ahead as they accelerate up to 200mph down the final straight from L'Epingle is the pit entry. The track disappears to the right into this very tight chicane. Getting the braking just right is very difficult, with few sighting points to judge it by. The exit is blind at this point and many drivers get the second (left-hand) part of the sequence wrong and then slam into the wall beyond.

Below **Track facts:** Looking down at the start/finish straight and the opening sequence of corners shows just how much water surrounds the circuit's island, with the Olympic rowing lake running behind the cramped paddock.

TRACK FACTS

Opened: 1978

Country: Canada

Location: Île de Notre Dame, Montreal

Active years in F1: 1978-1986, 1988-2008, 2010 onwards

Most wins/driver:
Michael Schumacher, 7
(1994, 1997-1998, 2000, 2002-2004)

Most wins/team: Ferrari, 10 (1978, 1983, 1985, 1995, 1997, 1998, 2000, 2002-2004)

Lap length: 2.710 miles

Number of turns: 14

Lap record: 1m13.622s, 132.511mph, Rubens Barrichello (Ferrari), 2004

A VIOLENT BARREL-ROLL

Thanks to the endless efforts to make racing cars safer, drivers today unlike their predecessors stand every chance of surviving accidents. Robert Kubica had reason to thank those responsible for these advances after the 2007 Canadian GP when his BMW Sauber clipped Jarno Trulli's Toyota on the approach to the hairpin, cannoned off a wall and disintegrated as it rolled back across the track. He escaped with just bruising.

BY THE SMALLEST OF MARGINS

The closest finish to a grand prix held here came in 2000 when Michael Schumacher won by 0.174 secs from Ferrari teammate Rubens Barrichello. The race was hit by rain midway and Barrichello worked his way past Giancarlo Fisichella to second but wasn't allowed to challenge for the lead. All too often, races here have been close in their first half before the circuit's car-breaking characteristics thinned the field.

ISLAND OF ADVENTURE

The Circuit Gilles Villeneuve has one of the sport's most unusual settings. Not only is it built on an island, but it runs alongside the rowing lake used at the 1976 Olympics and surrounds the pavilions built on the site of the world trade show, Expo 67.

MICHAEL'S MONTREAL MAGNIFICENCE

Michael Schumacher won three Canadian GPs in succession at Montreal between 2002 and 2004 for the best winning sequence the venue has known. Had he not been beaten by brother Ralf's Williams in 2001, his winning run would have stretched for five straight years. Such was Michael's success at the Circuit Gilles Villeneuve that he was only beaten twice there from 1997 to 2004, with Mika Hakkinen winning in 1999.

FERRARI LEADS THE WAY

Seven-time World Champion Michael Schumacher won seven times – once with Benetton and then six times with Ferrari – at the Circuit Gilles Villeneuve and this helped Ferrari to become the team that has won the most frequently here, with a tally of 10 triumphs. McLaren and Williams also have a strong record at the Canadian circuit, having claimed seven wins here apiece.

Above **Ferrari leads the way:** Michael Schumacher appeared to like winning in Montreal for Ferrari. The German maestro celebrated the fourth of his seven victories at the Circuit Gilles Villeneuve in 2000.

ZANDVOORT

Nestling in the sand dunes in this popular coastal resort near Amsterdam, Zandvoort is one of a roster of long-term F1 fixtures that have fallen from the calendar. Although reduced in length in 1989 it's still used for international racing, but it has been 26 years since it last hosted a World Championship round.

FOLLOWING THE FORM BOOK

Ferrari's mastery of the F2 rules adopted by the World Championship in 1952 meant that none of the other teams could match their pace. After Piero Taruffi won the opening round, Alberto Ascari started a winning run in Belgium and had added three more when he arrived at Zandvoort for the first World Championship Dutch GP. The Italian duly qualified on pole, as expected, and led every lap in a Ferrari one-two-three.

SAND ON TRACK SLOWS PLAY

One of the features of Zandvoort was its fast and open lap as it plotted a course over and around the sand dunes. Indeed, the fastest grand prix there, at the final

running of the Dutch GP in 1985, was at a fraction under 120mph. The slowest grand prix there was held 35 years earlier when Alberto Ascari won in his F2-spec Ferrari at an average speed of just 81.033mph, with only teammate Gisueppe Farina on the lead lap.

DEATH IN THE DUNES

Deaths in motor racing were all too frequent up to the 1970s and some stand out as being exceptionally shocking. Piers Courage died at Zandvoort in a fiery accident in 1970, and the Dutch circuit was the scene of another British death in 1973. Roger Williamson became trapped under his burning, inverted March but no officials attempted a rescue, leaving fellow driver David Purley to try and extricate the doomed driver.

Below **Race good, celebrations even better:** James Hunt triggers wild celebrations for the Hesketh team by scoring its one and only win in the 1975 Dutch GP.

RACE GOOD, CELEBRATIONS EVEN BETTER

Rain often adds to the excitement, and it fell in 1975 at the start of Zandvoort's most memorable race. Niki Lauda led for Ferrari but when the track started drying things became interesting. Having run fourth in his Hesketh, James Hunt was the first to pit for slicks and was ahead when Lauda, Jody Scheckter and Clay Regazzoni returned. Hunt then resisted intense pressure from Lauda for the next 60 laps to score his and the team's first wins.

Below **Track facts:** The long, long start/finish straight offers a superb place for overtaking where it feeds into the double right at Tarzan.

TRACK FACTS

Opened: 1948

Country: Holland

Location: 15 miles west of Amsterdam

Active years in F1: 1952-1953, 1955, 1958-1971, 1973-1985

Most wins/driver: Jim Clark, 4 (1963-1965, 1967)

Most wins/team: Ferrari, 8 (1952-1953, 1961, 1971, 1974, 1977, 1982-1983)

Lap length: 2.642 miles

Number of turns: 13

Lap record: 1m16.538s, 124.270mph, Alain Prost (McLaren), 1985

FASTEST AT THE FINISH

When the F1 circus arrived at Zandvoort in 1985 it wasn't known that this would be its final visit, but the circuit's finances weren't robust. None of this concerned Niki Lauda, though, as the McLaren driver advanced from 10th on the grid to hit the front at half-distance and then lead home his teammate Alain Prost. Lauda's win turned out to be the fastest in Zandvoort's history, at an average of 119.977mph.

Above **Fastest at the finish:** Niki Lauda's win in 1985 was achieved at an average speed of just under 120mph.

A GREAT PAIRING

The best victory sequence for a driver and a team at Zandvoort tally exactly, as the winning combination from 1963 to 1965 was Jim Clark and his Lotus. The Scot started from pole and led every lap in 1963 to win by a lap from Dan Gurney. In 1964 he got the jump on pole-sitter Gurney and led all the way. He had to work harder in 1965, as Richie Ginther led at first then Graham Hill hit the front before Clark took over.

SPLITTING THE HONOURS

Jim Clark's affinity for this high-speed circuit through the Dutch dunes is clear as he stands out as its most successful driver, with four wins. However, although his team, Lotus, won six times, Ferrari went two better to be the team with the most victories. The first of its eight came through Alberto Ascari on its first World Championship outing in 1952 and he won again in 1953. The last came through Rene Arnoux in 1983.

NEW MEANING TO HOME TURN

Zandvoort is one of many tracks that is a shadow of its former self, its original lay-out lost. Like Kyalami in South Africa, some of the site had to be sold off to realize funds to keep the circuit alive. So, sadly, houses are now built where the furthest reaches of the original lap used to flow.

HUGEN-HOLTZBOCHT

||||||||||||||||||||||||||||||||||||

Overlooked by the control tower, this dipping left-hander is far easier to get wrong than right. Many drivers fail to get onto the racing line as they've made a mistake at the preceding Gerlachbocht. They then struggle to be in position to apply the power as early as they would like past the apex into the uphill exit to the corner, thus hampering their speed down the very quick stretch of the lap that follows.

Below **Hugenholtzbocht:** Jim Clark pulls away from Jack Brabham in the 1967 Dutch GP to win for Lotus on the race debut of the engine that would revolutionize F1, the Ford Cosworth DFV.

IMOLA

For years, this circuit hosted Italy's "other" grand prix, under the honorary title of the San Marino GP. Running through orchards across the side of a hill, the circuit enjoyed a fine location, with every vantage point filled with red-clad *Tifosi* urging on their beloved Ferraris in the spring sunshine.

Below **Track facts:** The end of the lap, from lofty Variante Alta on the right, through the Rivazza corners, then back through Variante Bassa to the finish line.

TRACK FACTS

Opened: 1952

Country: Italy

Location: 20 miles south-east of Bologna

Active years in F1: 1980-2006

Most wins/driver: Michael Schumacher, 7 (1994, 1999-2000, 2002-2004, 2006)

Most wins/team: Ferrari, 8 (1982-1983, 1999-2000, 2002-2004, 2006) & Williams, 8 (1987, 1990, 1992-1993, 1995-1997, 2001)

Lap length: 3.065 miles

Number of turns: 15

Lap record: 1m20.411s, 137.230mph, Michael Schumacher (Ferrari), 2004

AN ITALIAN GP NOT AT MONZA

Imola played host to the Italian GP in 1980 as a result of the modifications that needed to be made to Monza following the massed accident that claimed Ronnie Peterson's life in 1978. Nelson Piquet won the race for Brabham by gaining two places at the start then hitting the front as Renault's Rene Arnoux and Jean-Pierre Jabouille hit trouble. From 1981, Imola would host the San Marino GP.

A RACE NO ONE WANTED TO WIN

The largest winning margin for a grand prix held at Imola was a lap in 1985 when Elio de Angelis won for Lotus. Ayrton Senna was set for victory but ran out of fuel with three laps to go, as did Stefan Johansson's Ferrari just after he took over at the front. McLaren's Alain Prost duly finished first, but was disqualified for being 2kg light. De Angelis, a lap clear of Thierry Boutsen's Arrows, was thus declared winner.

A CURSED MEETING

There will hopefully never by a meeting again like the one that Imola endured in 1994. Rubens Barrichello was lucky to survive a shunt in his Jordan in practice. Then Roland Ratzenberger was killed in qualifying. On race day JJ Lehto stalled and was hit by Pedro Lamy, firing debris into the grandstand. Then Ayrton Senna had his fatal accident before Michele Alboreto's Minardi shed a wheel in the pits, hitting a cluster of mechanics.

FERRARI AT THE LAST

As the World Championship spread its wings to take in venues in the Middle East and Asia it became untenable for Italy to host two grands prix. Imola, the more outdated circuit, was dropped and the final San Marino GP was held in 2006. Michael Schumacher started from pole for Ferrari, but Fernando Alonso gave chase for Renault and the *Tifosi* could relax only when the Spaniard pitted earlier than expected and Michael sent them home happy.

WILLIAMS RULES THE ROOST

Ferrari fans had every reason to be delighted with the prolific Michael Schumacher as he claimed six wins at Imola to add to his victory here for Benetton in 1994 to secure the highest number of wins at this parkland circuit. However, wins for Nigel Mansell, Riccardo Patrese, Alain Prost, Damon Hill, Heinz-Harald Frentzen and Ralf Schumacher helped Williams to be the team with the highest victory tally at what was the San Marino GP, with eight.

A HOME FROM HOME

Imola is one of a few circuits that have hosted grands prix named after other countries. The principality of San Marino after which its grand prix was named is 50 miles away. Likewise, Dijon-Prenois in France hosted the Swiss GP in 1982 and the Nürburgring hosted the Luxembourg GP in 1997 and 1998.

Left **Italian circuit, British wins:** David Coulthard celebrates winning for McLaren in 1998, the last of 15 straight wins at Imola for British teams.

ITALIAN CIRCUIT, BRITISH WINS

Between 1984 and 1998 British teams enjoyed a run of 15 wins at Imola – from Alain Prost's win in 1984 for McLaren to David Coulthard's victory for the same team in 1998. Williams won seven times during this period, McLaren six and both Lotus and Benetton once apiece, blocking out the Ferraris the *Tifosi* would have been cheering on. There was at least some Italian success on the driving front, with Elio de Angelis winning in 1985 and Riccardo Patrese in 1990.

Right **A sting in the tail:** The relationship between Gilles Villeneuve and Didier Pironi never recovered after the Ferrari drivers disagreed on team orders in 1982. *Below* **Acque Minerali:** This aerial shot shows the downhill plunge from Pinatella and the twisting exit back uphill to Variante Alta.

A STING IN THE TAIL

Imola's most memorable race was the 1982 San Marino GP. As a result of a power struggle only the FISA teams turned up. This meant a 14-car grid headed by the Renaults of Rene Arnoux and Alain Prost then the Ferraris of Gilles Villeneuve and Didier Pironi. The Renaults failed and Villeneuve and Pironi put on a show for the fans until Pironi grabbed the lead on the final lap and kept it, sending Villeneuve into a fury as he swore that team orders had been broken.

ACQUE MINERALI

The setting for this difficult, two-part corner is sublime, the track dipping and rising through wooded parkland. The downhill approach in sixth gear leads into a right-hand kink, then the track bottoms out for the tight right that leads immediately into a left-hand flick as the track feeds back uphill again. Brabham's Riccardo Patrese crashed out of the race here in 1983, having taken the lead of the San Marino GP with five laps to go.

INTERLAGOS

Although rough around the edges, Interlagos remains one of the world's great racing circuits, with its dipping, twisting lap providing scope for the brave to overtake. Often a late-season race, Interalgos has been made all the more exciting by hosting some classic title shoot-outs.

THE WORST WEATHER

When rain arrives in Brazil, as it often has throughout the history of the Brazilian GP, it hits hard. In 1993, the water lay so deep at some points on the circuit that drivers struggled not to aquaplane. Aguri Suzuki spun on the start/finish straight and even multiple World Champion Alain Prost rotated when he came upon the scene of Christian Fittipaldi's spun Minardi. Ayrton Senna overcame a stop-go penalty to win on this very wet day.

THE FAST AND THE SLOW

Bad weather and accidents are the main reasons for speeds being kept in check at Interlagos. The slowest Brazilian GP held at this undulating circuit was won by Jordan's Giancarlo Fisichella in 2003 at an average winning speed of 95.009mph

after the race spent its first eight laps behind a safety car. Conversely, the fastest grand prix here was won by Ferrari's Michael Schumacher in 2004 at an average of 129.566mph.

HALF A SECOND, TWO BROTHERS

The closest finish to a Brazilian GP at Interlagos was when Michael Schumacher won in 2002 ahead of his brother Ralf whose Williams had chased him home, losing out by just 0.588 secs. It was the first outing for the Ferrari F2002 and although Ralf could close in on the Ferrari he couldn't find a way past, perhaps wisely being wary as Michael had

clashed with Ralf's teammate Juan Pablo Montoya on lap 1.

FEW ACHIEVE DOMINANCE

One unusual feature of Interlagos's history is that no driver has ever won at the circuit in the São Paulo suburbs more than two years in a row. Emerson Fittipaldi won in 1973 and 1974, then Michael Schumacher in 1994 and 1995, Mika Hakkinen in 1998 and 1999 and Juan Pablo Montoya in 2004 and 2005. No driver has ever had three straight wins. Ferrari's three wins from 2006 to 2008 is the best sequence.

Left **Half a second, two brothers:** Michael Schumacher (*left*) was chased to the finish in 2002 by brother Ralf.

Above **Track facts:** The circuit sits in a natural amphitheatre as is clear when viewing from above the Curva do Sol and looking back towards the Senna S.

TRACK FACTS

Opened: 1940

Country: Brazil

Location: 9 miles south of Sao Paulo

Active years in F1: 1973-1977, 1979-1980, 1990 onwards

Most wins/driver: Michael Schumacher, 4 (1994, 1995, 2000, 2002)

Most wins/team: Ferrari, 8 (1976, 1977, 1990, 2000, 2002, 2006, 2007, 2008)

Lap length: 2.667 miles

Number of turns: 15

Lap record: 1m11.473s, 134.837mph, Juan Pablo Montoya (Williams), 2004

Below right **A popular home win:** Emerson Fittipaldi leads away from pole position to score for Lotus in the 1973 Brazilian GP.

FERRADURA

||||||||||||||||||||||||||||||||||||||

There is gradient change aplenty at the home of the Brazilian GP, and Ferradura is one of the trickiest of these. It's approached up the climb from Descida do Lago, then the track arcs gently to the right, but it's made difficult by the fact that it's at the crest of this hill before a level run from its exit to the next turn, Laranja. Taken in fifth gear, it's easy for drivers to carry too much speed in and spin.

RUNNING TO FORM

Even the quickest of examinations of a Formula 1 history book will reveal that Michael Schumacher is way out clear in the number of grand prix victories, with 91, so it's likely that he will be the driver with the most wins at any of the contemporary circuits. Interlagos is no different and his tally of four wins is the greatest. Likewise, Ferrari and McLaren, the teams at the top of the victories chart, have eight and seven wins each.

BETWEEN THE LAKES

The name Interlagos means "between the lakes" and the original 4.946-mile circuit crossed the lake at the foot of its hillside site twice. The shorter track, introduced in 1990, crosses the lake only once, at Descida do Lago.

Below **Ferradura:** Many drivers, even Michael Schumacher, have got their entry to the righthander wrong.

A POPULAR HOME WIN

After holding a non-championship race in 1972, a Brazilian GP at Interlagos had World Championship blessing for 1973. Emerson Fittipaldi was the nation's hope and he qualified second behind his Lotus teammate Ronnie Peterson. Fittipaldi took the lead at the start and fellow Brazilian Carlos Pace leapt into second in his Surtees, but was soon demoted. Fittipaldi was untouchable though and his was a popular win

SENNA, BUT ONLY JUST

Ayrton Senna had won plenty of races but never at home, and it was starting to get to him. Having won 1991's opening race in Phoenix, he put his McLaren on pole at Interlagos (as he had in the three preceding years). Senna made the race truly memorable for the home fans as he led every lap, until he hit gearbox trouble and had to run the final seven laps in sixth gear, just holding off Riccardo Patrese's Williams.

HOCKENHEIM

Seen at first as flat-out and boring, Hockenheim was also unloved as it claimed the life of Jim Clark. However, it hosted some classic German GPs and opinions began to change. Then, sadly, its lap was cut short in 2002 and the racing has never been as good again.

A CLASSIC AFTER A VENUE SWAP

The Grand Prix Drivers' Association boycotted racing at the Nürburging in 1970 as it said safety improvements hadn't been made, so the German GP was held at Hockenheim instead. Jochen Rindt and Jacky Ickx were the pacesetters for Lotus and Ferrari respectively and Ickx grabbed pole, but he and Rindt swapped the lead in a five-car slipstreaming bunch before Rindt made a break with two laps remaining.

HOME ALONE

The largest winning margin for a grand prix at Hockenheim came in 1987 when Nelson Piquet gained victory in a race of high attrition as his Williams crossed the line 99.591 secs ahead of Stefan Johansson's McLaren. The closest race here was the first one, in 1970, when Jochen Rindt's Lotus crossed the line just 0.7 secs ahead of Jacky Ickx's Ferrari, although there have been team one-twos marginally closer.

Below **Track facts:** Multi-coloured grandstand seats mark the stadium section from the Mobil 1 Kurve at the top of the photo to Nordkurve at the bottom right.

READY, STEADY, GO... STOP!

Luciano Burti was fortunate to survive an aerobatic crash on the run to the first corner in the 2001 German GP. The massed accident, the worst in the circuit's history, was triggered by Michael Schumacher's Ferrari suddenly slowing with a gear problem. Unsighted, Burti's Prost couldn't avoid it, flying over Enrique Bernoldi's Arrows. The red flag flew and those with spare cars were able to take the restart.

TRACK FACTS

Opened: 1929

Country: Germany

Location: 15 miles south of Heidelberg

Active years in F1: 1970, 1977-1984, 1986-2006, 2008, 2010

Most wins/driver: Michael Schumacher, 4 (1995, 2002, 2004, 2006)

Most wins/team: Ferrari, 9 (1977, 1982-1983, 1994, 1999-2000, 2002, 2004, 2006) & Williams, 9 (1979, 1986-1987, 1991-1993, 1996, 2001, 2003)

Lap length: 2.842 miles

Number of turns: 17

Lap record: 1m14.917s, 138.685mph, Kimi Raikkonen (McLaren) 2004

Below **Ready, steady, go...stop!:** The world turned upside down for Luciano Burti in 2001 when the Prost driver crashed into Michael Schumacher's stuttering Ferrari on the run to the first corner and flipped, fortunately without injury.

A TRICKY TRACK TO WIN ON

Hockenheim was a circuit that didn't yield to the same driver twice until its 11th grand prix, when Nelson Piquet scored his second win there. Ayrton Senna then scored three in a row before Michael Schumacher became the most successful visitor when he took his fourth win in 2006. Of the teams, Ferrari is out front with Fernando Alonso's win there in 2010 being its 11th, putting it two ahead of Williams.

CUTTING THE SPEED

The original Hockenheim circuit, with its 215mph straights, produced races with high average speeds. The highest came in 2001 when Ralf Schumacher achieved a winning average in his Williams of 146.176mph. The shortened circuit layout, used from 2002, has a highest average of 134.124mph, achieved by Michael Schumacher in his Ferrari in 2004 before aerodynamics were restricted and engine life extended from 2005.

A RACE OF TWISTS AND TURNS

One of Hockenheim's greatest races came in 1987 when Nelson Piquet, Ayrton Senna, Nigel Mansell and Alain Prost were fighting for honours.

Senna blasted his Lotus into the lead ahead of Mansell's Williams. Senna was soon demoted to fourth and it turned into a battle between Prost and Mansell until the Williams' engine failed. With four laps to go, Prost's McLaren had alternator failure and Piquet won the day.

THREE IN A ROW, TIMES THREE

Ayrton Senna enjoyed a period of superiority at Hockenheim at the end of the 1980s. Having just joined McLaren from Lotus, he recorded the best victory sequence by winning in 1988, 1989 and 1990. Williams also enjoyed a hat-trick of wins at Hockenheim directly after that when Nigel Mansell was triumphant in 1991 and 1992, followed by Alain Prost taking the third in his final title-winning year, 1993.

Above **A tricky track to win on:** Fernando Alonso celebrates in 2010 after giving Ferrari its 11th win at Hockenheim. *Below* **Sudkurve:** Rene Arnoux's Ferrari flashes through the final corner of the lap in 1983 chased by Andrea de Cesaris's Alfa Romeo.

ALMOST TWO MILES LOST

Until 1965, Hockenheim's lap was 4.779 miles long and ran anticlockwise. Then an autobahn was built across its old lay-out, and the area now behind the pits grandstands was lost. The next chop came for 2002, with the forest loop curtailed and the lap length cut from 4.239 miles to just 2.842.

SUDKURVE

The final corner of a lap of Hockenheim circuit is right at the foot of the giant grandstands and it's a surprisingly difficult corner. Despite being only a third-gear, 90-degree right-hander, it's awkward as it follows so closely after the previous corner, Elf Kurve, and failure to get in position to take the proper line through here, hampers a driver's speed all the way past the pits to Nordkurve and on to Einfahrt Parabolika.

FORMULA 1 STATISTICS

Michael Schumacher's phenomenal Formula 1 career has put him at the top of pretty much every table of driver records and it has helped Ferrari to top the tables too. However, the statistics reveal some perhaps forgotten names, emphasising how the world's most spectacular sport has ebbed and flowed as teams and drivers have shone brightly then waned or, sadly, been extinguished. **Note:** Statistics correct to the start of 2011

DRIVERS RECORDS

STARTS

306	Rubens Barrichello	158	Martin Brundle
269	Michael Schumacher		Olivier Panis
256	Riccardo Patrese		Mark Webber
247	David Coulthard	157	Kimi Raikkonen
237	Jarno Trulli	152	John Watson
230	Giancarlo Fisichella	149	Rene Arnoux
210	Gerhard Berger	147	Eddie Irvine
208	Andrea de Cesaris		Derek Warwick
204	Nelson Piquet	146	Carlos Reutemann
201	Jean Alesi	144	Emerson Fittipaldi
199	Alain Prost	135	Jean-Pierre Jarier
194	Michele Alboreto	134	Felipe Massa
190	Jenson Button	132	Eddie Cheever
187	Nigel Mansell		Clay Regazzoni
180	Ralf Schumacher	128	Mario Andretti
176	Graham Hill	126	Jack Brabham
175	Jacques Laffite	123	Ronnie Peterson
174	Nick Heidfeld	119	Pierluigi Martini
171	Niki Lauda	116	Damon Hill
165	Jacques Villeneuve		Jacky Ickx
163	Thierry Boutsen		Alan Jones
162	Mika Hakkinen	114	Keke Rosberg
	Johnny Herbert		Patrick Tambay
161	Ayrton Senna	112	Denny Hulme
159	Fernando Alonso		Jody Scheckter
	Heinz-Harald Frentzen		

WINS

91	Michael Schumacher	11	Rubens Barrichello
51	Alain Prost		Felipe Massa
41	Ayrton Senna		Jacques Villeneuve
31	Nigel Mansell	10	Gerhard Berger
27	Jackie Stewart		James Hunt
26	Fernando Alonso		Ronnie Peterson
25	Jim Clark		Jody Scheckter
	Niki Lauda		Sebastian Vettel
24	Juan Manuel Fangio	9	Jenson Button
23	Nelson Piquet	8	Denny Hulme
22	Damon Hill		Jacky Ickx
20	Mika Hakkinen	7	Rene Arnoux
18	Kimi Raikkonen		Juan Pablo Montoya
16	Stirling Moss	6	Tony Brooks
14	Jack Brabham		Jacques Laffite
	Emerson Fittipaldi		Riccardo Patrese
	Lewis Hamilton		Jochen Rindt
	Graham Hill		Ralf Schumacher
13	Alberto Ascari		John Surtees
	David Coulthard		Gilles Villeneuve
12	Mario Andretti		Mark Webber
	Alan Jones		
	Carlos Reutemann		

Left **Starts:** When he retired in 1975, Graham Hill held the record for the most starts in F1 but, by the end of the 2010 season, 15 drivers had surpassed his total of 176 with Rubens Barrichello leading the way on 306 starts.

Above **Wins:** Michael Scumacher heads for his first win at Spa-Francorchamps in 1992 for Benetton, and would go on to add 90 more.

WINS IN ONE SEASON

13	Michael Schumacher	2004			Kimi Raikkonen	2005
11	Michael Schumacher	2002			Ayrton Senna	1991
9	Nigel Mansell	1992			Jacques Villeneuve	1997
	Michael Schumacher	1995		6	Mario Andretti	1978
	Michael Schumacher	2000			Alberto Ascari	1952
	Michael Schumacher	2001			Jim Clark	1965
8	Mika Hakkinen	1998			Juan Manuel Fangio	1954
	Damon Hill	1996			Damon Hill	1994
	Michael Schumacher	1994			James Hunt	1976
	Ayrton Senna	1988			Nigel Mansell	1987
7	Fernando Alonso	2005			Kimi Raikkonen	2007
	Fernando Alonso	2006			Michael Schumacher	1998
	Jim Clark	1963			Michael Schumacher	2003
	Alain Prost	1984			Michael Schumacher	2006
	Alain Prost	1988			Ayrton Senna	1989
	Alain Prost	1993			Ayrton Senna	1990

POINTS

1441	Michael Schumacher
829	Fernando Alonso
798.5	Alain Prost
654	Rubens Barrichello
614	Ayrton Senna
579	Kimi Raikkonen
541	Jenson Button
535	David Coulthard
496	Lewis Hamilton
485.5	Nelson Piquet
482	Nigel Mansell
464	Felipe Massa
420.5	Niki Lauda
420	Mika Hakkinen
411.5	Mark Webber
385	Gerhard Berger
381	Sebastian Vettel
360	Damon Hill
	Jackie Stewart
329	Ralf Schumacher
310	Carlos Reutemann
307	Juan Pablo Montoya
289	Graham Hill
281	Emerson Fittipaldi
	Riccardo Patrese
277.5	Juan Manuel Fangio
275	Giancarlo Fisichella
274	Jim Clark
273	Robert Kubica
261	Jack Brabham
255	Jody Scheckter
248	Denny Hulme
246.5	Jarno Trulli
242	Jean Alesi

POLE POSITIONS

68	Michael Schumacher
65	Ayrton Senna
33	Jim Clark
	Alain Prost
32	Nigel Mansell
29	Juan Manuel Fangio
26	Mika Hakkinen
24	Niki Lauda
	Nelson Piquet
20	Fernando Alonso
	Damon Hill
18	Mario Andretti
	Rene Arnoux
	Lewis Hamilton
17	Jackie Stewart
16	Stirling Moss
	Kimi Raikkonen
15	Felipe Massa
	Sebastian Vette;
14	Alberto Ascari
	Rubens Barrichello
	James Hunt
	Ronnie Peterson
13	Jack Brabham
	Graham Hill
	Jacky Ickx
	Juan Pablo Montoya
	Jacques Villeneuve
12	Gerhard Berger
	David Coulthard
10	Jochen Rindt
8	Riccardo Patrese
	John Surtees

FASTEST LAPS

75	Michael Schumacher
41	Alain Prost
35	Kimi Raikkonen
30	Nigel Mansell
28	Jim Clark
25	Mika Hakkinen
24	Niki Lauda
23	Juan Manuel Fangio
	Nelson Piquet
21	Gerhard Berger
19	Damon Hill
	Stirling Moss
	Ayrton Senna
18	Fernando Alonso
	David Coulthard
17	Rubens Barrichello
15	Clay Regazzoni
	Jackie Stewart
14	Jacky Ickx
13	Alberto Ascari
	Alan Jones
	Riccardo Patrese
12	Rene Arnoux
	Jack Brabham
	Felipe Massa
	Juan Pablo Montoya
11	John Surtees

Above **Drivers' titles:** Sebastian Vettel become the youngest ever champion when he was crowned in 2010 at the age of just 23 years and 134 days.

TITLES

7	Michael Schumacher
5	Juan Manuel Fangio
4	Alain Prost
3	Jack Brabham
	Niki Lauda
	Nelson Piquet
	Ayrton Senna
	Jackie Stewart
2	Fernando Alonso*
	Alberto Ascari
	Jim Clark
	Emerson Fittipaldi
	Mika Hakkinen
	Graham Hill
1	Mario Andretti
	Jenson Button
	Giuseppe Farina
	Lewis Hamilton
	Mike Hawthorn
	Damon Hill
	Phil Hill
	Denis Hulme
	James Hunt
	Alan Jones
	Nigel Mansell
	Kimi Raikkonen
	Jochen Rindt
	Keke Rosberg
	Jody Scheckter
	John Surtees
	Sebastian Vettel
	Jacques Villeneuve

* This figure is gross tally, i.e. including scores that were later dropped.

CONSTRUCTOR RECORDS

STARTS

- 812 Ferrari
- 685 McLaren
- 604 Williams
- 490 Lotus
- 430 Toro Rosso (+ Minardi)
- 418 Tyrrell
- 409 Prost
- 394 Brabham
- 383 Arrows
- 339 Force India (+ Jordan then Midland then Spyker)
- 317 Benetton
- 306 BMW Sauber
- 282 Renault
- 242 Red Bull (+Stewart + Jaguar Racing)
- 230 March
- 197 BRM
- 169 Honda Racing (+ BAR)
- 132 Osella

Below **Wins:** Jean-Pierre Beltoise splashes his way to victory in the 1972 Monaco GP for the last of BRM's 11 grand prix wins.

Right **Pole positions:** Jack Brabham started claiming poles in a car bearing his own name in 1966, the year in which he also made history by becoming the only driver to become world champion in a car of his own.

WINS

- 215 Ferrari
- 168 McLaren
- 113 Williams
- 79 Lotus
- 35 Brabham
      Renault
- 27 Benetton
- 23 Tyrrell
- 17 BRM
- 16 Cooper
- 15 Red Bull (+ Stewart)
- 11 Brawn (+ Honda)
- 10 Alfa Romeo
- 9 Ligier
     Maserati
     Matra
     Mercedes
     Vanwall
- 4 Force India (+ Jordan)
- 3 March
     Wolf
- 1 BMW Sauber
     Eagle
     Hesketh
     Honda Racing (+ BAR)
     Penske
     Porsche
     Scuderia Toro Rosso
     Shadow
     Stewart

WINS IN ONE SEASON

15	Ferrari	2002	8	Benetton	1994
	Ferrari	2004		Brawn GP	2009
	McLaren	1988		Ferrari	2003
12	McLaren	1984		Lotus	1978
	Williams	1996		McLaren	1991
11	Benetton	1995		McLaren	2007
10	Ferrari	2000		Renault	2005
	McLaren	2005		Renault	2006
	McLaren	1989		Williams	1997
	Williams	1992	7	Ferrari	1952
	Williams	1993		Ferrari	1953
9	Ferrari	2001		Ferrari	2008
	Ferrari	2006		Lotus	1963
	Ferrari	2007		Lotus	1973
	McLaren	1998		McLaren	1999
	Red Bull	2010		McLaren	2000
	Williams	1986		Tyrrell	1971
	Williams	1987		Williams	1991
				Williams	1994

POLE POSITIONS

205	Ferrari	9	Prost (+ Ligier)
145	McLaren	8	Brawn (+ Honda)
126	Williams		Mercedes
107	Lotus	7	Vanwall
51	Renault	5	March
39	Brabham	4	Matra
21	Red Bull (+ Jaguar)	3	Force India (+ Jordan)
16	Benetton		Shadow
14	Tyrrell		Toyota
12	Alfa Romeo	2	Lancia
11	BRM	1	BAR
	Cooper		BMW Sauber
10	Maserati		Scuderia Toro Rosso

FASTEST LAPS

223	Ferrari
142	McLaren
130	Williams
71	Lotus
40	Brabham
35	Benetton
31	Renault
20	Tyrrell
15	BRM
	Maserati
14	Alfa Romeo
13	Cooper
12	Matra
	Red Bull
11	Prost
9	Mercedes
7	March
6	Brawn GP (+ Honda)
	Vanwall

POINTS

4473.5	Ferrari
3816.5	McLaren
2675	Williams
1352	Lotus
1309	Renault
877.5	Benetton
854	Brabham
842.5	Red Bull (+ Stewart/ Jaguar Racing)
617	Tyrrell
541	BMW Sauber
439	BRM
424	Prost (+ Ligier)
339	Force India (+ Jordan/ Midland/ Spyker)
333	Cooper
326	Honda Racing (+ BAR)
278.5	Toyota
171.5	March
167	Arrows
155	Matra

TITLES

15	Ferrari
9	Williams
8	McLaren
7	Lotus
2	Brabham
	Cooper
	Renault
1	Benetton
	Brawn
	BRM
	Matra
	Red Bull
	Tyrrell
	Vanwall

N.B. To avoid confusion, the Renault stats listed are based on the team that evolved from Benetton in 2002 and include those stats that have happened since plus those from Renault's first spell in F1 between 1977 and 1985. The figures for Benetton and Toleman from which it metamorphosed in 1986 are listed as Benetton. Conversely, the stats for Red Bull include those of the Stewart and Jaguar Racing teams from which it evolved. Likewise, Force India's stats include those of Jordan and Midland Spyker; and Scuderia Toro Rosso those of Minardi.

ONE-TWOS FINISHES

1	Ferrari	78
2	McLaren	47
3	Williams	32
4	Brabham	8
	Tyrrell	8
6	Red Bull	7
	Lotus	7
8	BRM	5
	Mercedes	5
10	Alfa Romeo	4
	Brawn	4
12	Benetton	2
	Cooper	2
	Matra	2
	Renault	2
16	BMW Sauber	1
	Jordan	1
	Ligier	1
	Maserati	1

Below **One-two finishes:** Didier Pironi leads Gilles Villeneuve (both Ferrari 126C2s) across the line in 1st and 2nd positions respectively at Imola in 1982, but Villeneuve claimed a pre-race deal had been broken.

INDEX

PICTURE CREDITS

The publishers would like to thank the following sources for their kind permission to reproduce the pictures in this book. The page numbers for each of the photographs are listed below, giving the page on which they appear in the book and any location indicator (C-centre, T-top, B-bottom, L-left, R-right).

Getty Images: /Sascha Schuermann/AFP: 172; /Mark Thompson: 181B

LAT Photographic: 4BR, 5, 5L, 12-13, 14T, 16B, 17R, 18B, 21R, 21B, 22B, 23B, 24B, 25TR, 25L, 26T, 26B, 27T, 28T, 30R, 31T, 32C, 32B, 33T, 35B, 38T, 38B, 39C, 39B, 40T, 40B, 41B, 44C, 45T, 46, 47B, 48BL, 49C, 49B, 51R, 52L, 52R, 54T, 54B, 55R, 56T, 56BR, 57L, 58TR, 58B, 59L, 60T, 62C, 63R, 66TL, 67T, 67B, 68T, 68B, 69B, 70R, 71T, 71BR, 72R, 72B, 73C, 73B, 75TR, 75B, 78-79, 82R, 82B, 83TR, 84-85, 86, 87T, 87L, 87BR, 88-89, 90TL, 90B, 91T, 91B, 92-93, 94L, 94BR, 95C, 95B, 96-97, 98T, 98B, 99T, 99L, 99R, 100-101, 102TL, 102R, 102B, 103, 104-105, 106TR, 106BL, 107TL, 107R, 107B, 108-109, 110, 111T, 111L, 111C, 112-113, 114TL, 114B, 115T, 115C, 115BR, 116-117, 118T, 118R, 119, 120-121, 125T, 125B, 126-127, 128B, 129TL, 129B, 130-131, 132B, 133T, 133C, 134-135, 136T, 136L, 136B, 137C, 137B, 138-139, 140R, 140BL, 141TL, 141B, 142-143, 145B, 146-147, 148TL, 148C, 148BR, 149T, 149B, 150-151, 152TL, 152R, 153T, 153B, 154-155, 156T, 156B, 157T, 157B, 158-159, 160TR, 160BL, 160BR, 161T, 161B, 164R, 165T, 166BR, 167B, 168B, 169R, 169B, 170, 171TR, 171R, 171B, 174C, 174B, 175B, 176R, 176B, 177R, 177B, 179C, 180C, 181R, 182B, 183B, 184T, 184B, 186R, 186BL, 187; /Lorenzo Bellanca: 42-43, 83BR, 165B; /Charles Coates: Front Endpaper, 4BC, 10-11, 31B, 37BR, 132T, 144B, 173T, 180B, Back Endpaper; /Michael Cooper: 37T; /Glenn Dunbar: 18T, 20B, 29B, 37C, 66B, 145T; /Steve Etherington: 9, 33B, 41TR, 48R, 53R, 64-65, 69T, 70B, 77T, 80-81, 122-123, 124, 128T, 144C, 162-163, 167T, 179TL; /Andrew Ferraro: 4R, 34BR, 36B, 45C, 47T, 74T, 76R, 77R, 77BL, 185; /Colin McMaster: 168R; /Alastair Staley: 47TL; / Steven Tee: 2, 6-7, 27C, 50T, 118BL, 129TR, 166BL, 183T

Press Association Images: /AP: 53B; /Victor R. Caivano/AP: 63B; /Antonio Calanni/AP: 74B; /DPA: 17B, 28B, 45B, 73T; /David Davies: 22T, 35C, 59BR; /Steve Etherington/Empics Sport: 20R; /Tom Hevezi/PA Archive: 62B; /John Marsh/Empics Sport: 14B, 16T, 36T, 51B, 53T, 55TR, 61R, 76B; /Steve Mitchell/Empics Sport: 19T, 55BR; /PA Archive: 15T, 23C; /Alberto Pellaschiar/AP: 50B; /Martin Rickett/PA Archive: 27B; /Daniel Roland/ AP: 182R; /S&G and Barratts/Empics Sport: 19B; /Michael Sohn/AP: 61T; /Peter Steffen/DPA: 24T, 30B; / Sutton Motorsport: 15B, 29T, 34L, 56BL, 57B; /Rui Vieira/PA Archive: 60B

Sutton Motorsport Images: 164B, 173B, 175T, 178, 179B

Topfoto.co.uk: 44B

Every effort has been made to acknowledge correctly and contact the source and/or copyright holder of each picture and Carlton Books Limited apologises for any unintentional errors or omissions that will be corrected in future editions of this book.

ABOUT THE AUTHOR

||||||||||||||||||||||||||||||||||||||||||||

Bruce Jones has been covering motor racing for more than a quarter of a century. He has written countless books on the subject, from Formula 1 to the broadest spectrum of world motor sport, with titles aimed at all ages. As a journalist he worked on *Autosport* in the mid-1980s, a magazine acknowledged as the voice of motor sport the world over, going on to be Editor in the mid-1990s.

In addition to his writing, Bruce has been a pitlane interviewer for FOM Television, also conducting the official post-race TV interviews. Branching into event commentary, he regularly broadcasts at the Le Mans 24 Hours and, his favourite event of the year, the Goodwood Revival historic race meeting.